How about a trip to...

How about a trip to…

Alaska

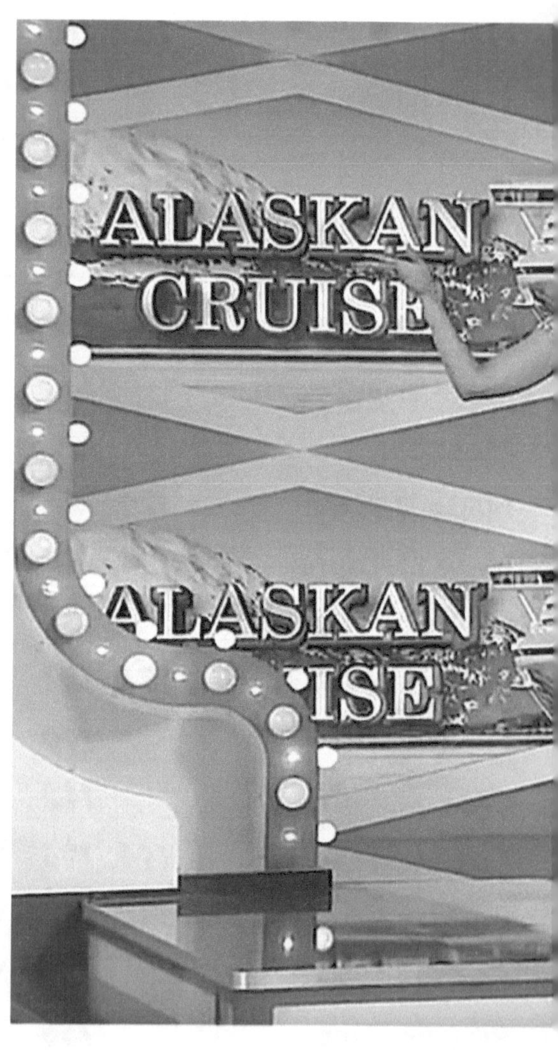

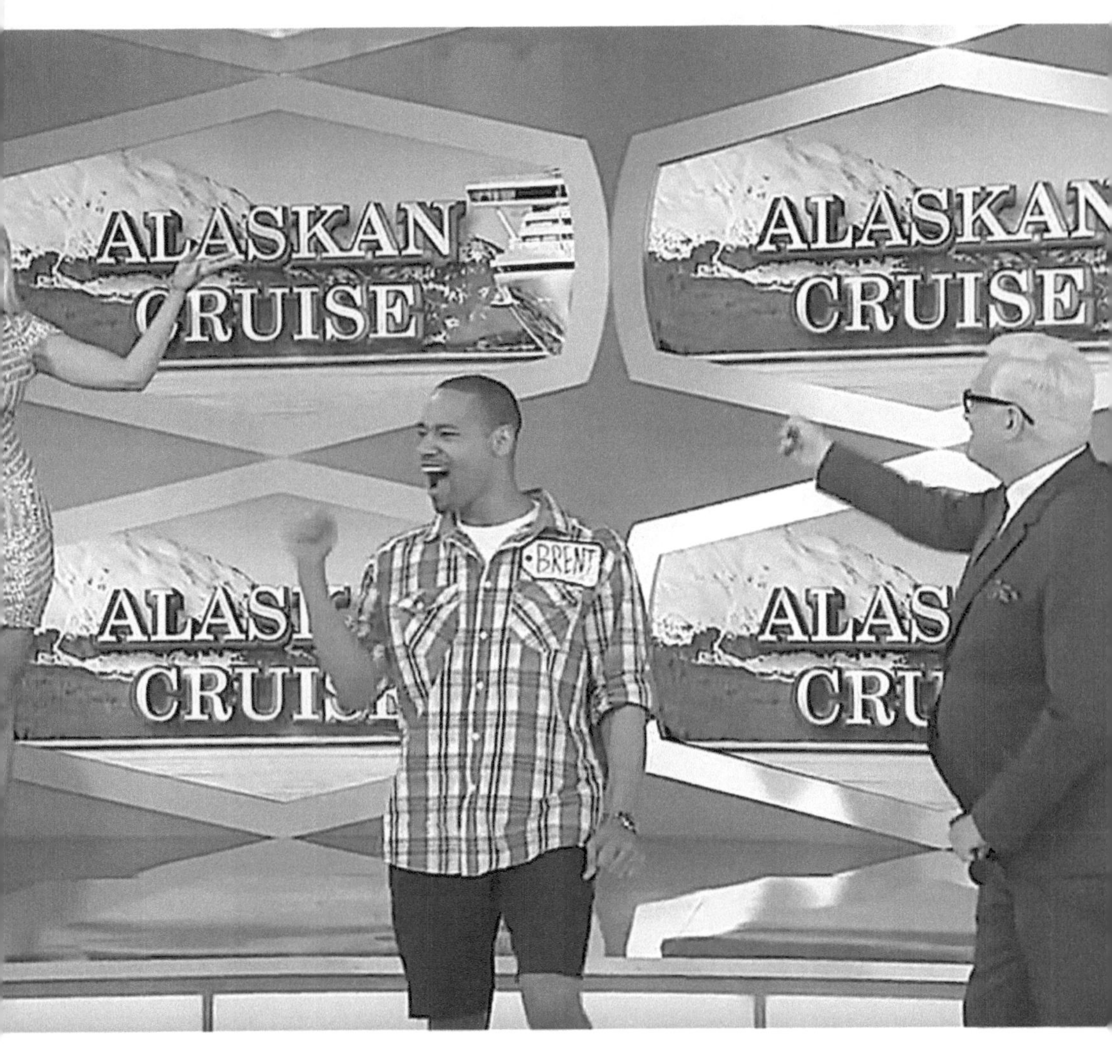

ALASKAN CRUISE
ALASKAN CRUISE
ALASKAN CRUISE
ALAS CRU
BRENT

Argen-
tina

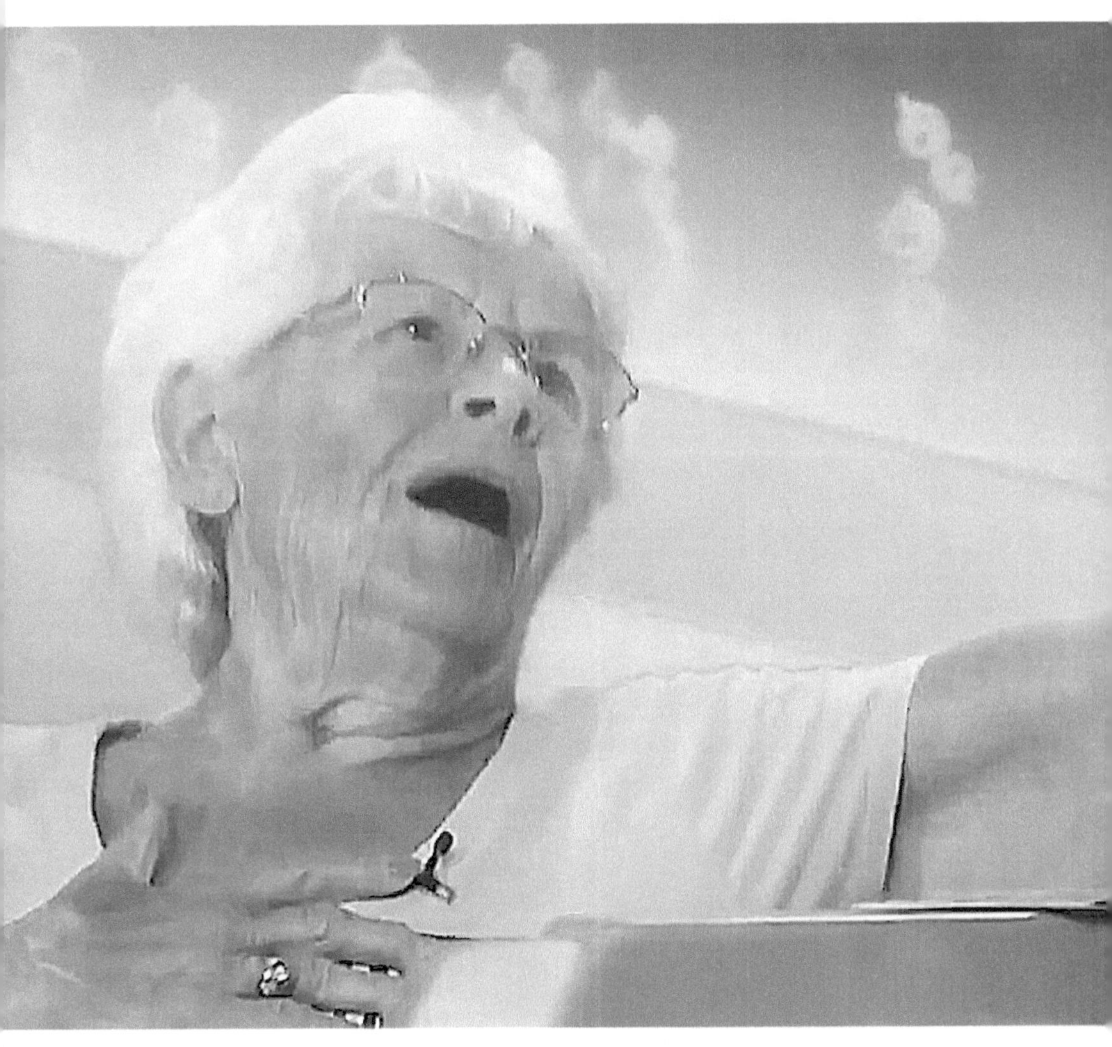

Ari-
zona

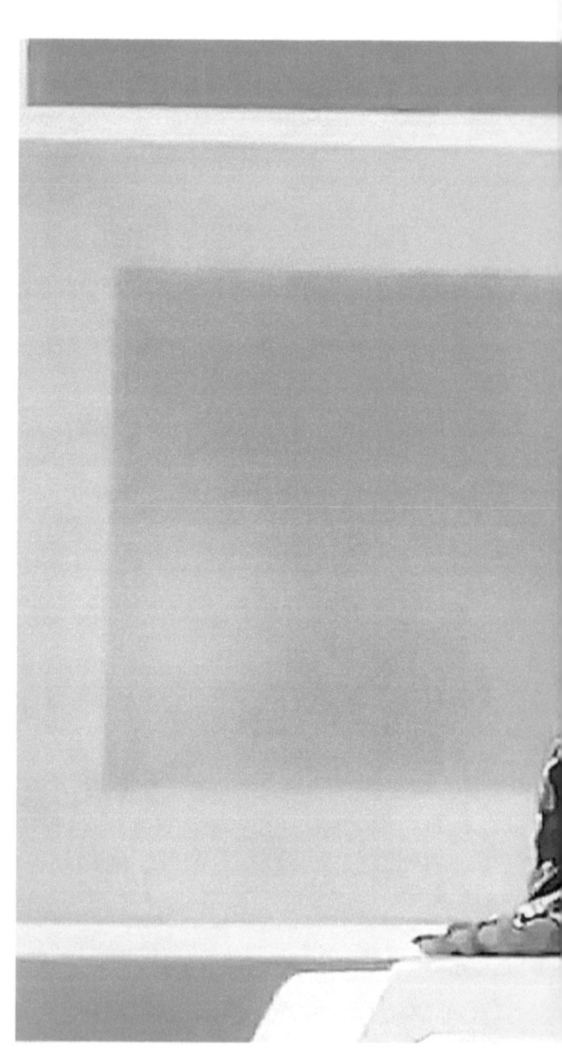

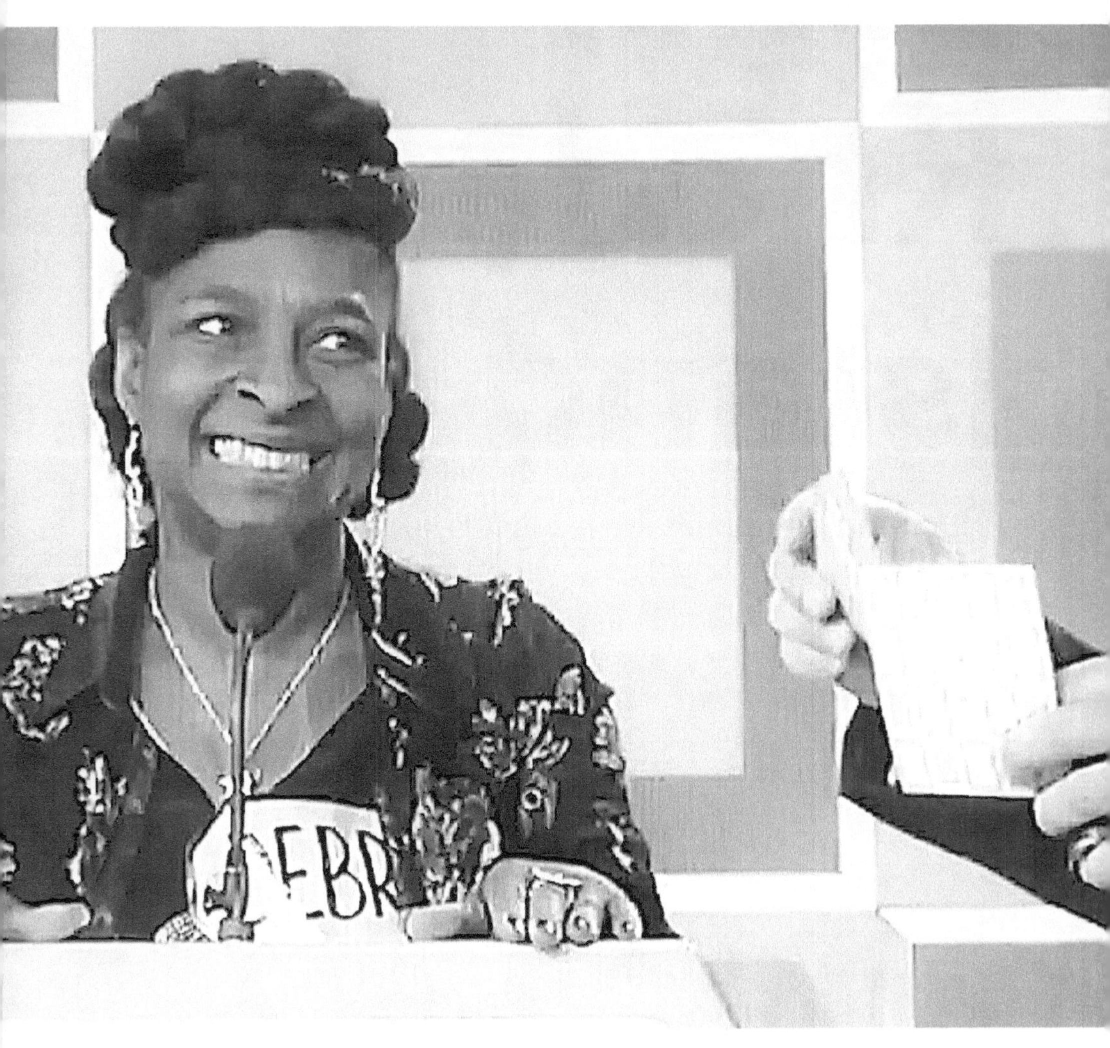

Ari-zona/ Rhode Island

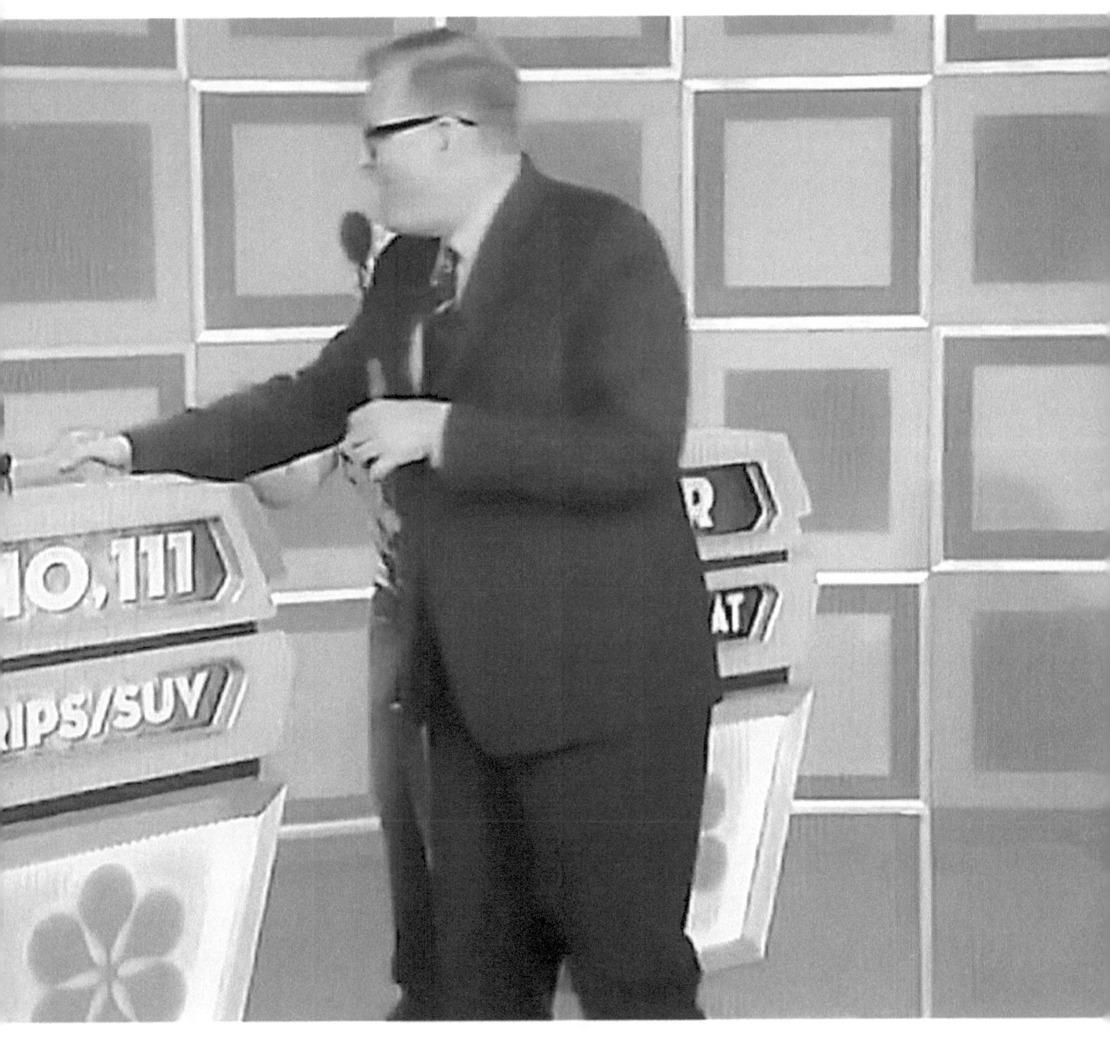
10,111
RIPS/SUV
R
AT

Austin

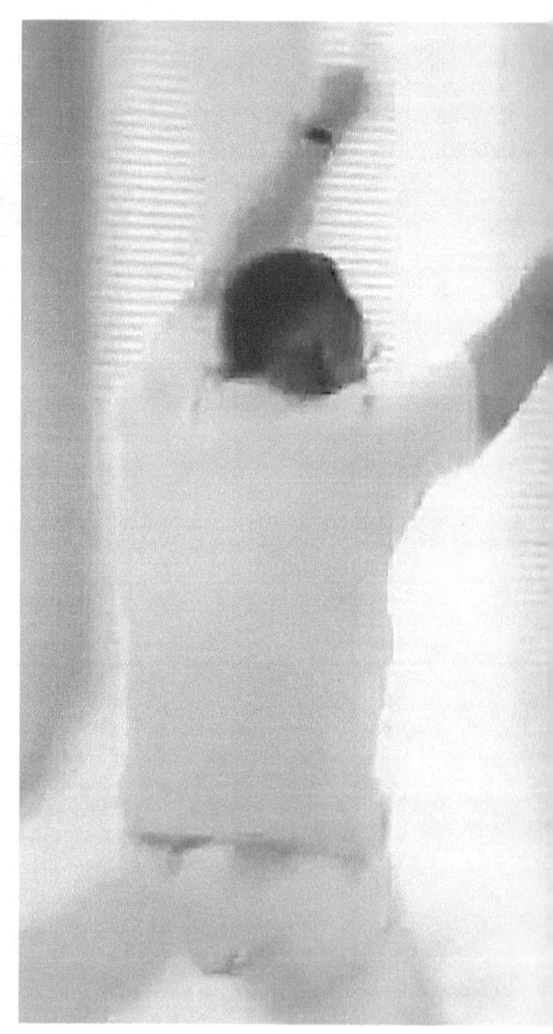

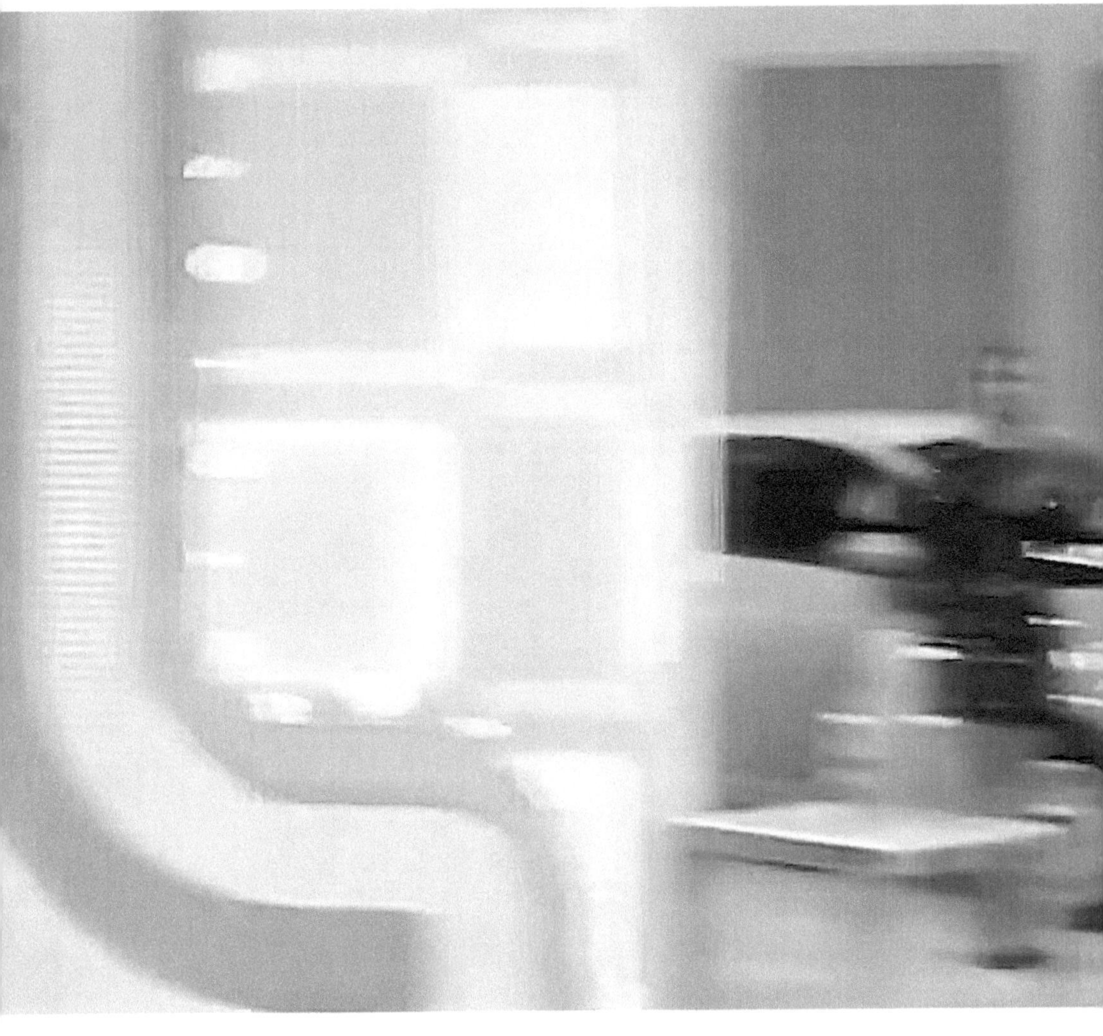

Aus-tralia

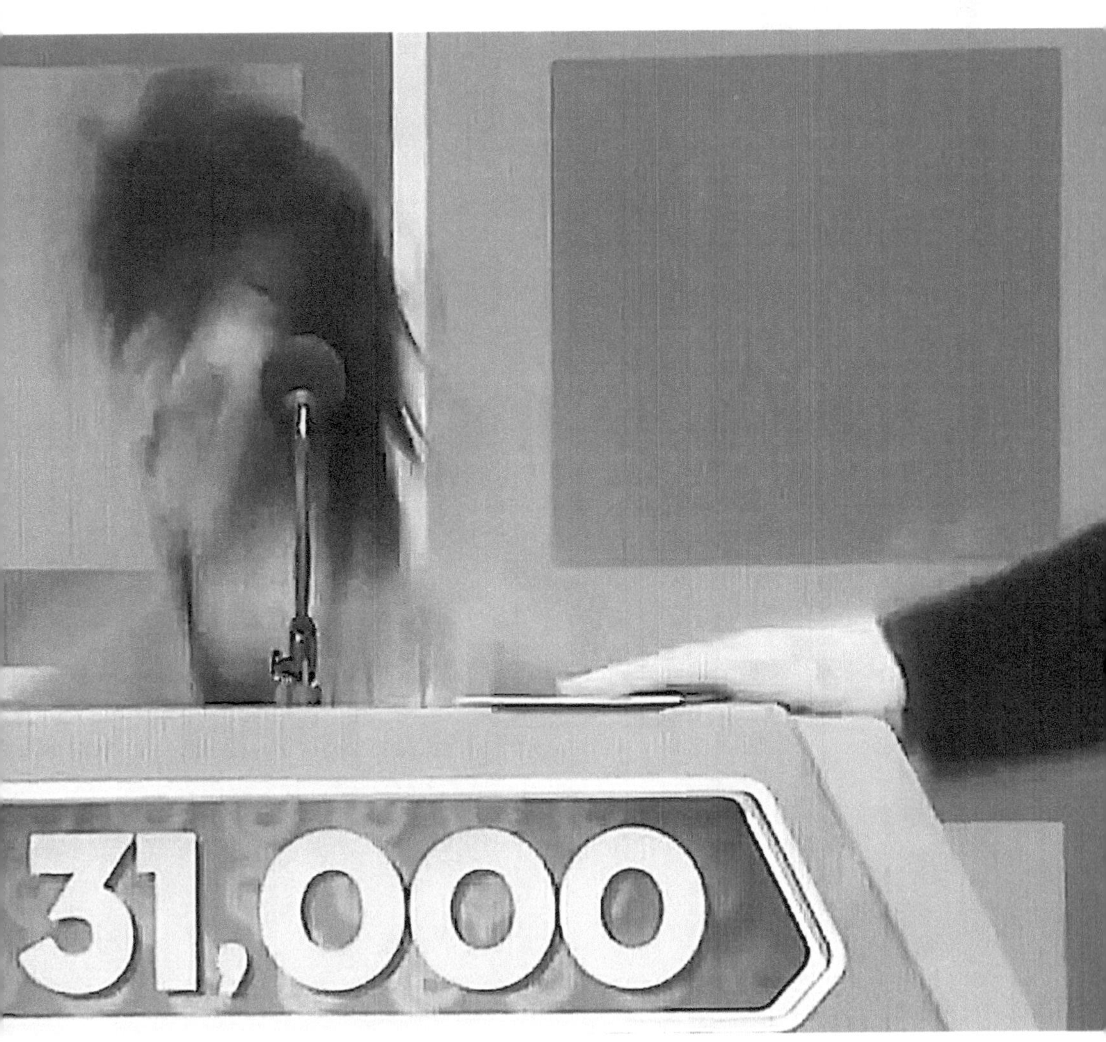
31,000

Australia/ Houston

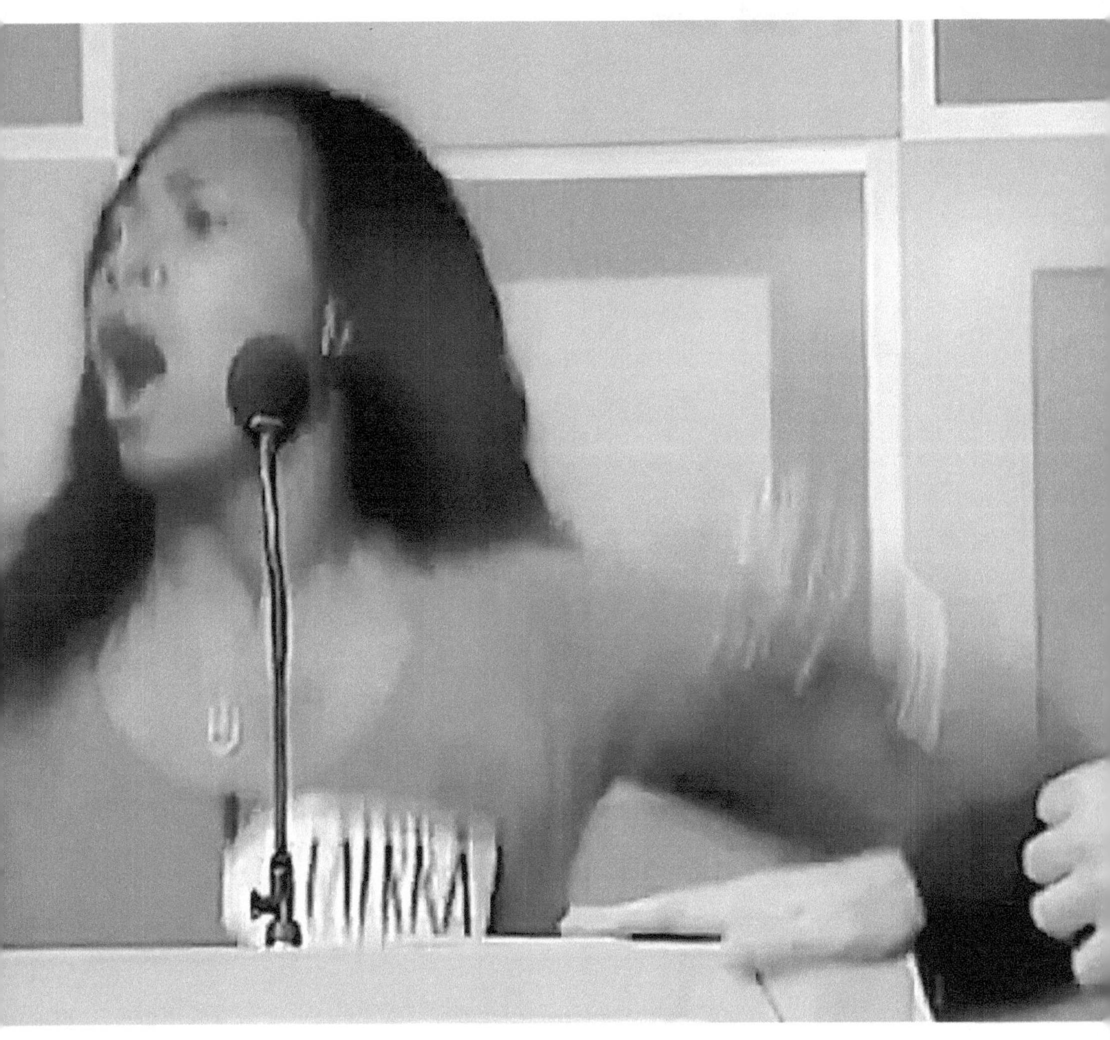

Baha-
mas

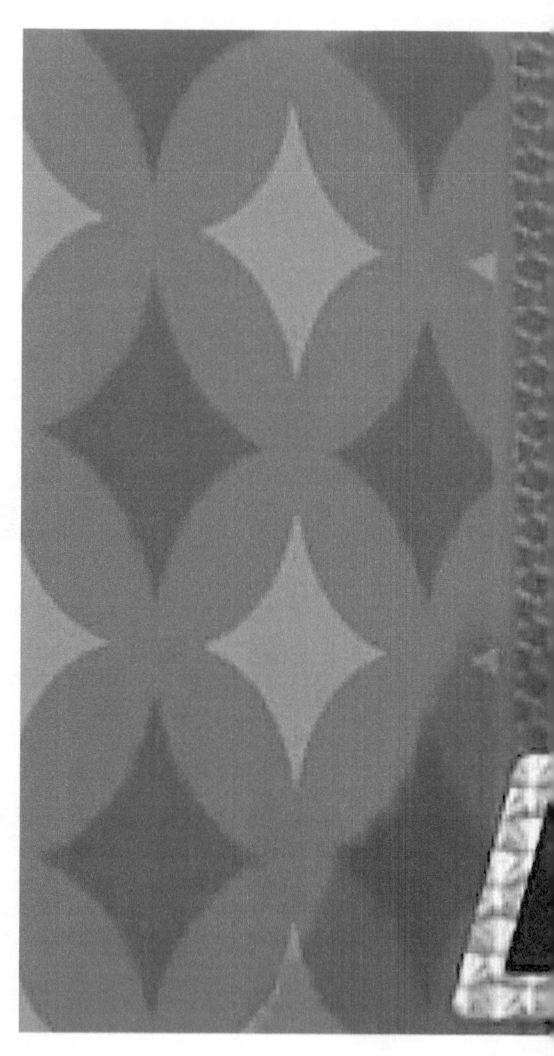

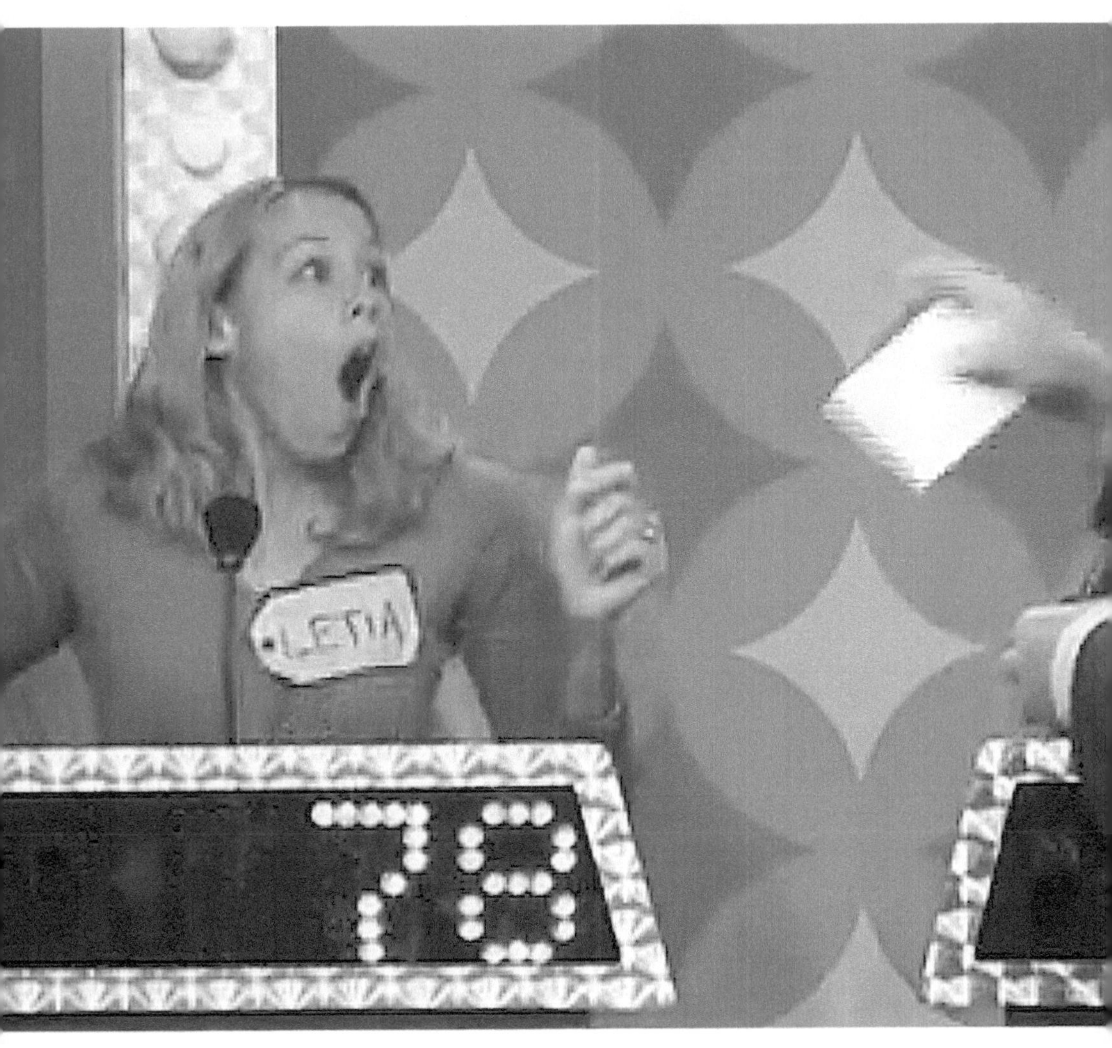

Baha-mas

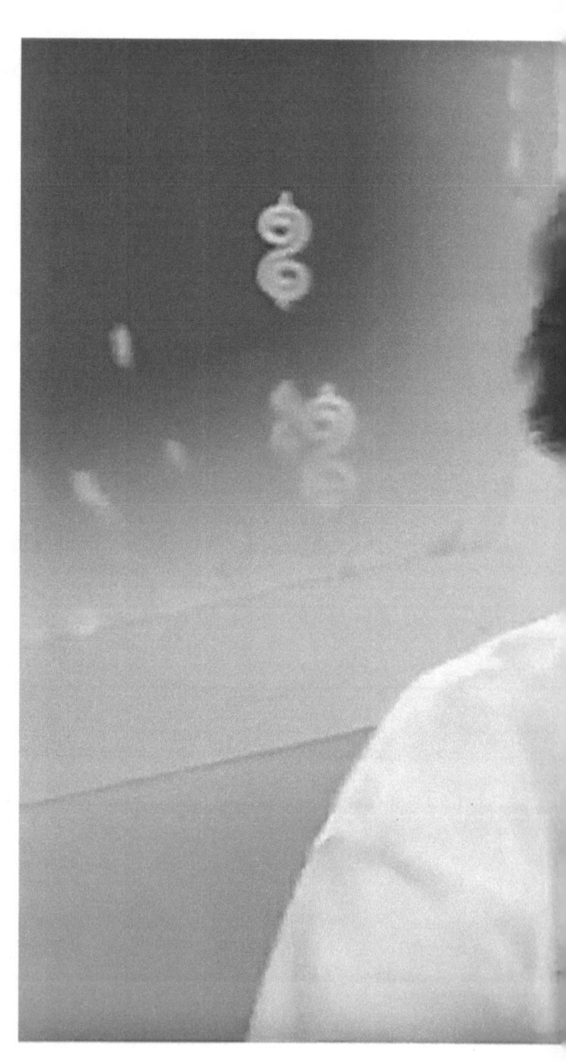

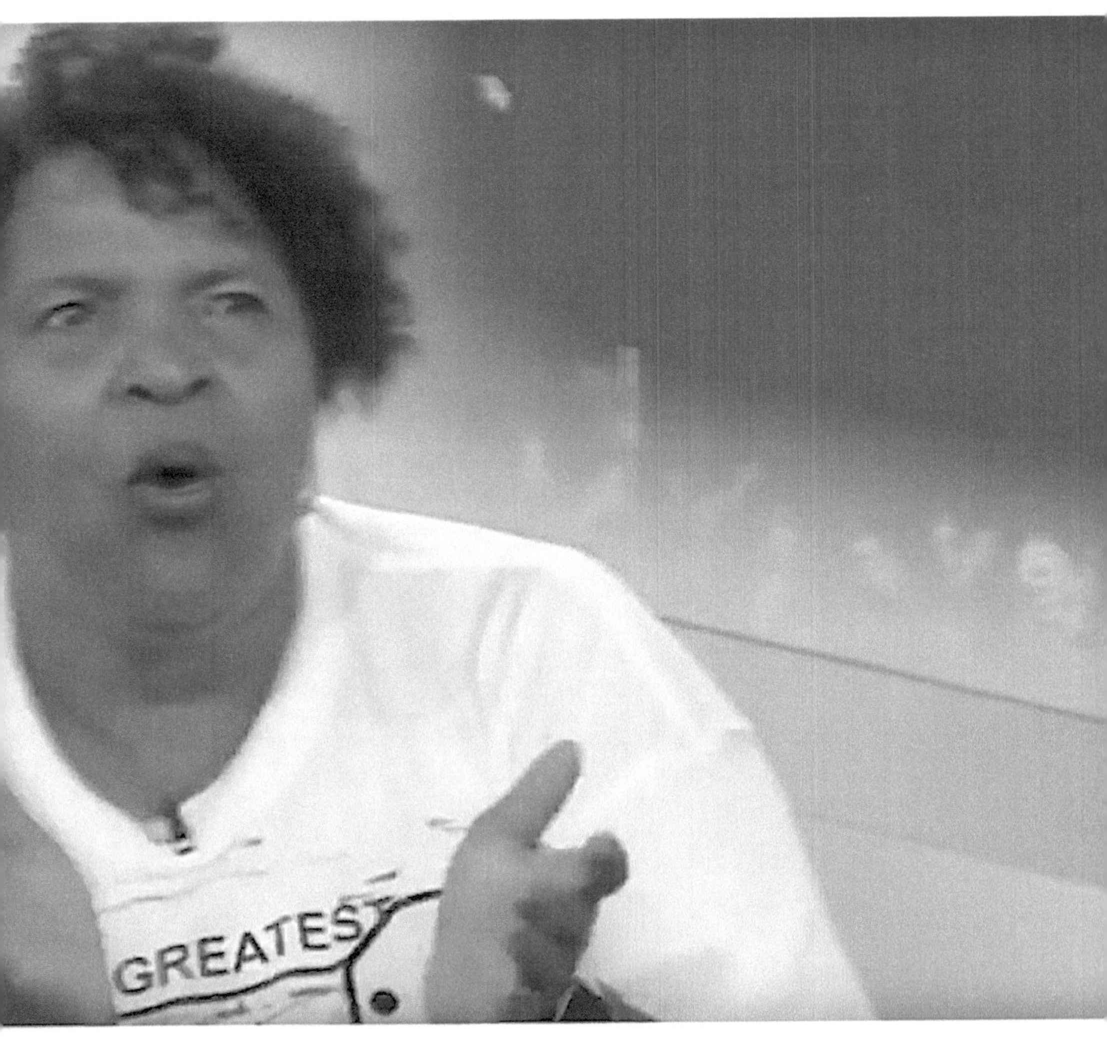
GREATEST

Bali

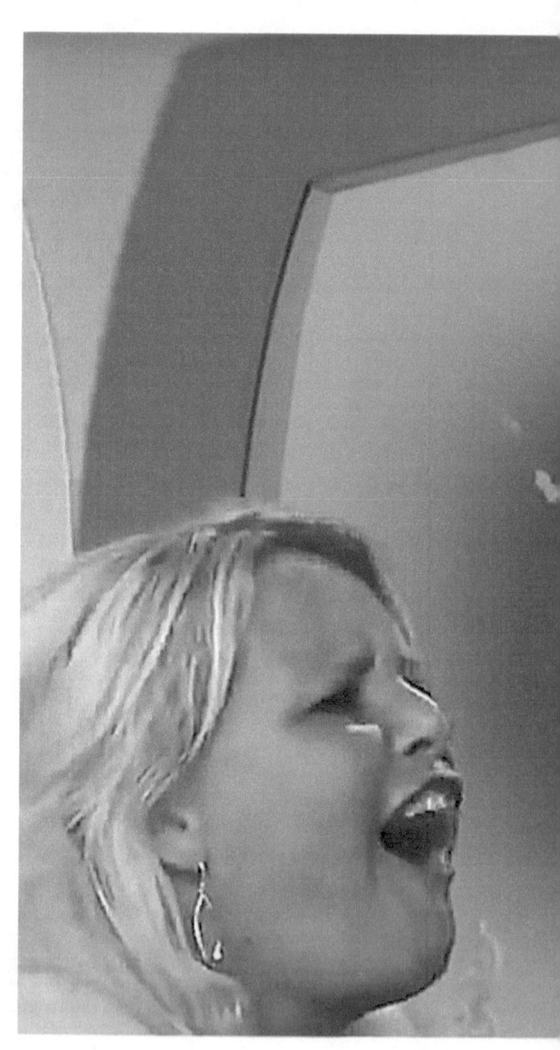

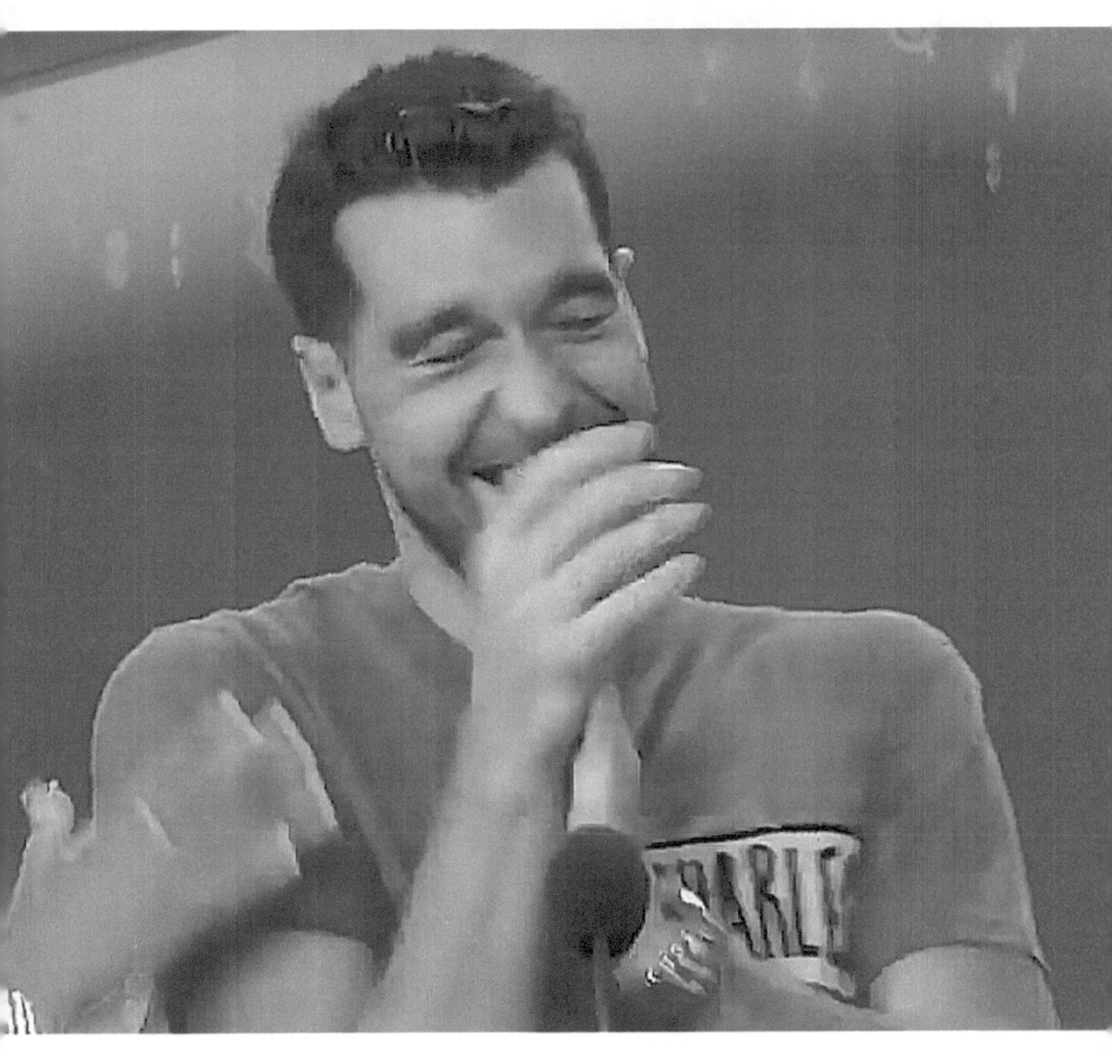

Belize/ Ecua- dor

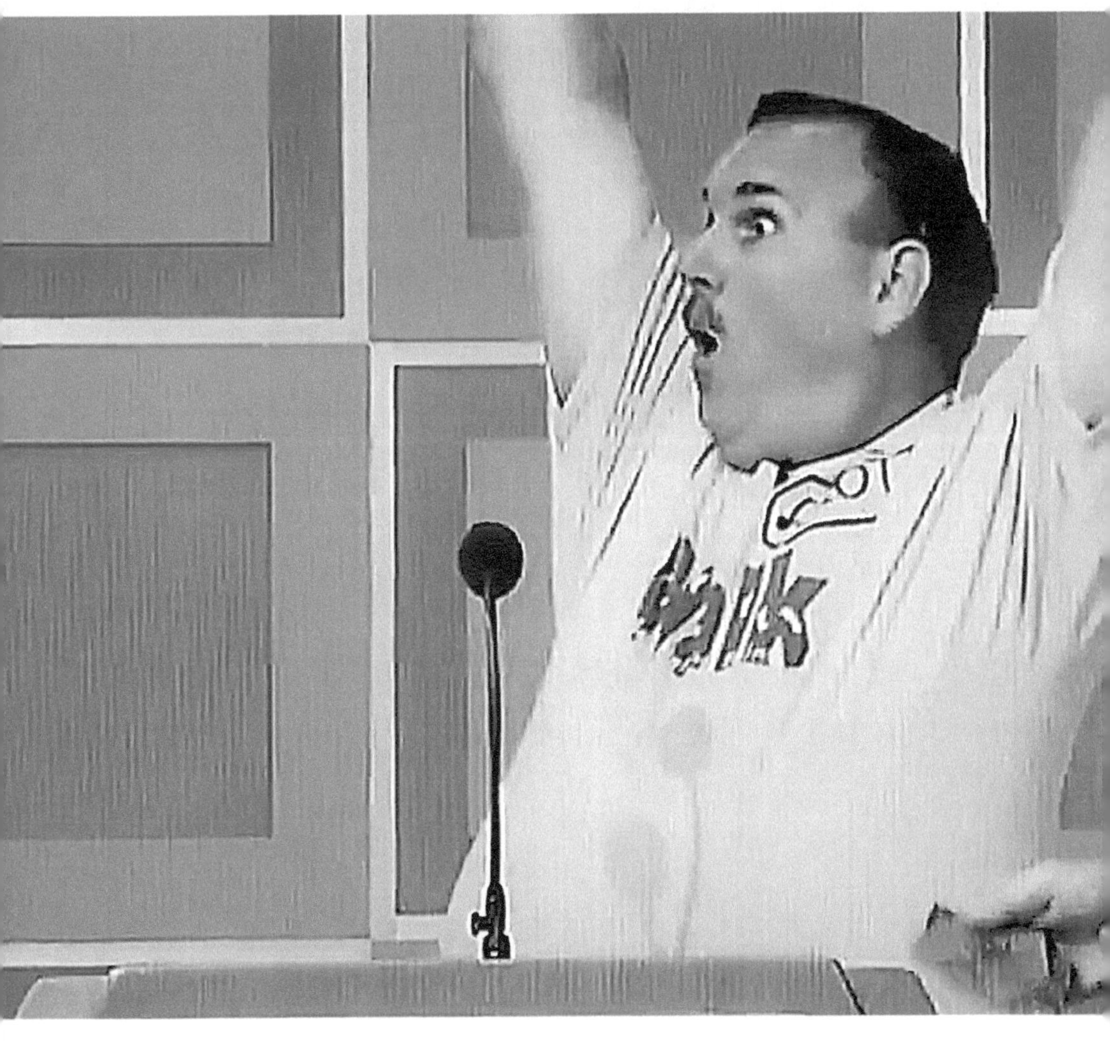

Bora Bora

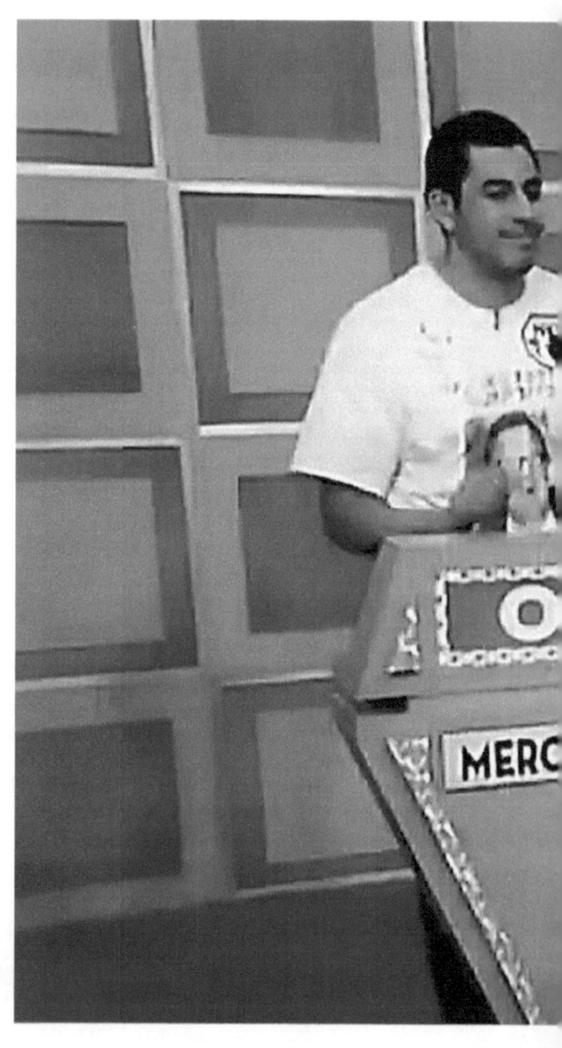

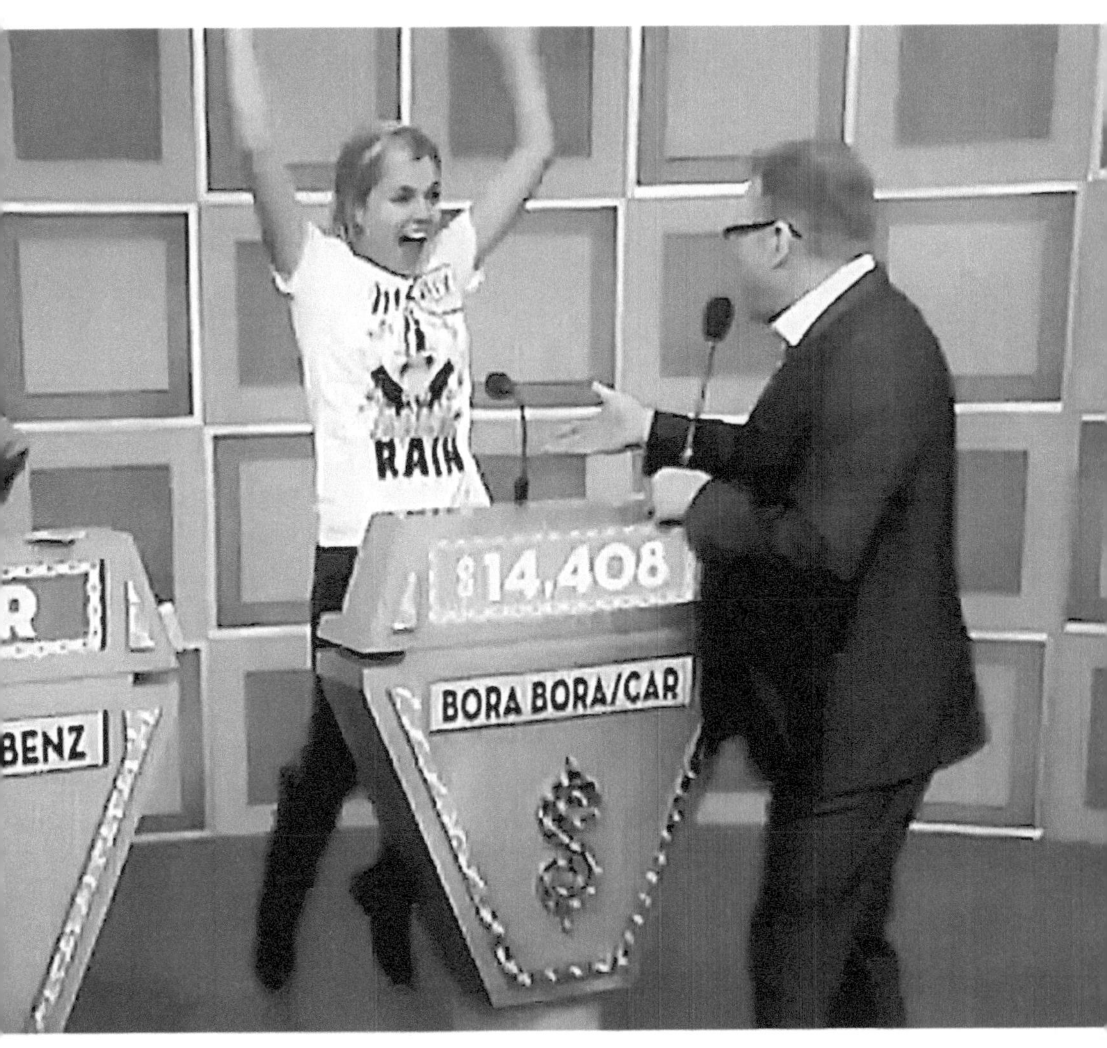

BENZ
$14,408
BORA BORA/CAR

Boston

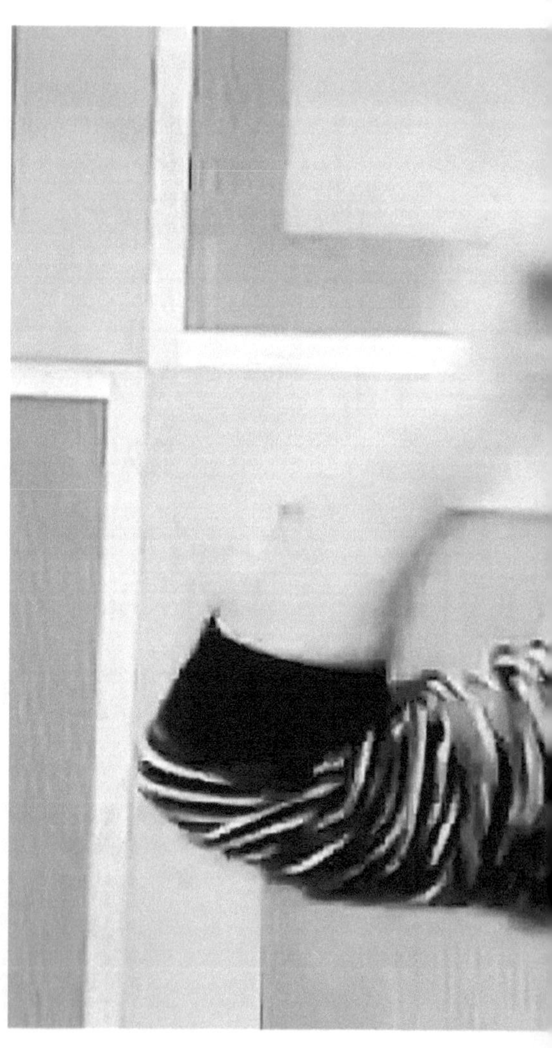

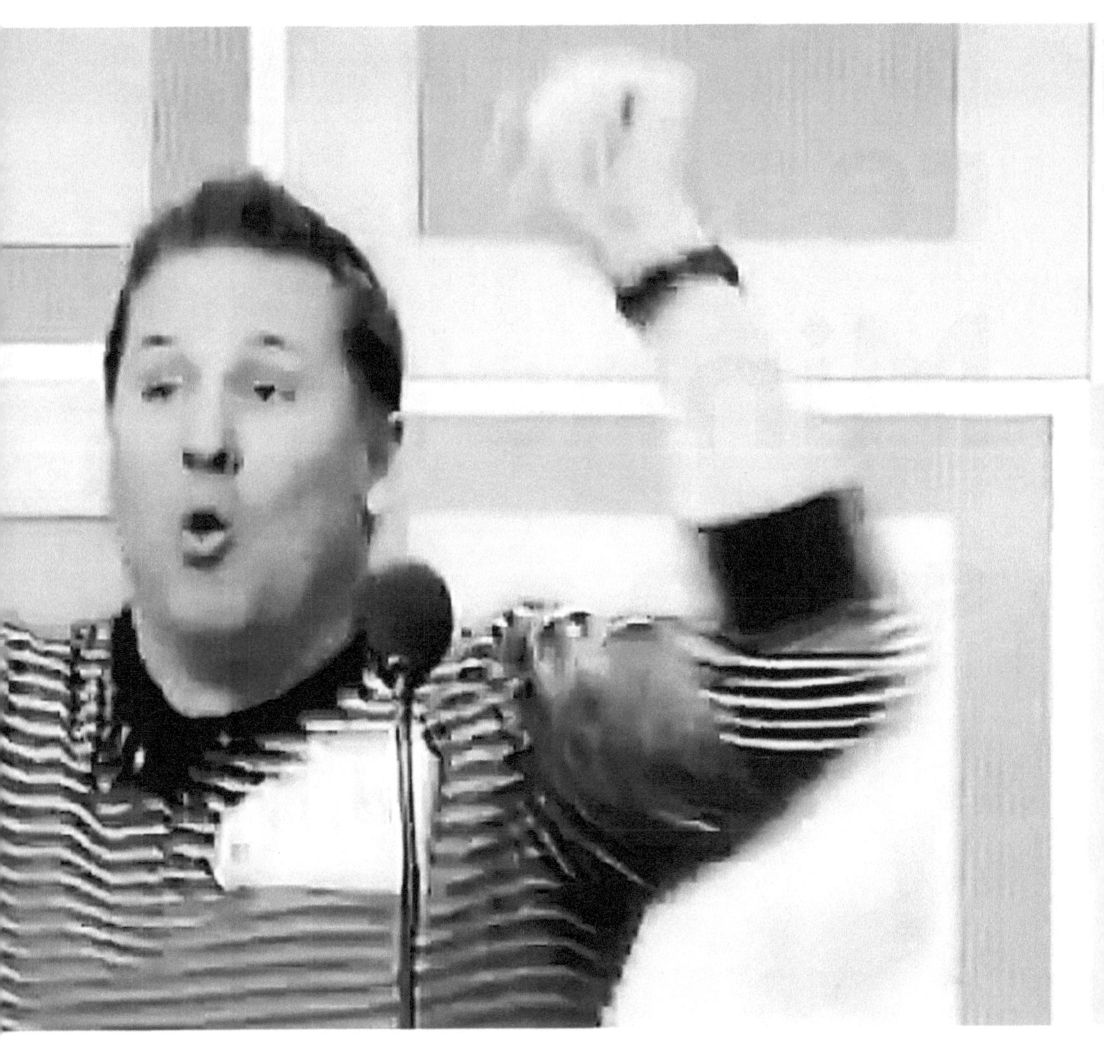

Buenos Aires/ Minnesota

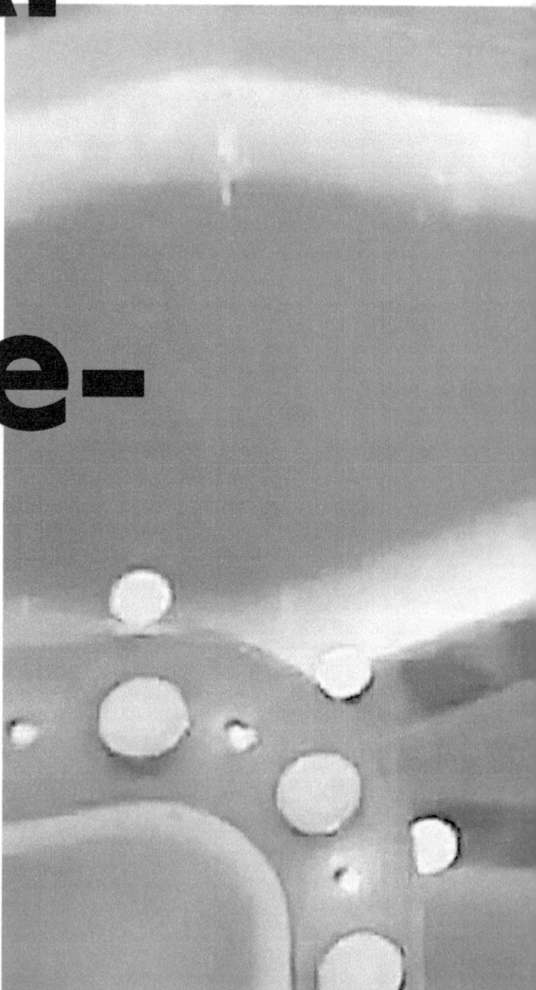

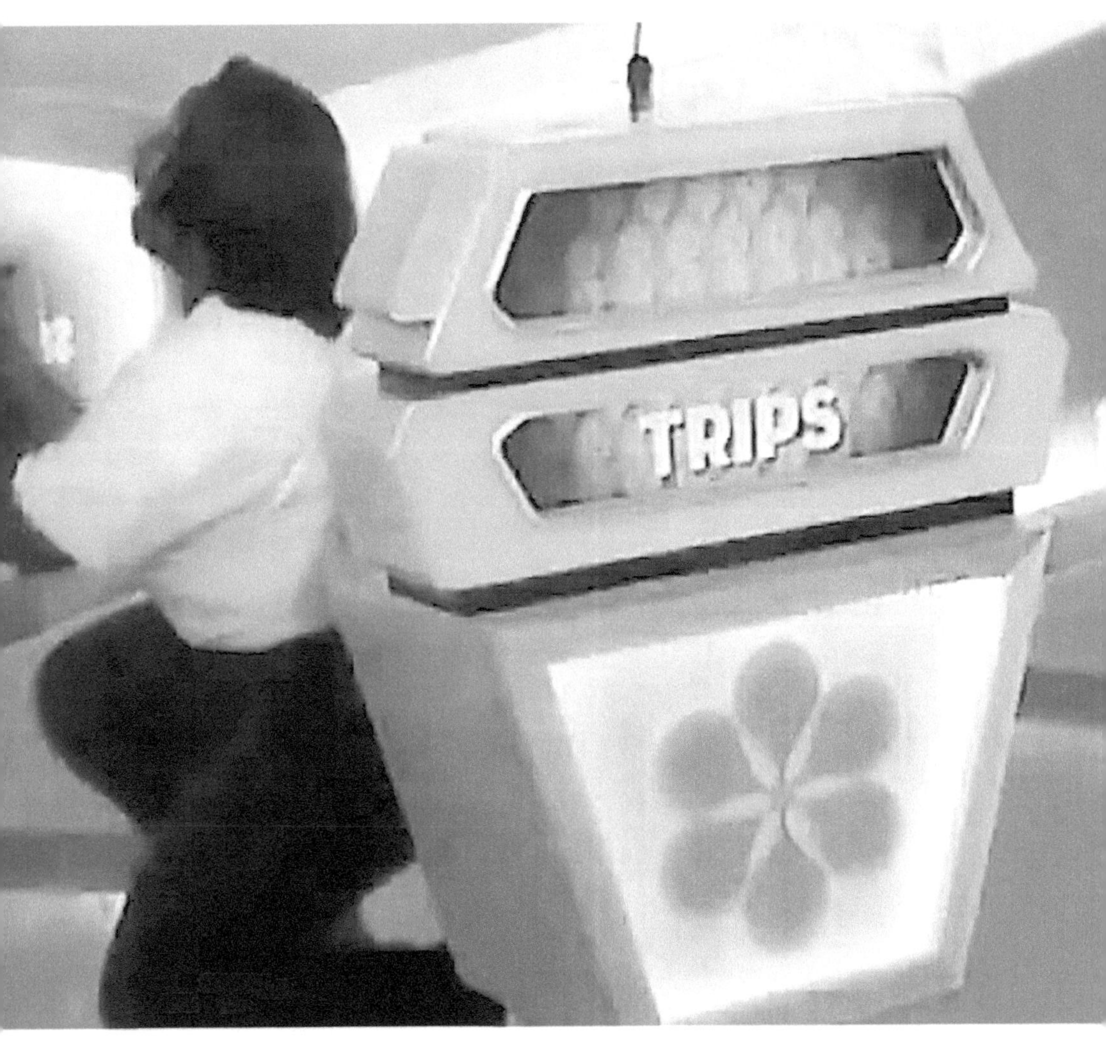
TRIPS

Cabo San Lucas

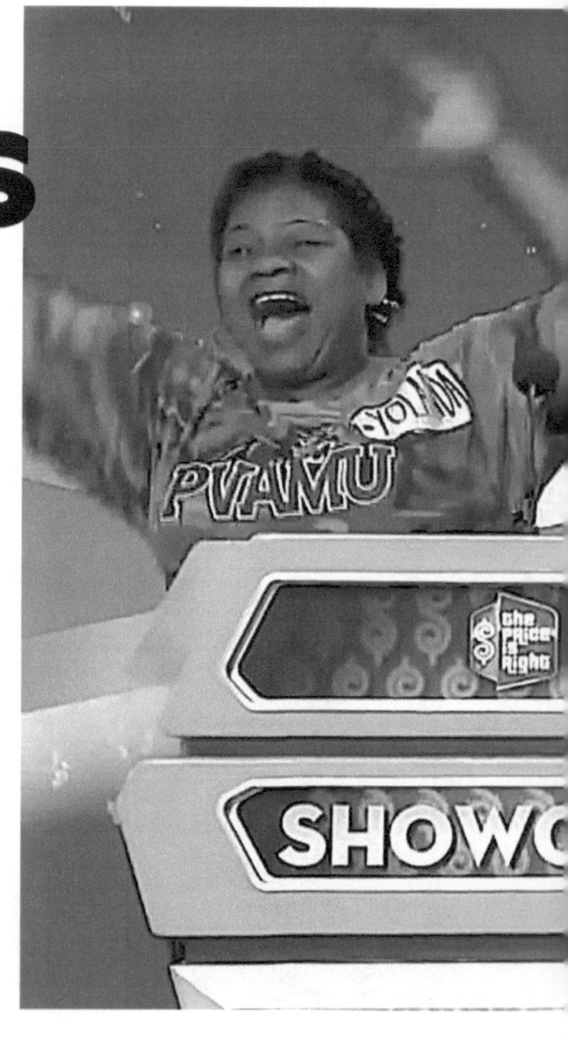

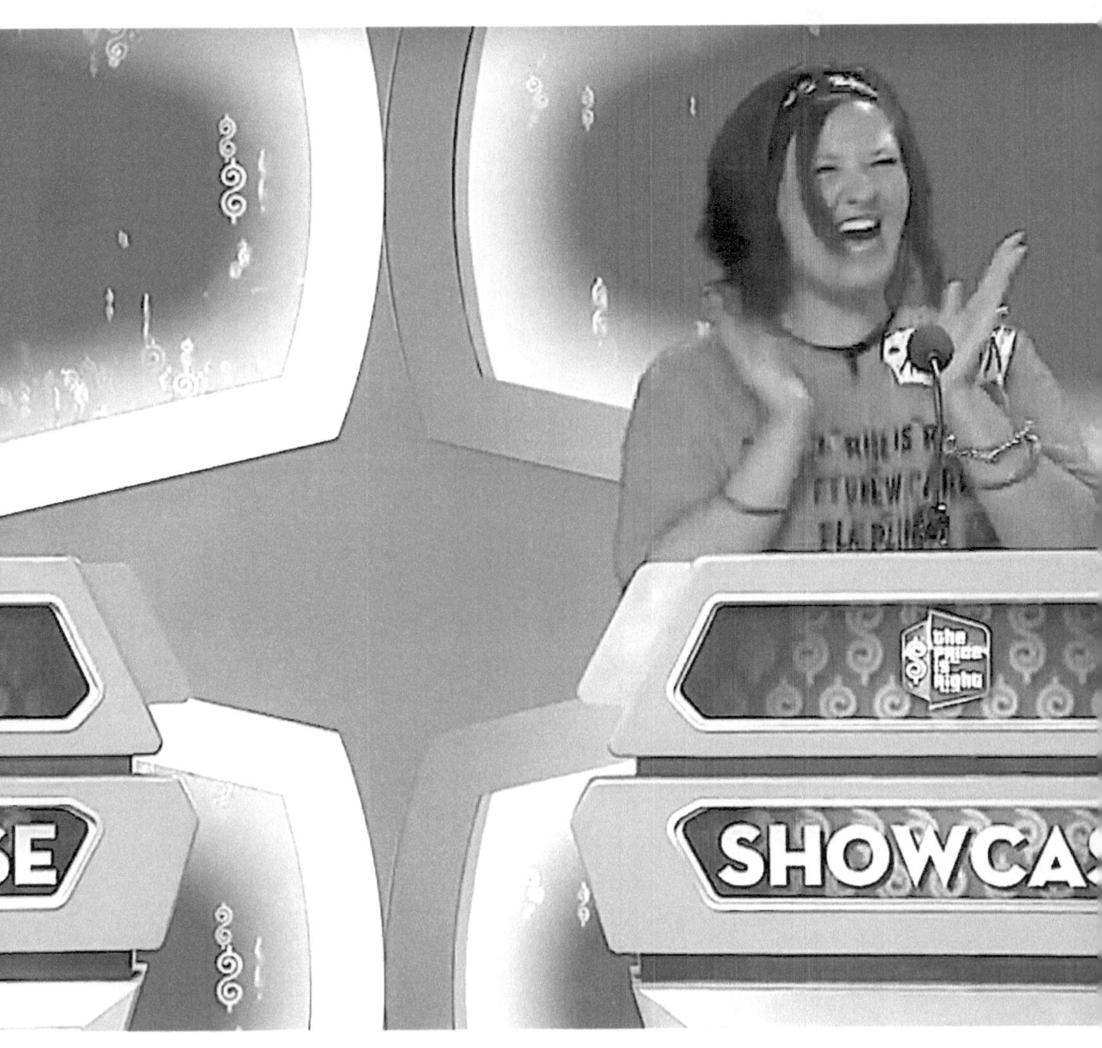
SHOWCA
SE
the price is right

Cana-da

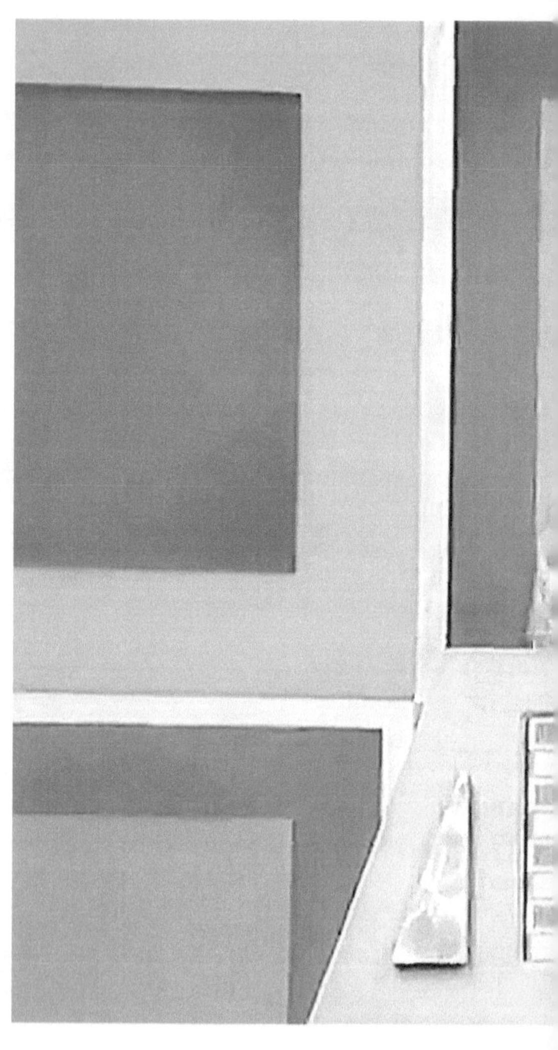

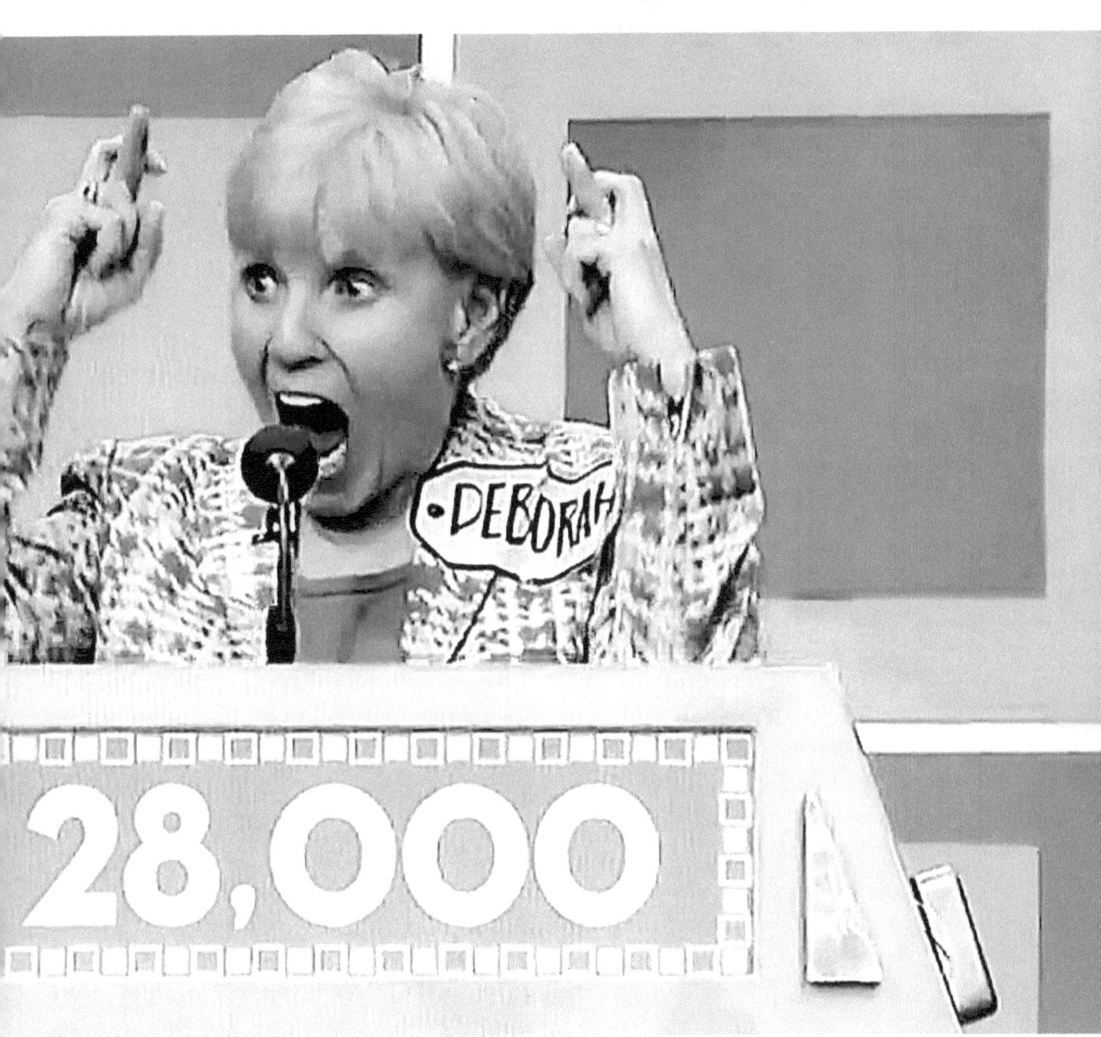

DEBORAH
28,000

Char-
lotte

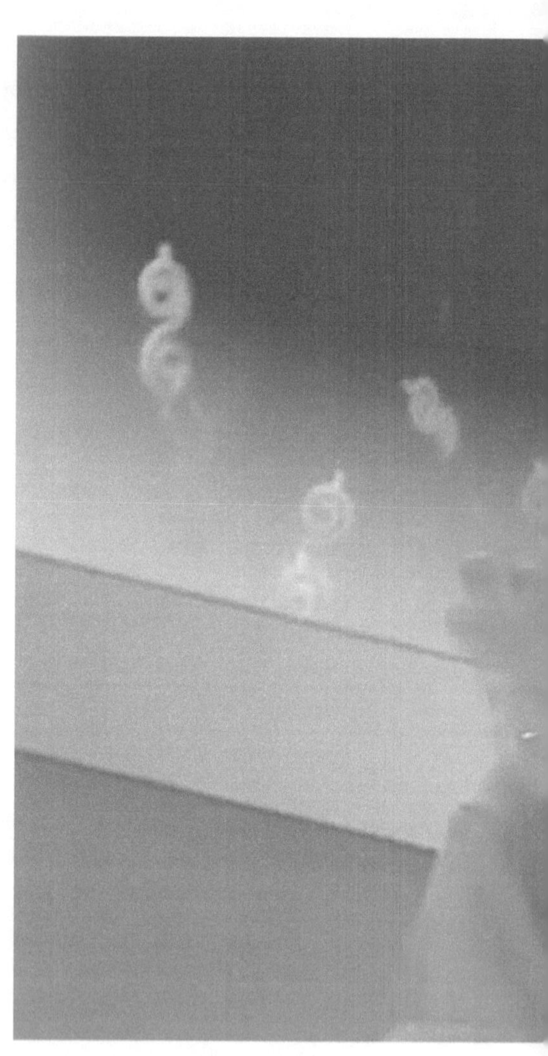

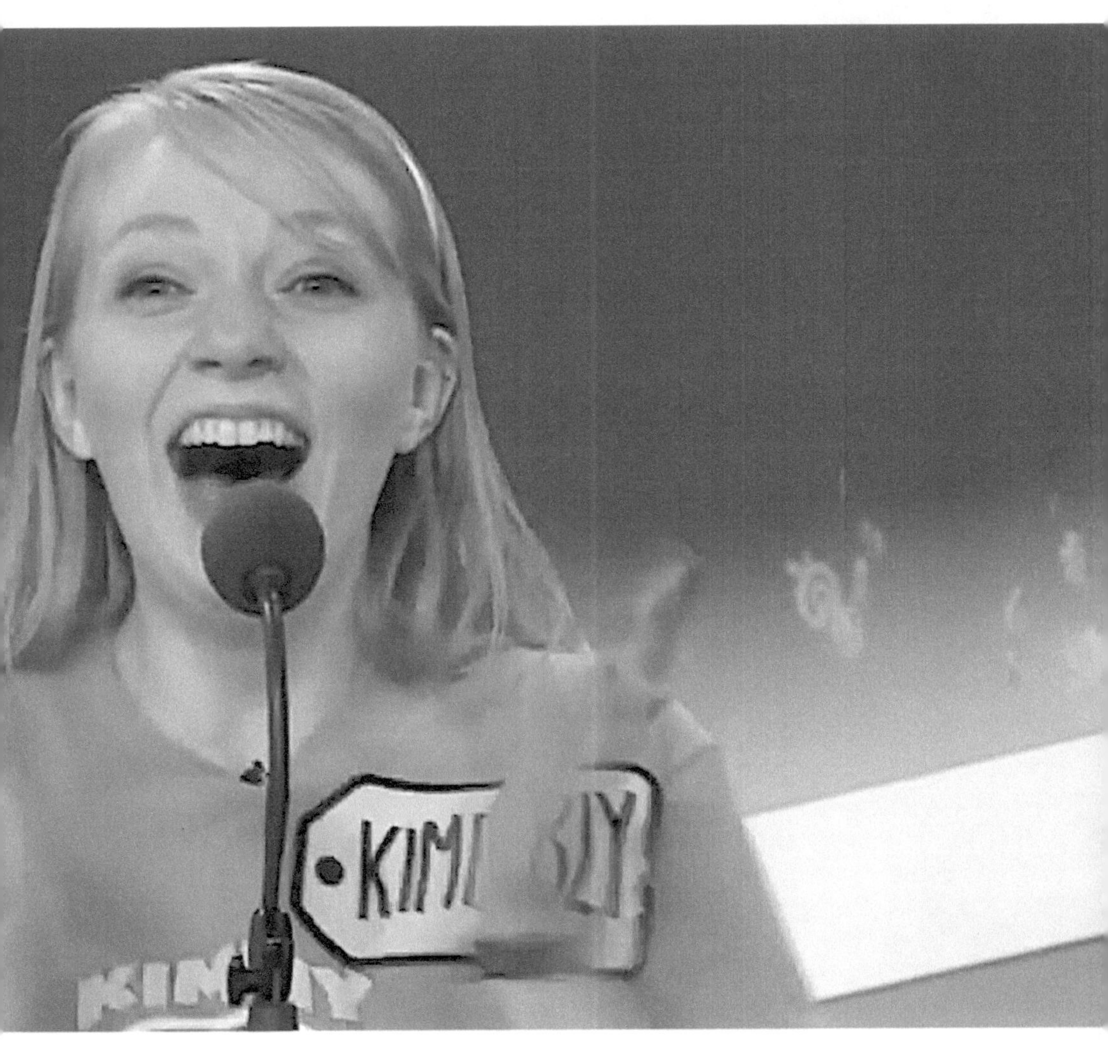

KIMBERLY
KIMBERLY

Chica-
go

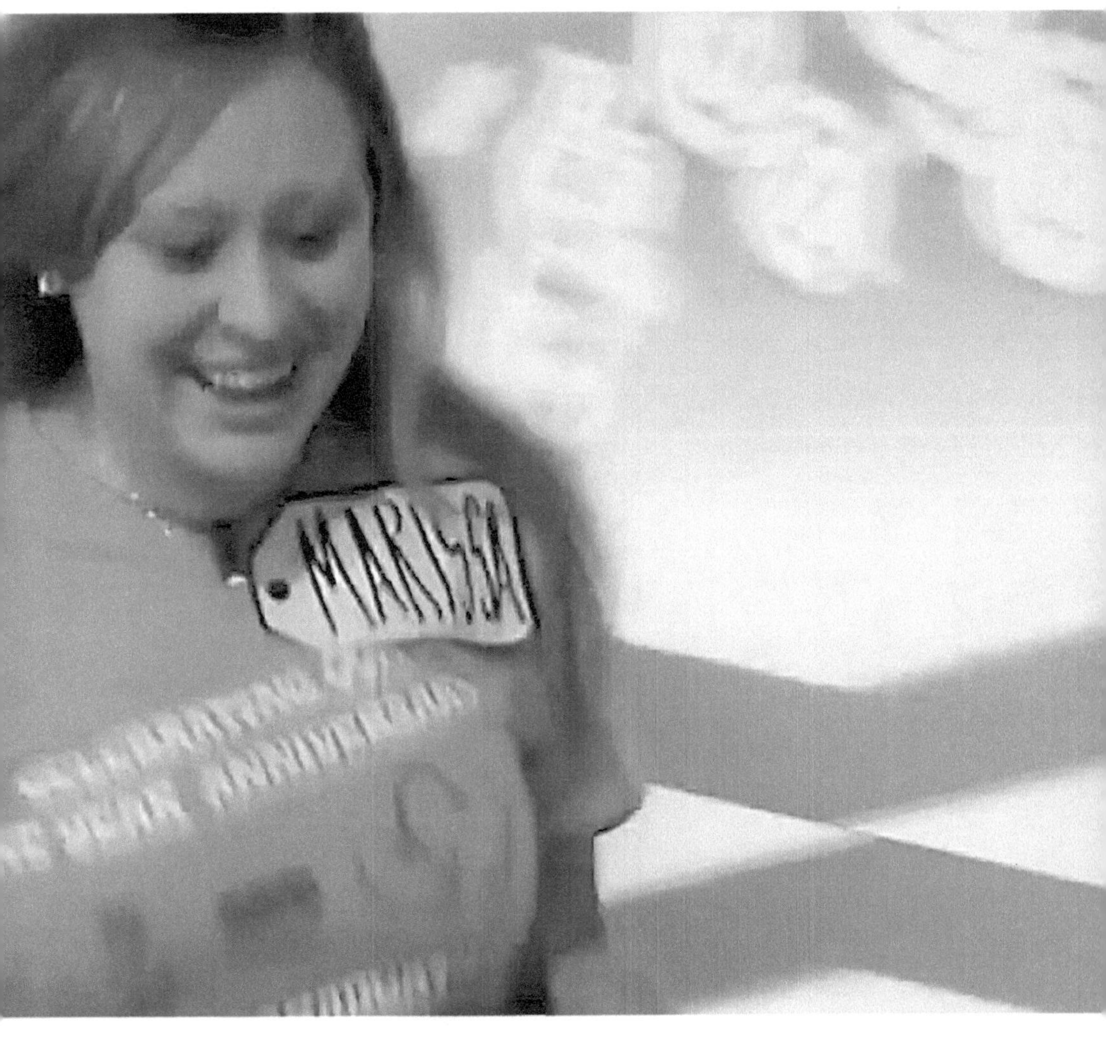

MARISSA

Coachella

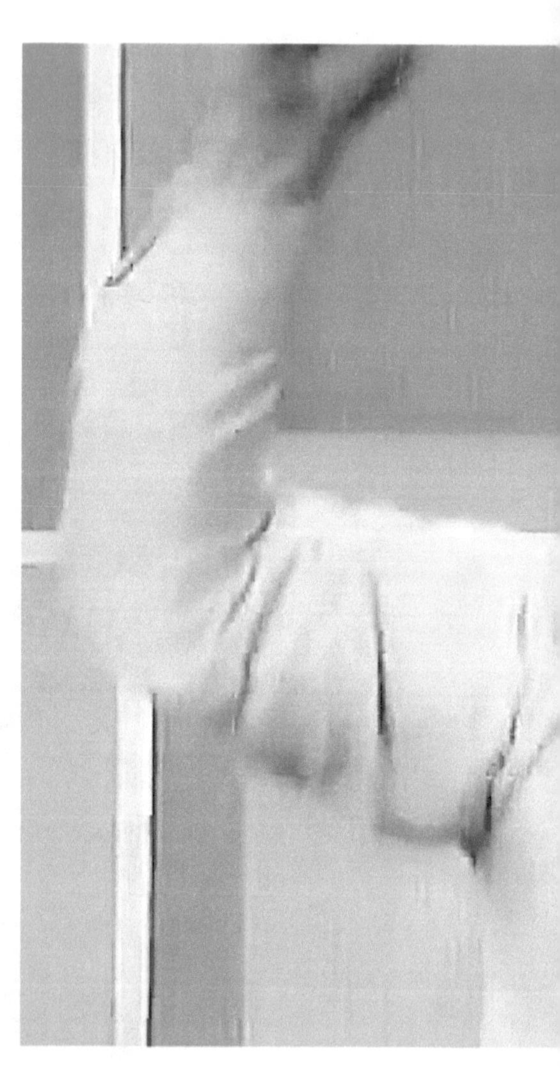

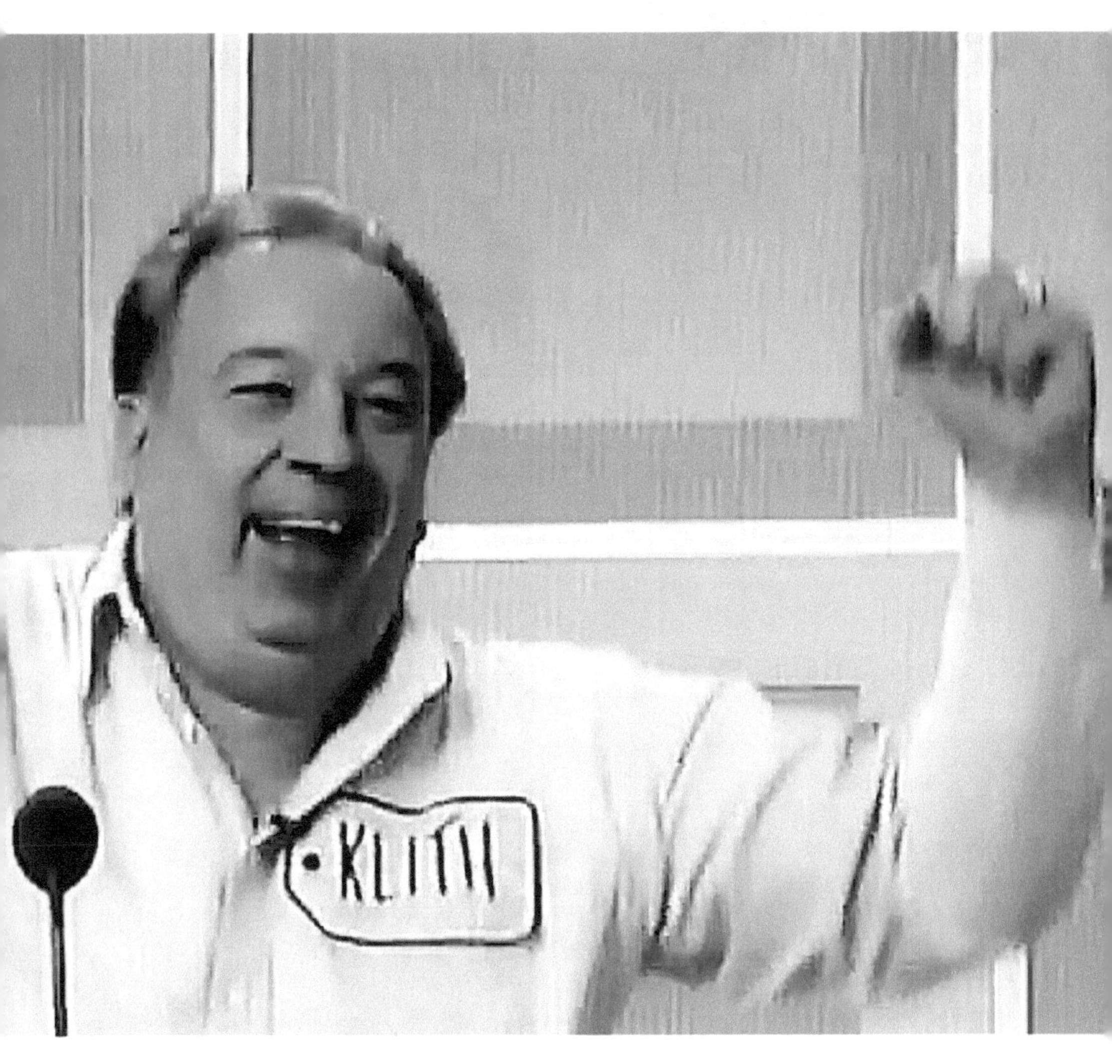

43

Costa Rica

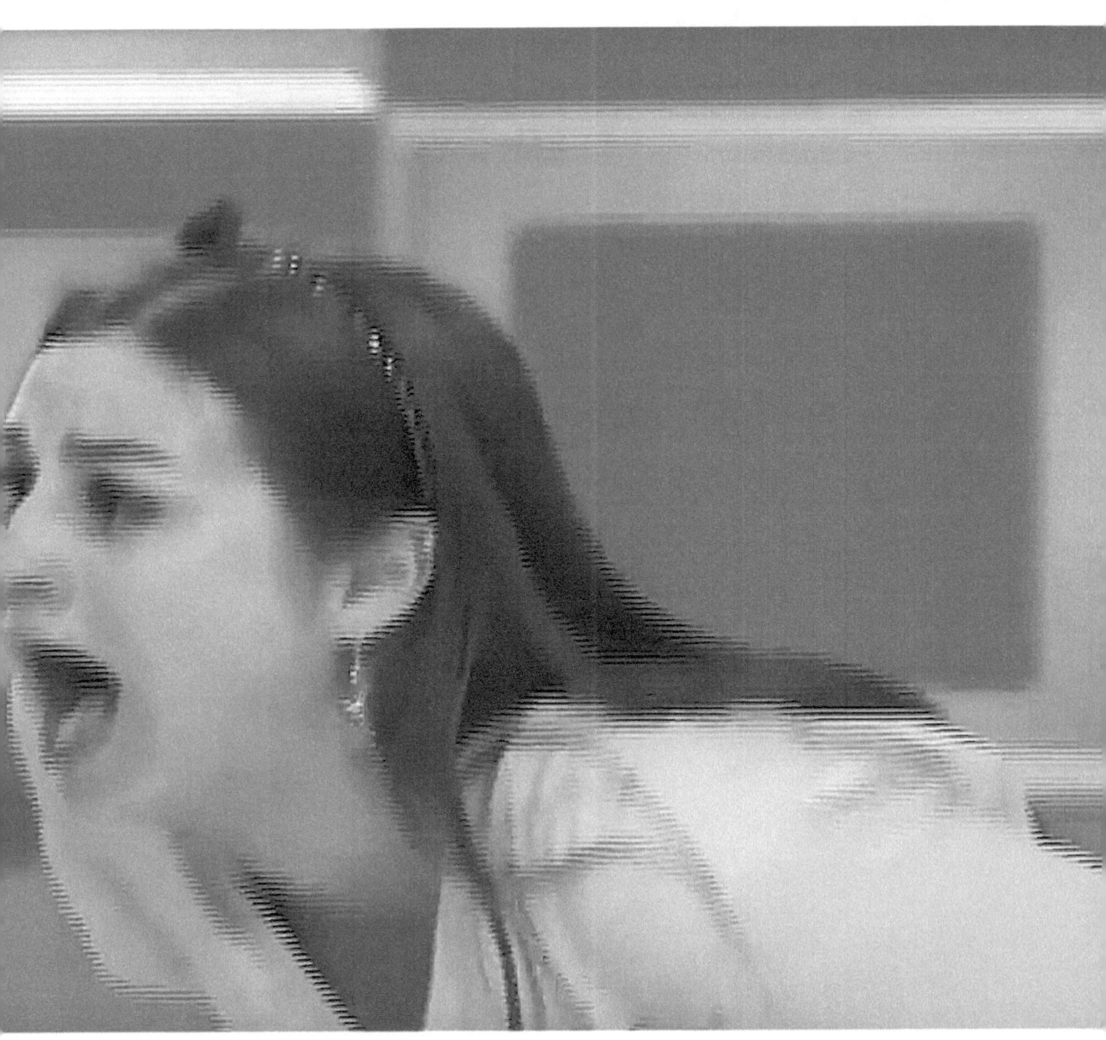

Costa Rica

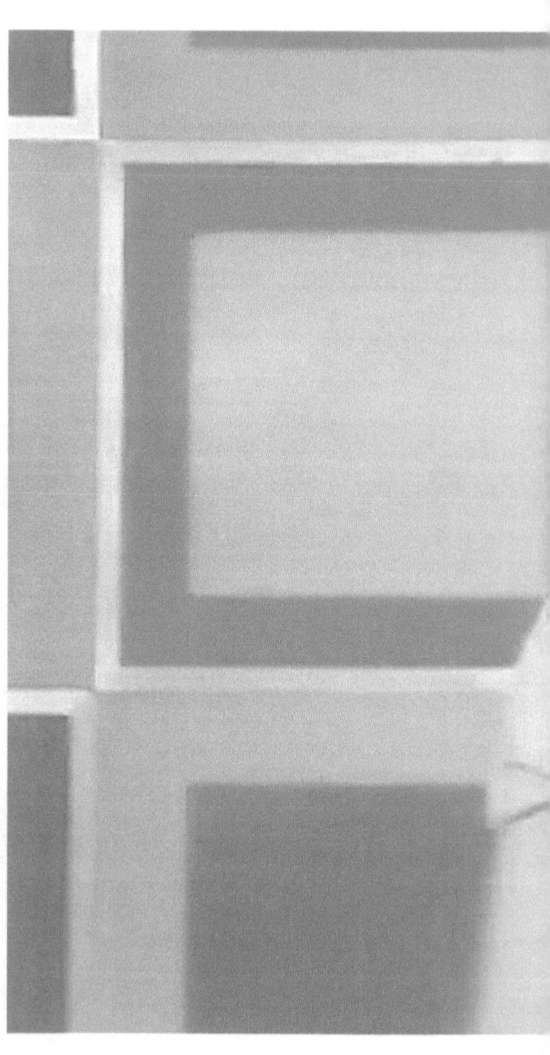

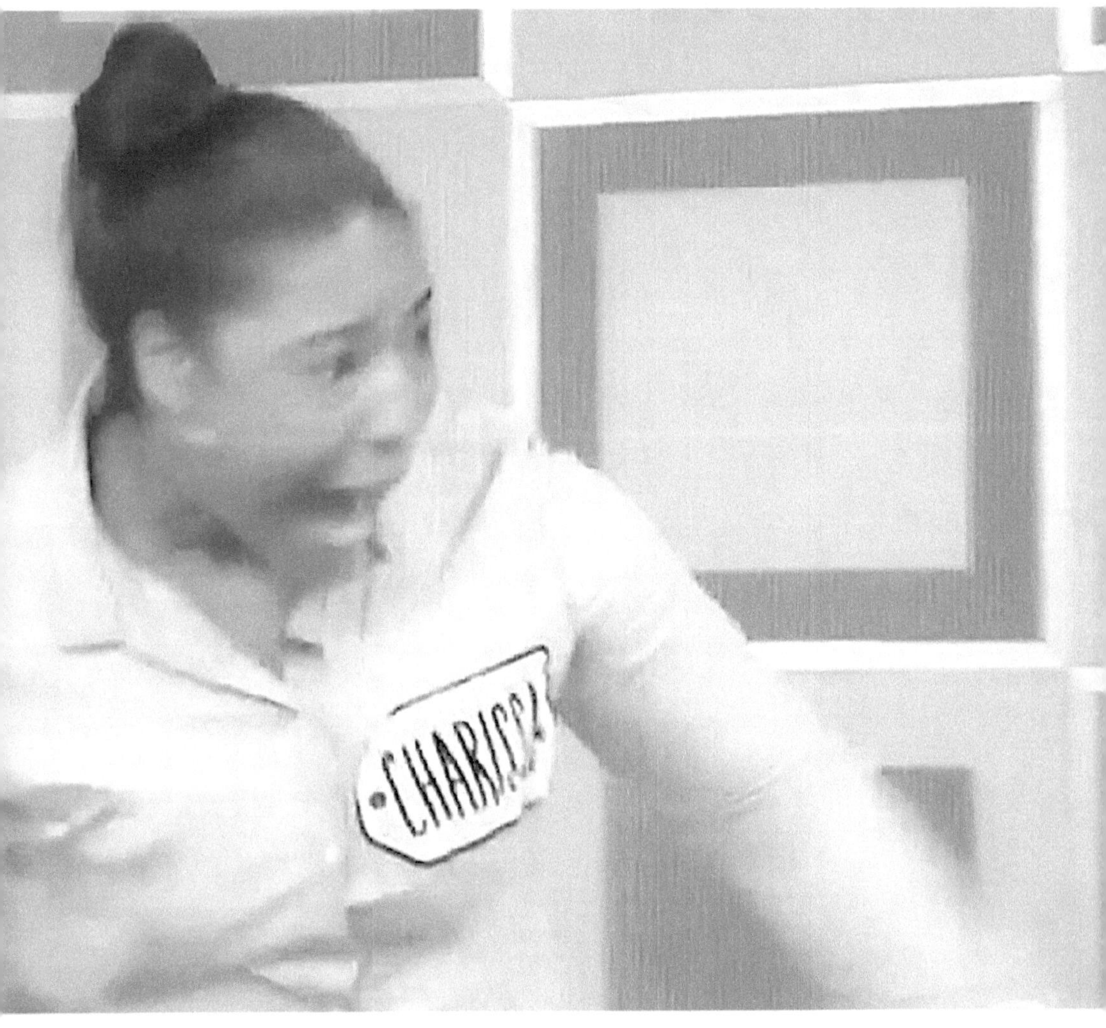

CHARISSE

Costa Rica

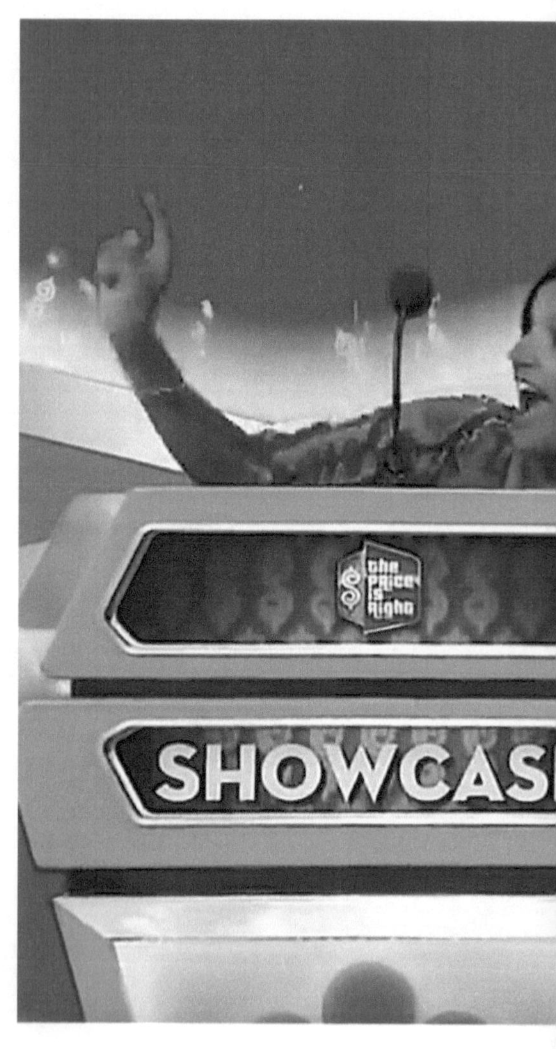

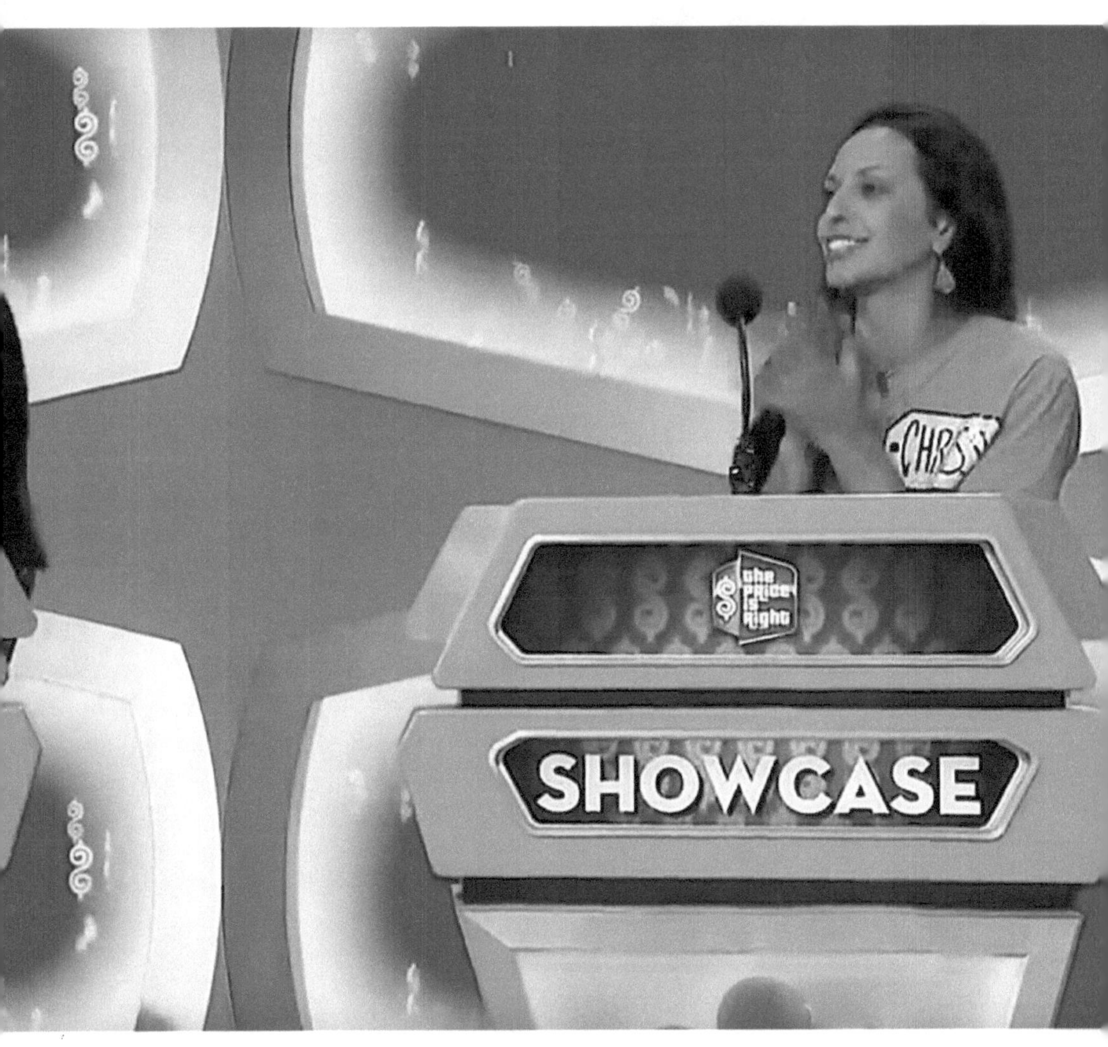

49

Cozu-
mel

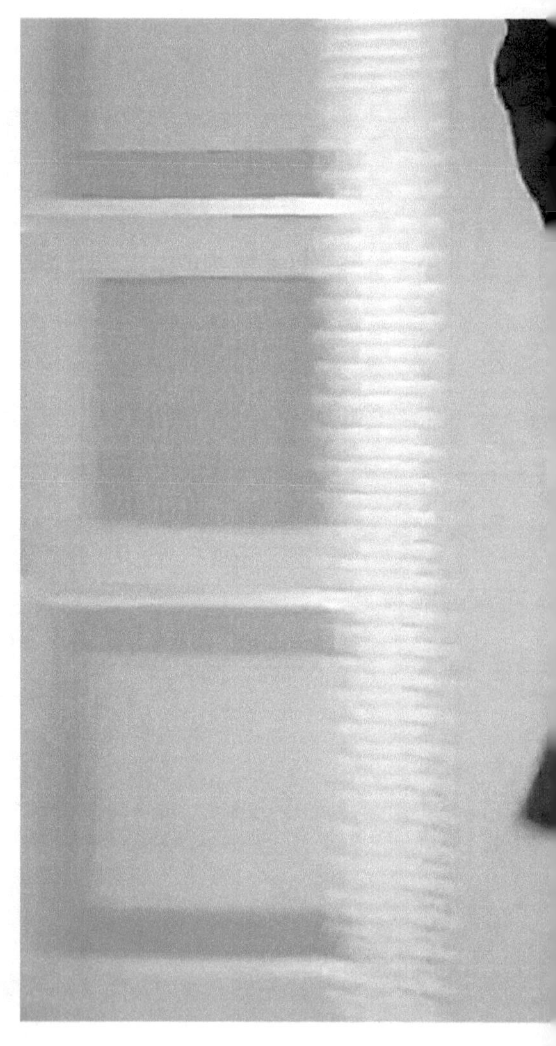

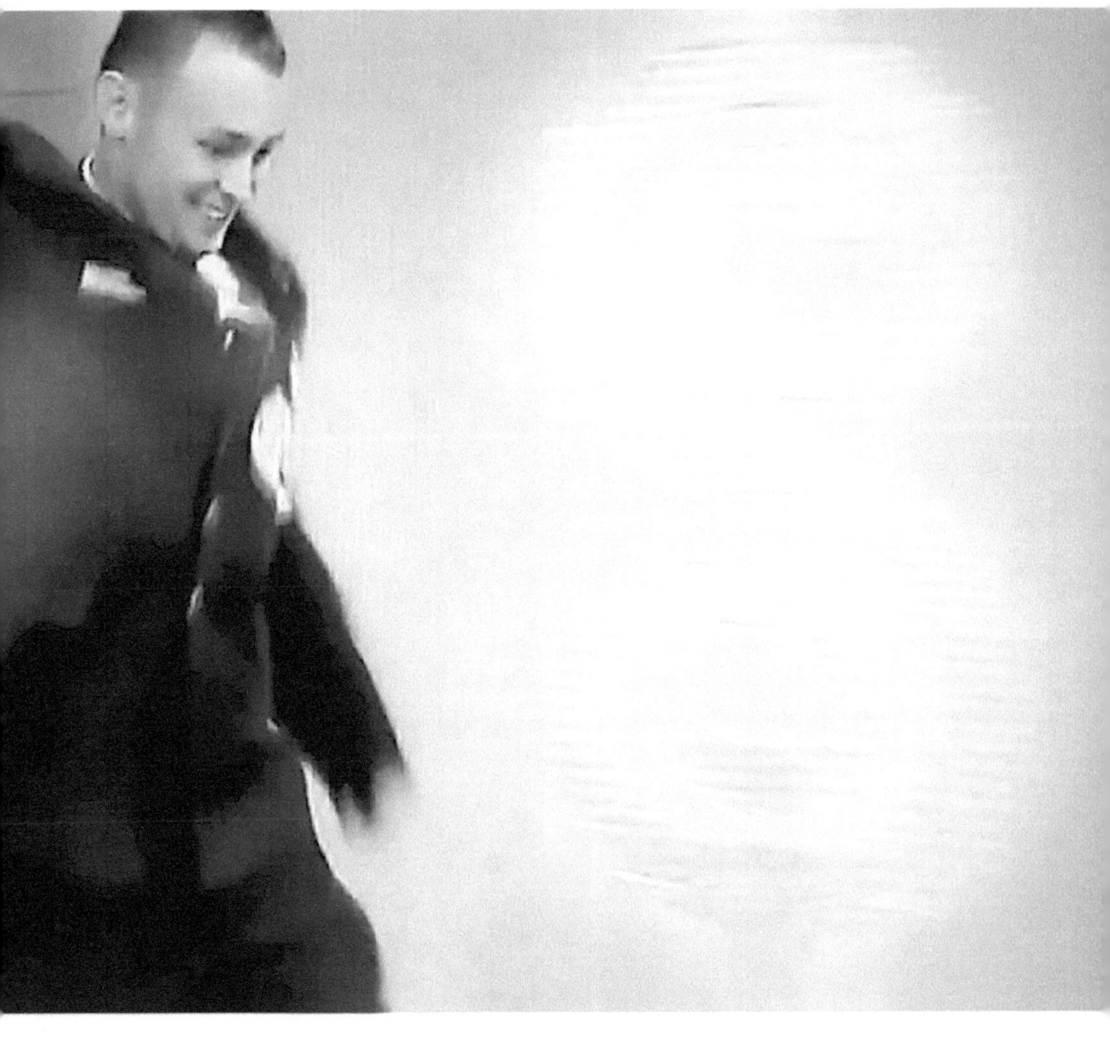

Croa-
tia

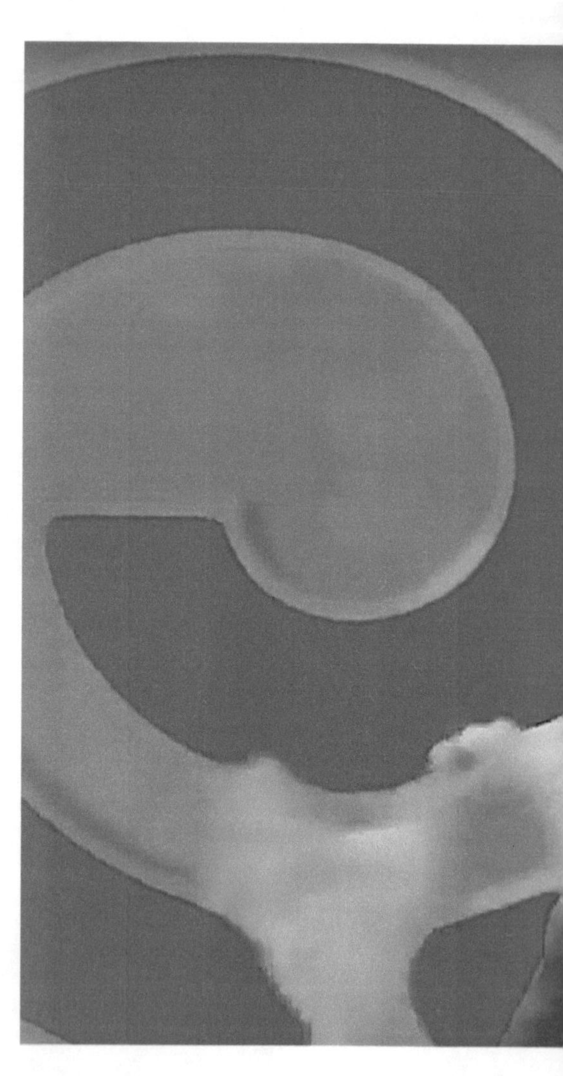

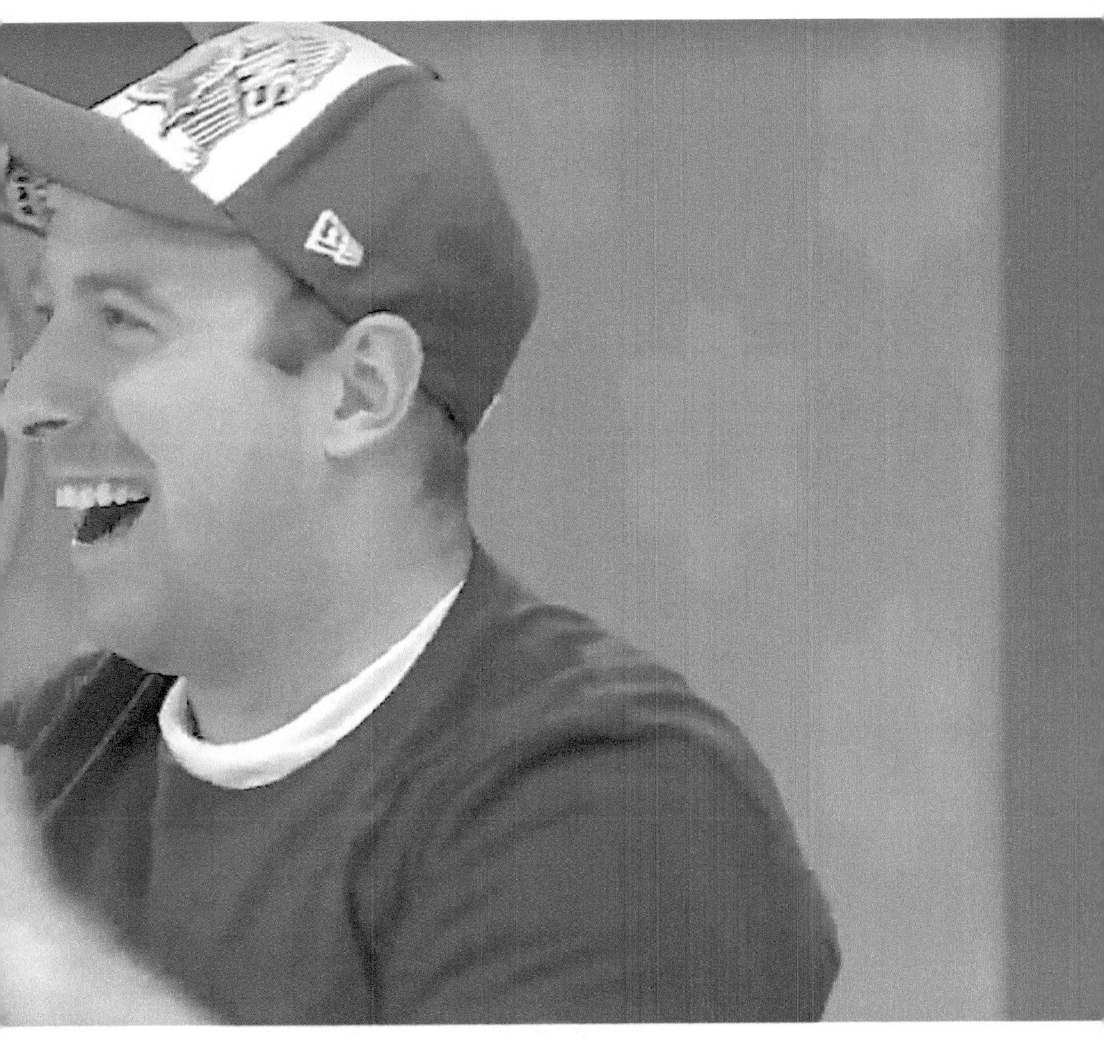

Florida

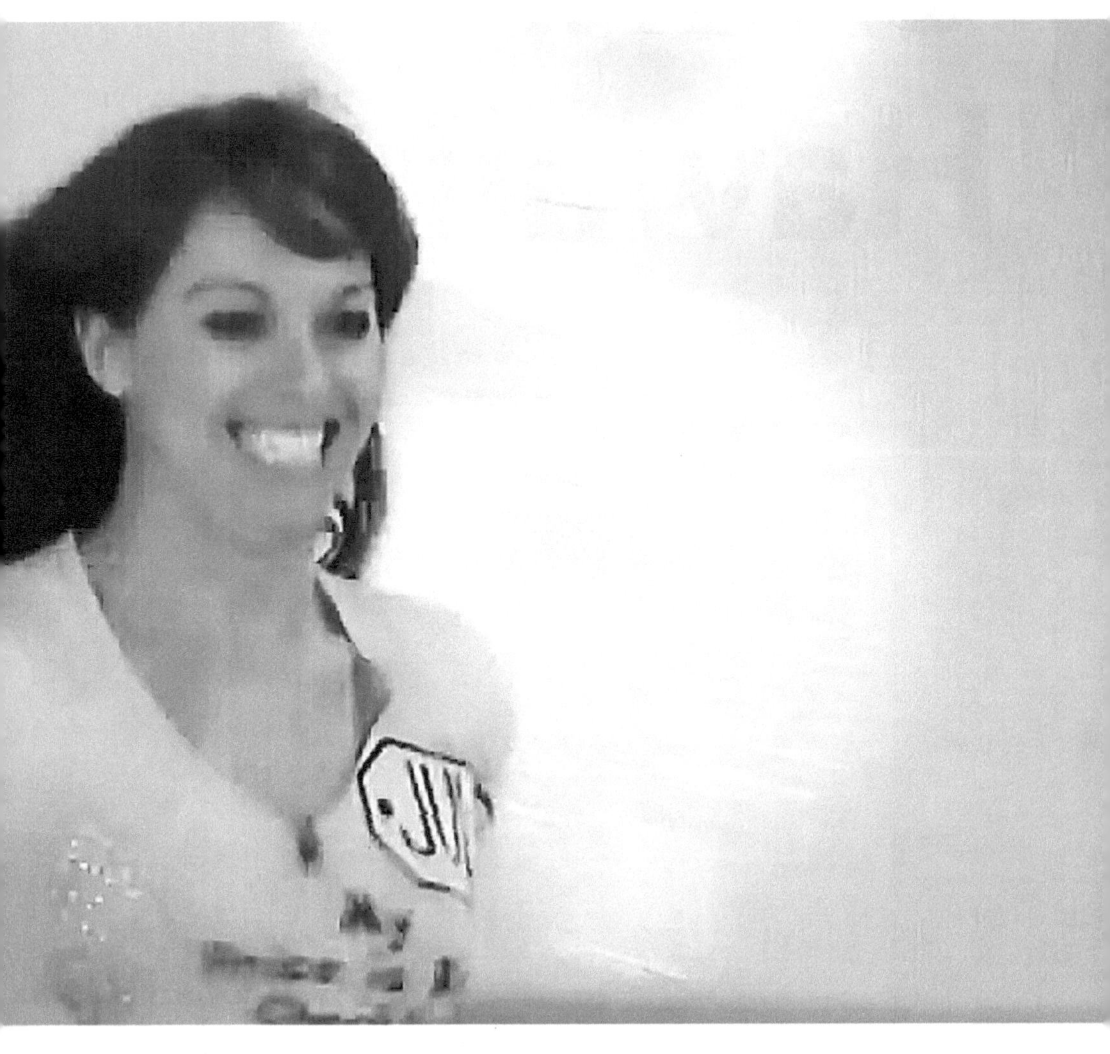

France/
Utah/
Hawaii

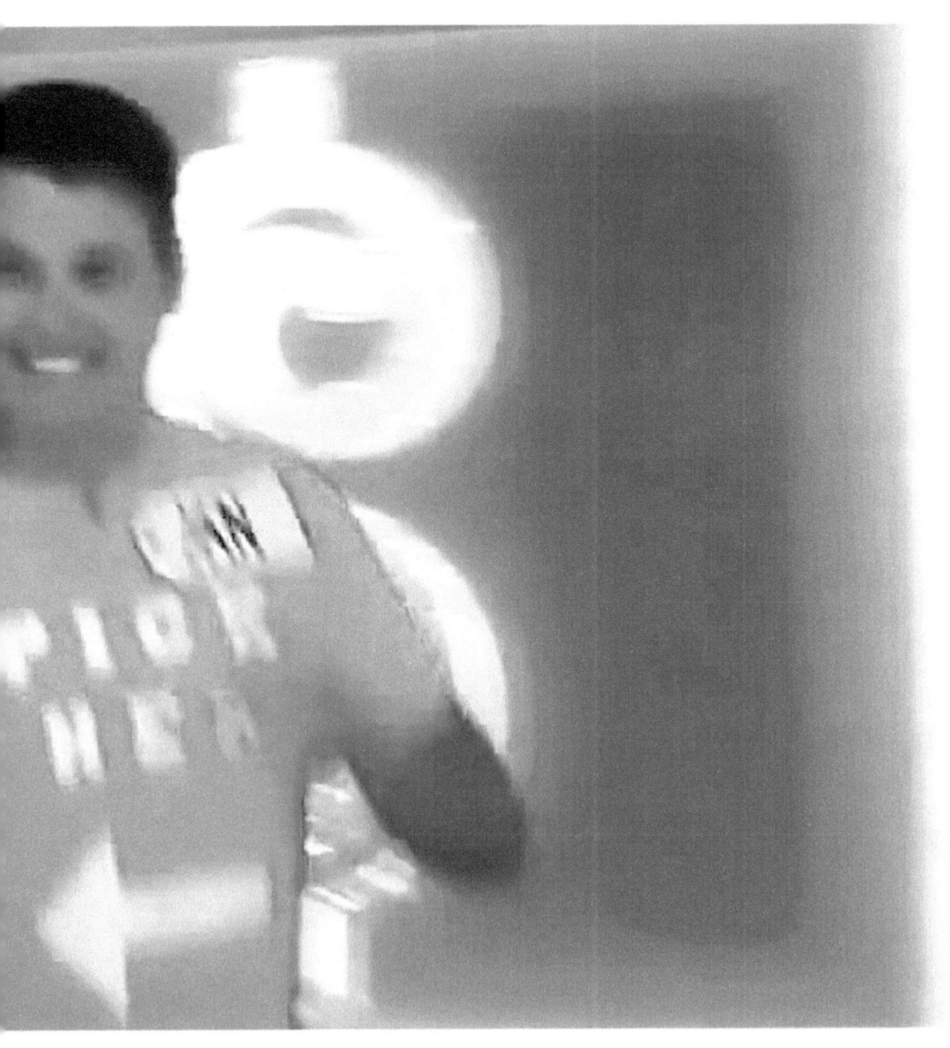

Grand Canyon/ Greece/ Dubai

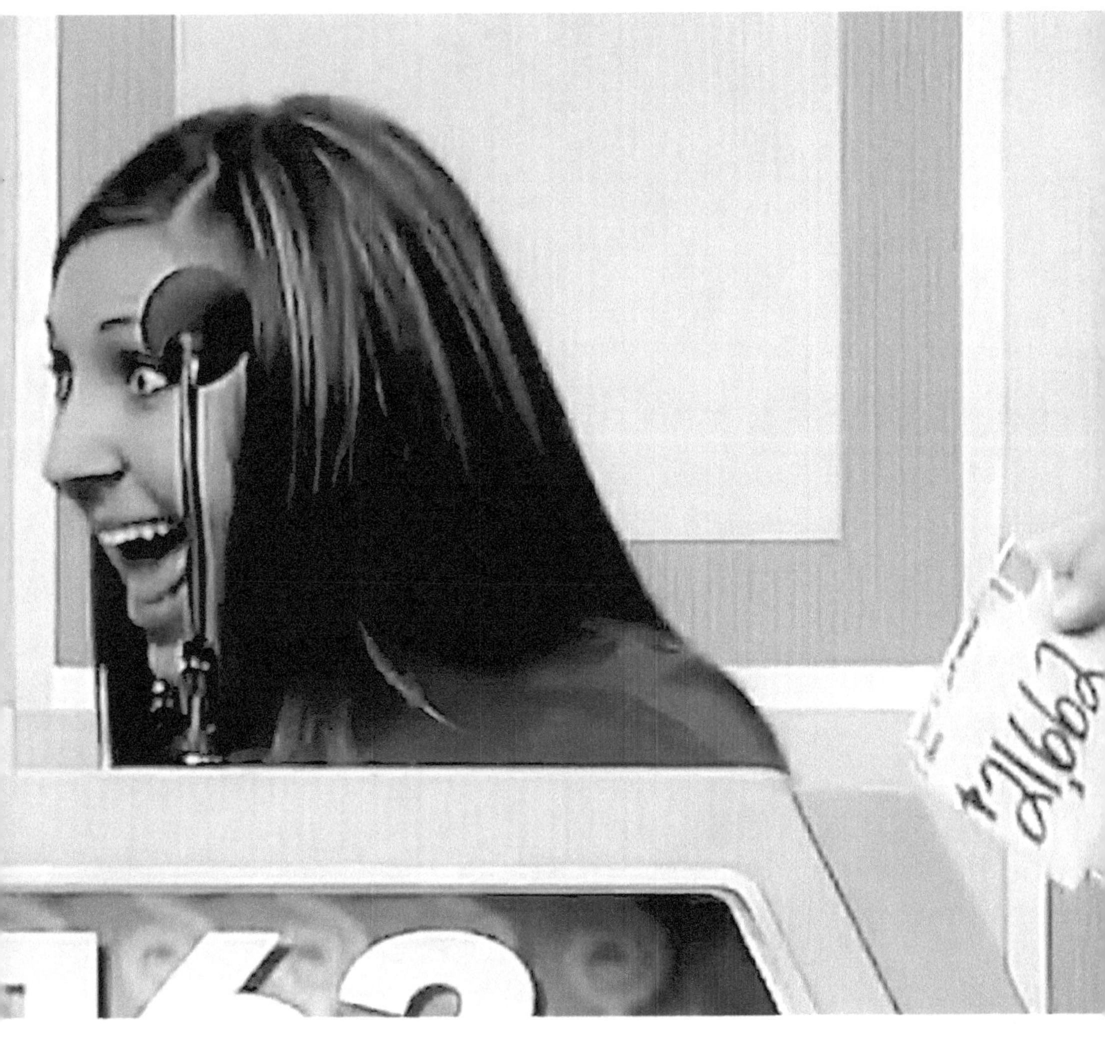

Grena-
dines

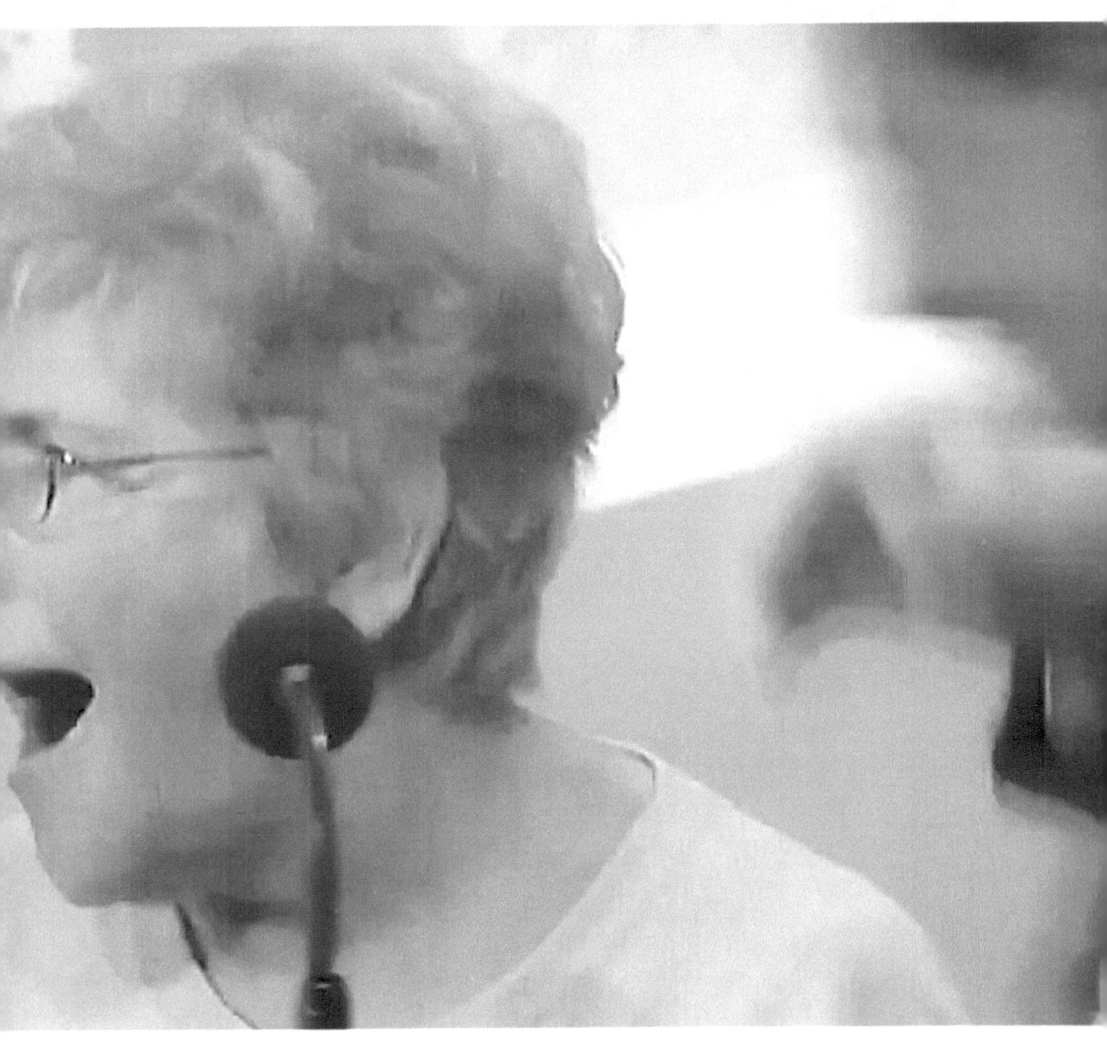

Hamp-
tons

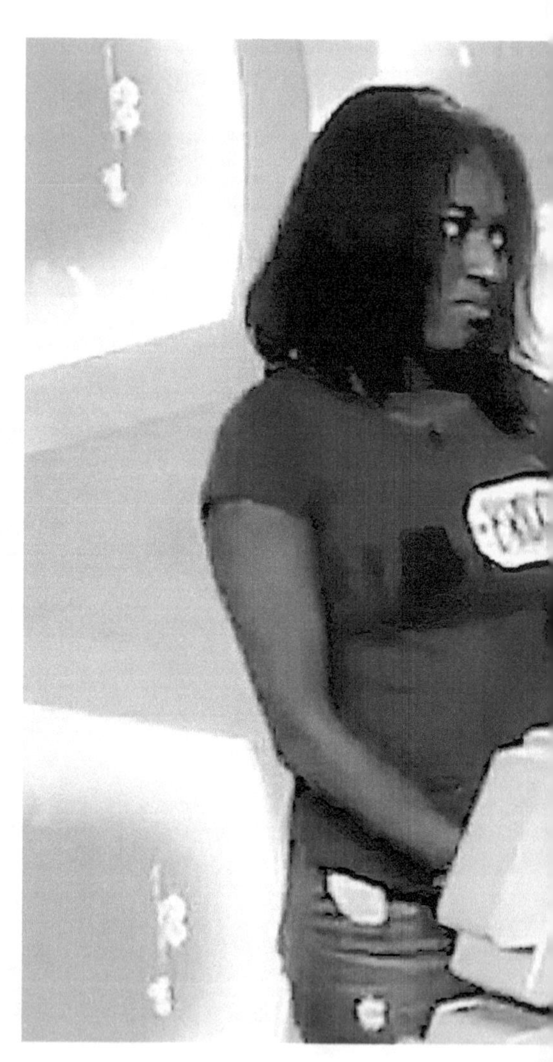

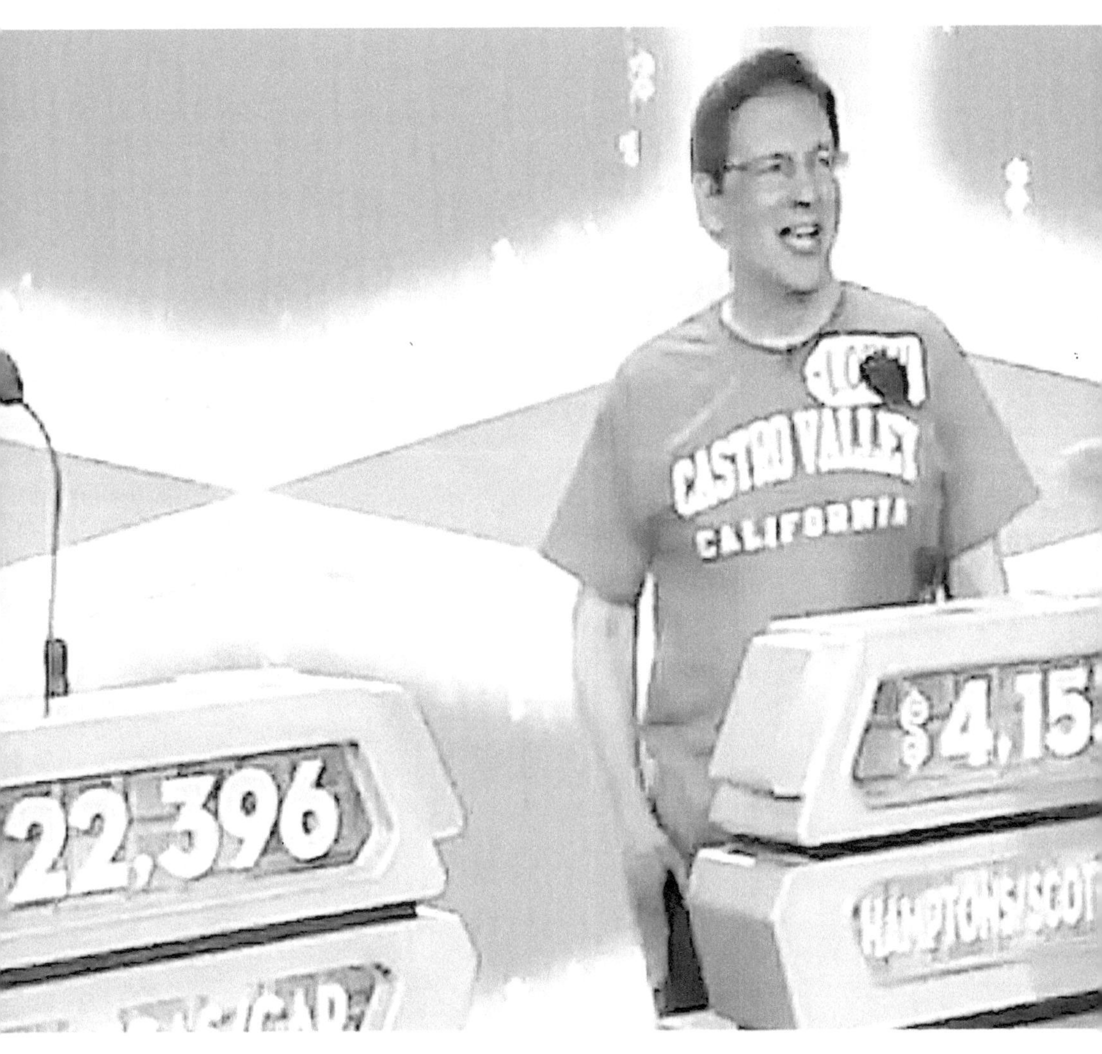

63

Hamp-
tons

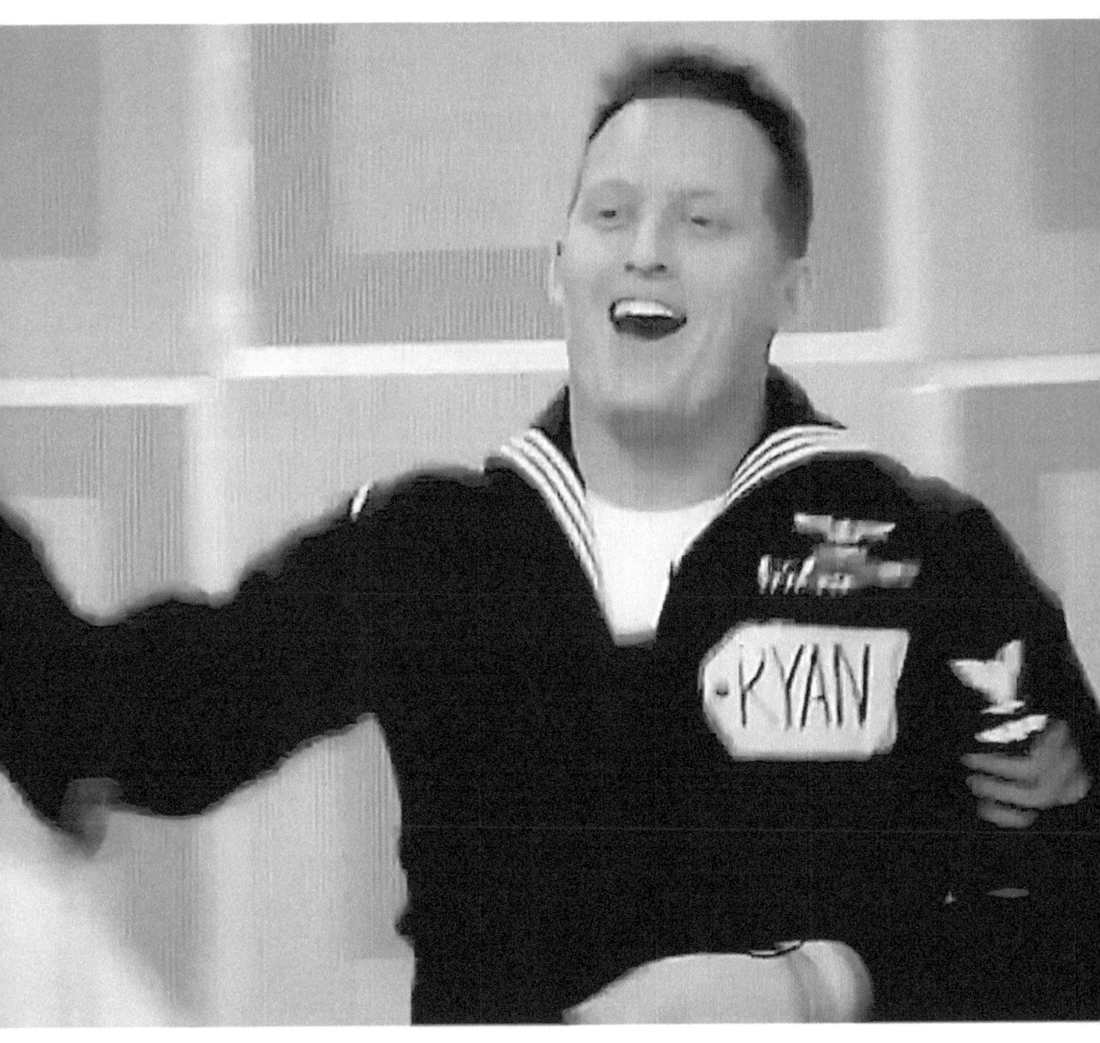
RYAN

Hawaii

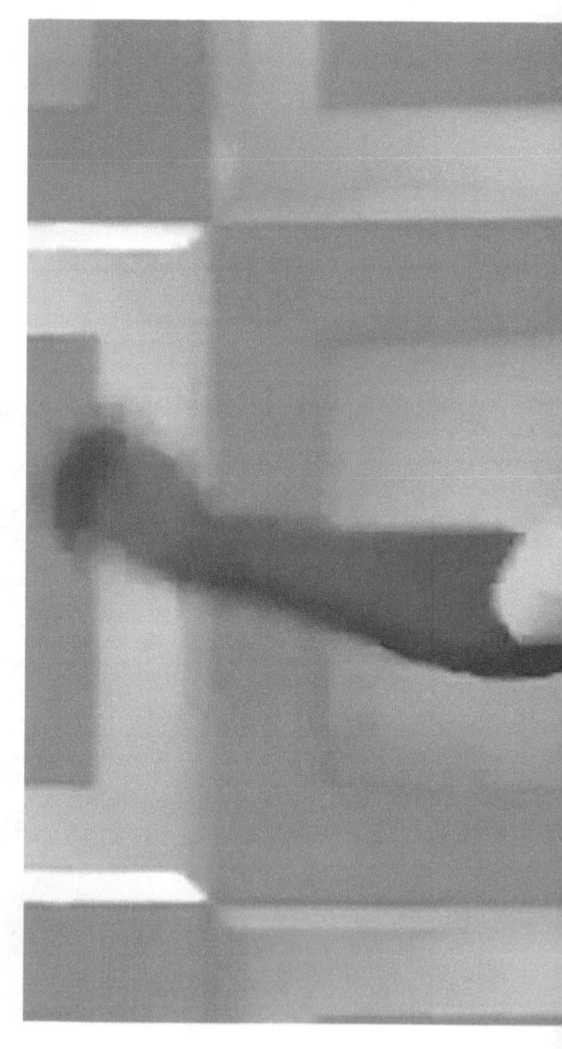

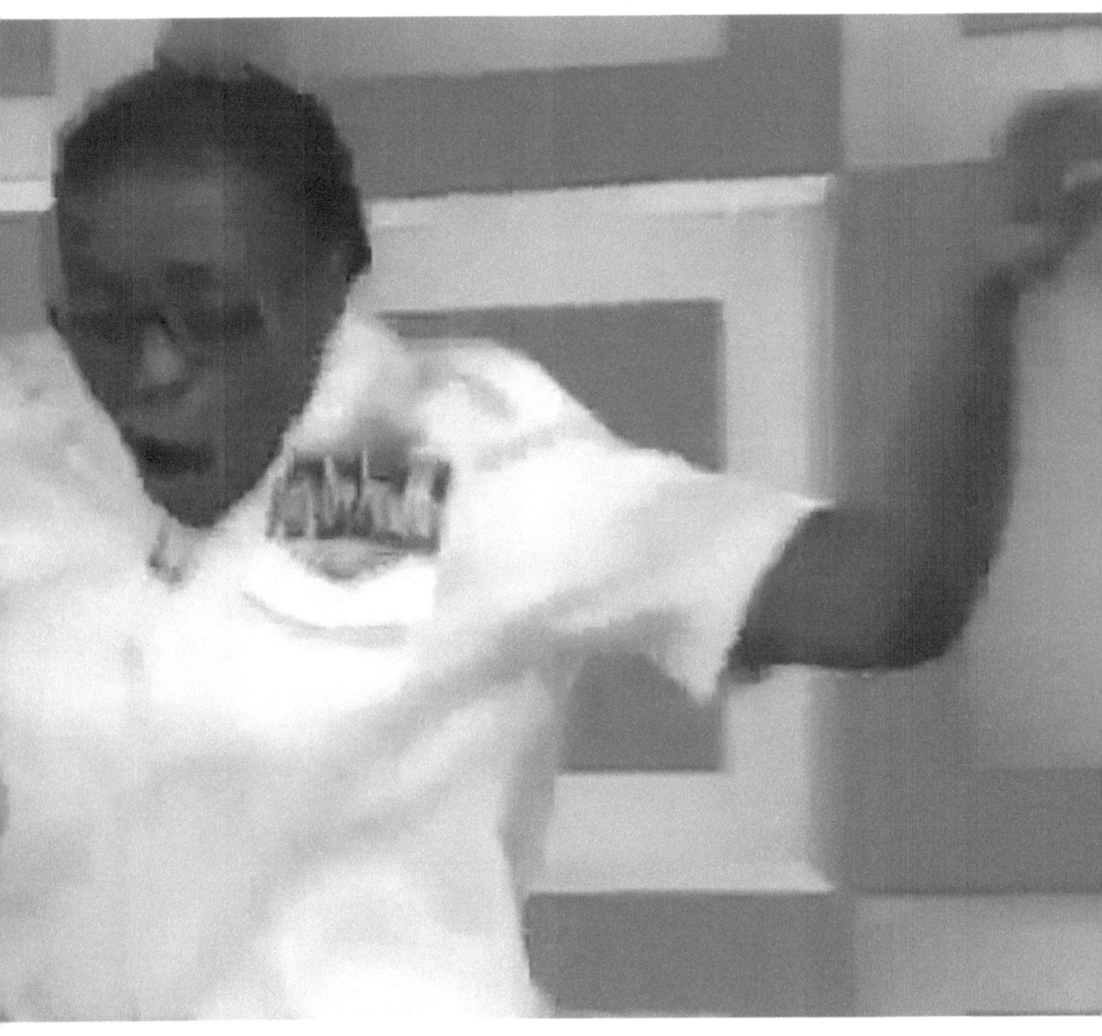

Hawaii

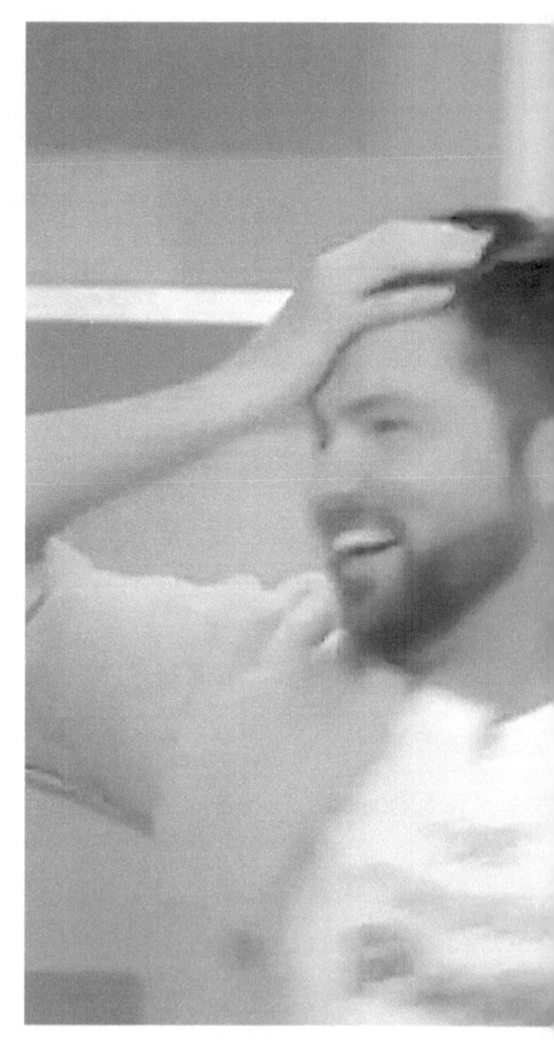

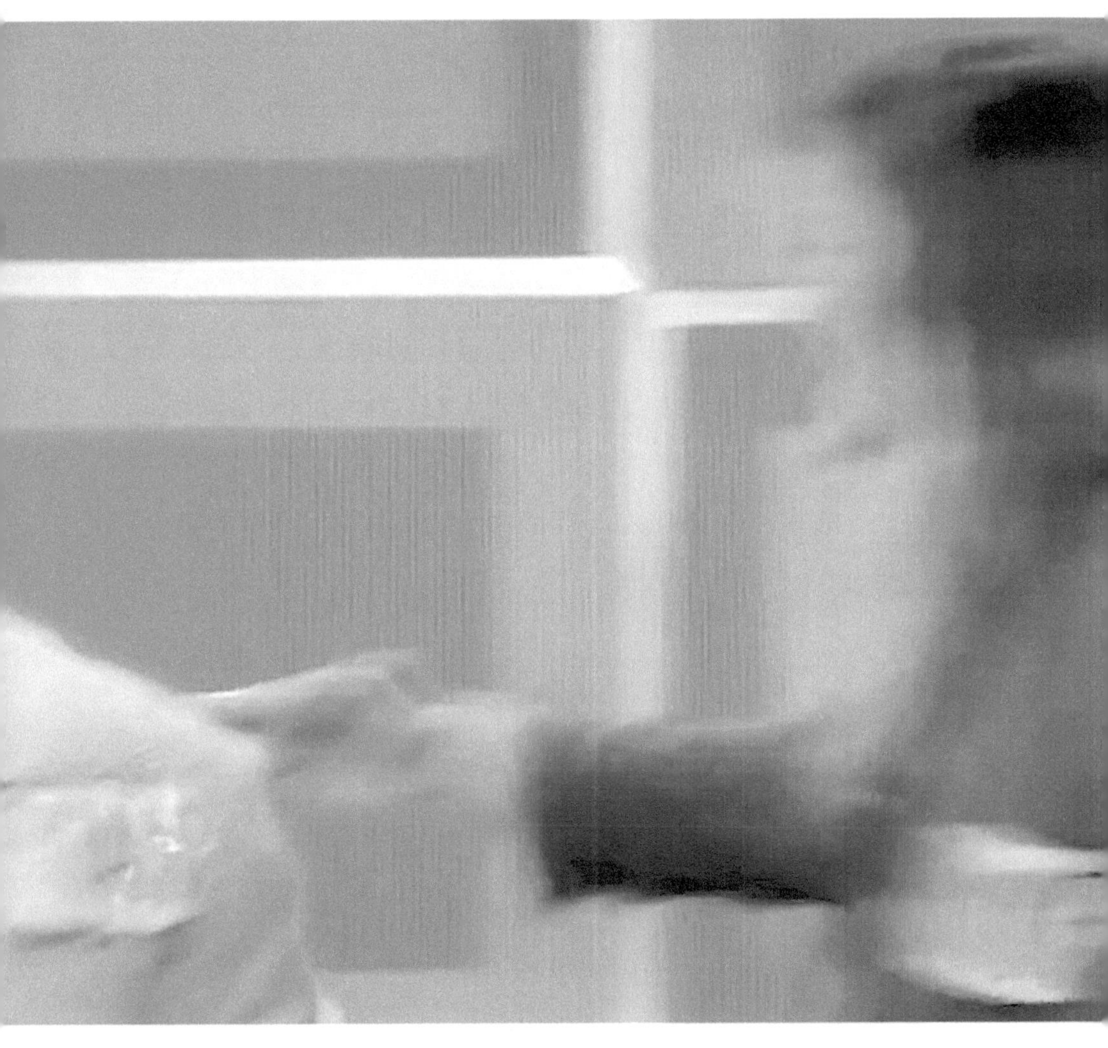

Hawaii

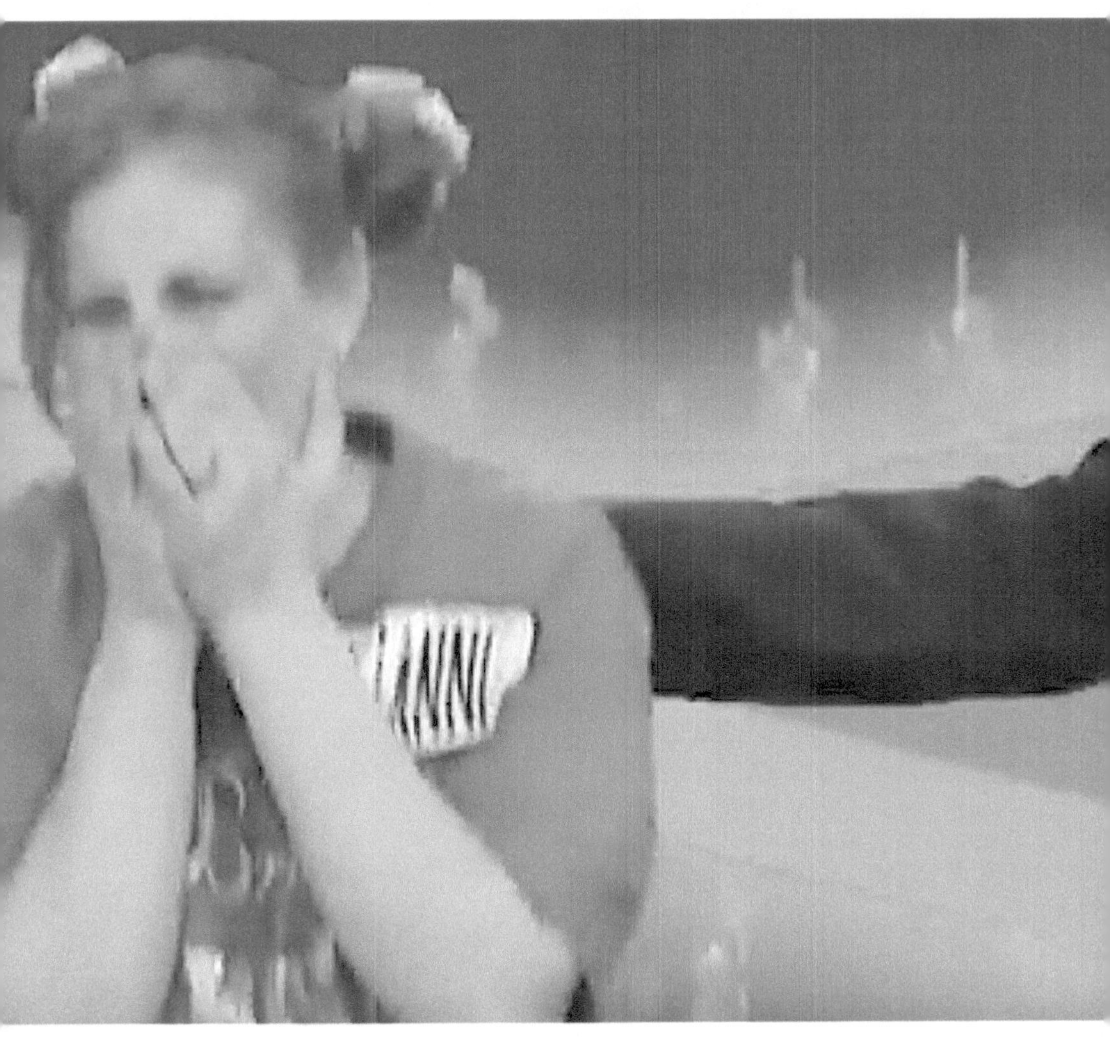

Hong Kong

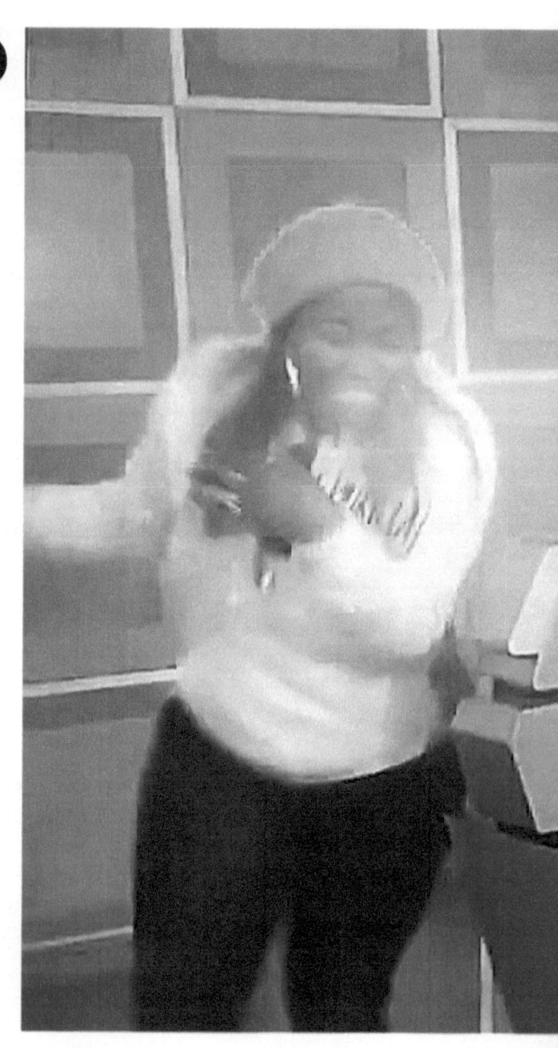

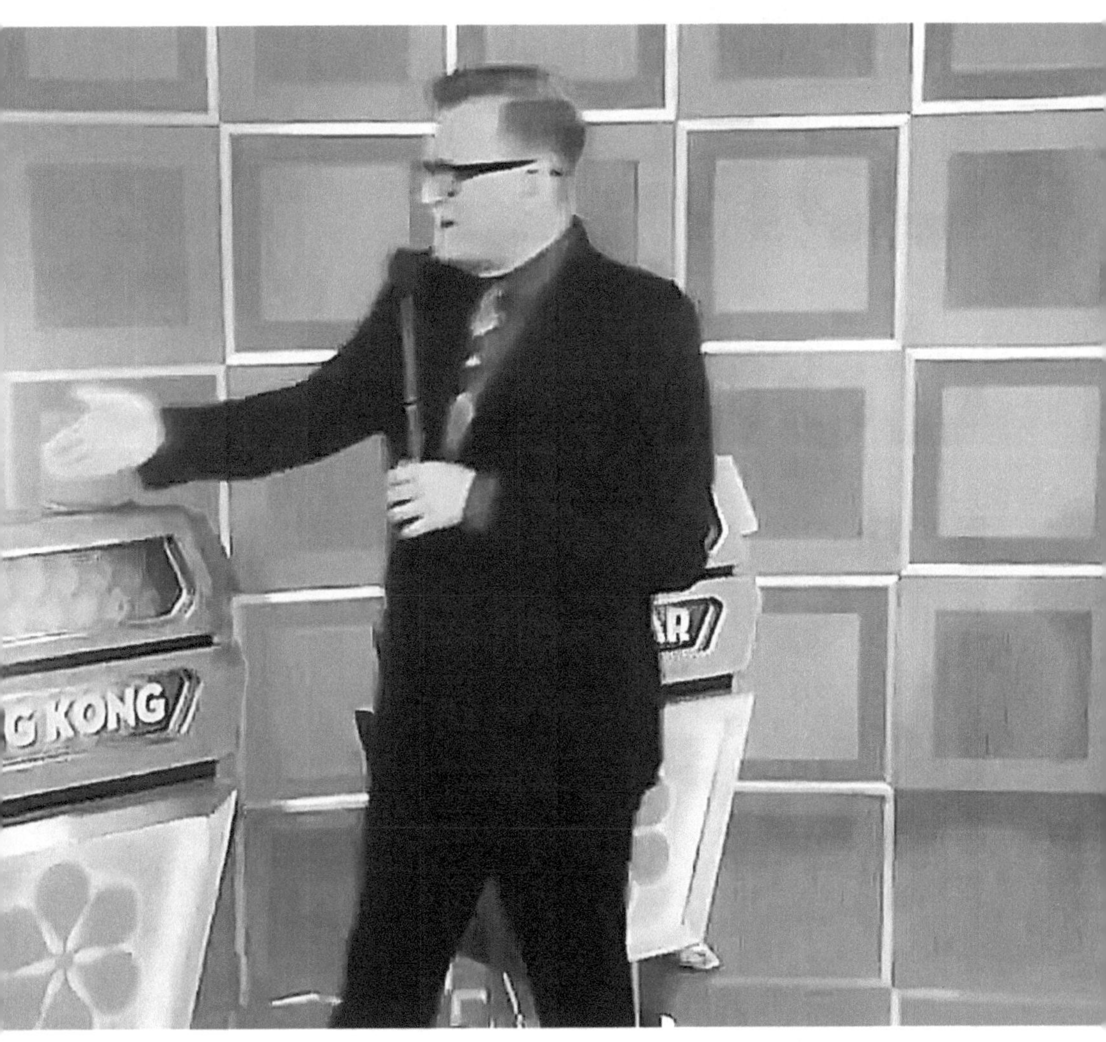

G KONG
AR

Houston/ London/ Hong Kong

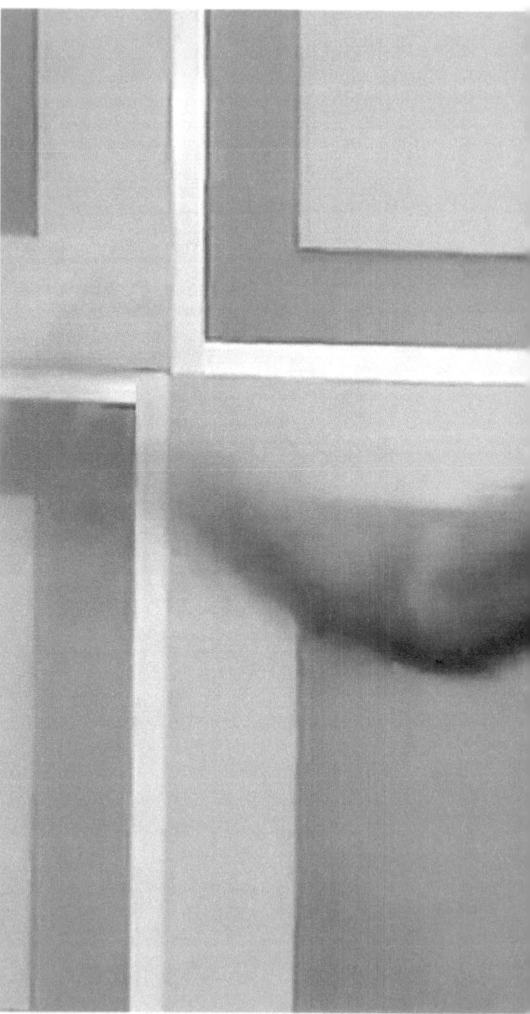

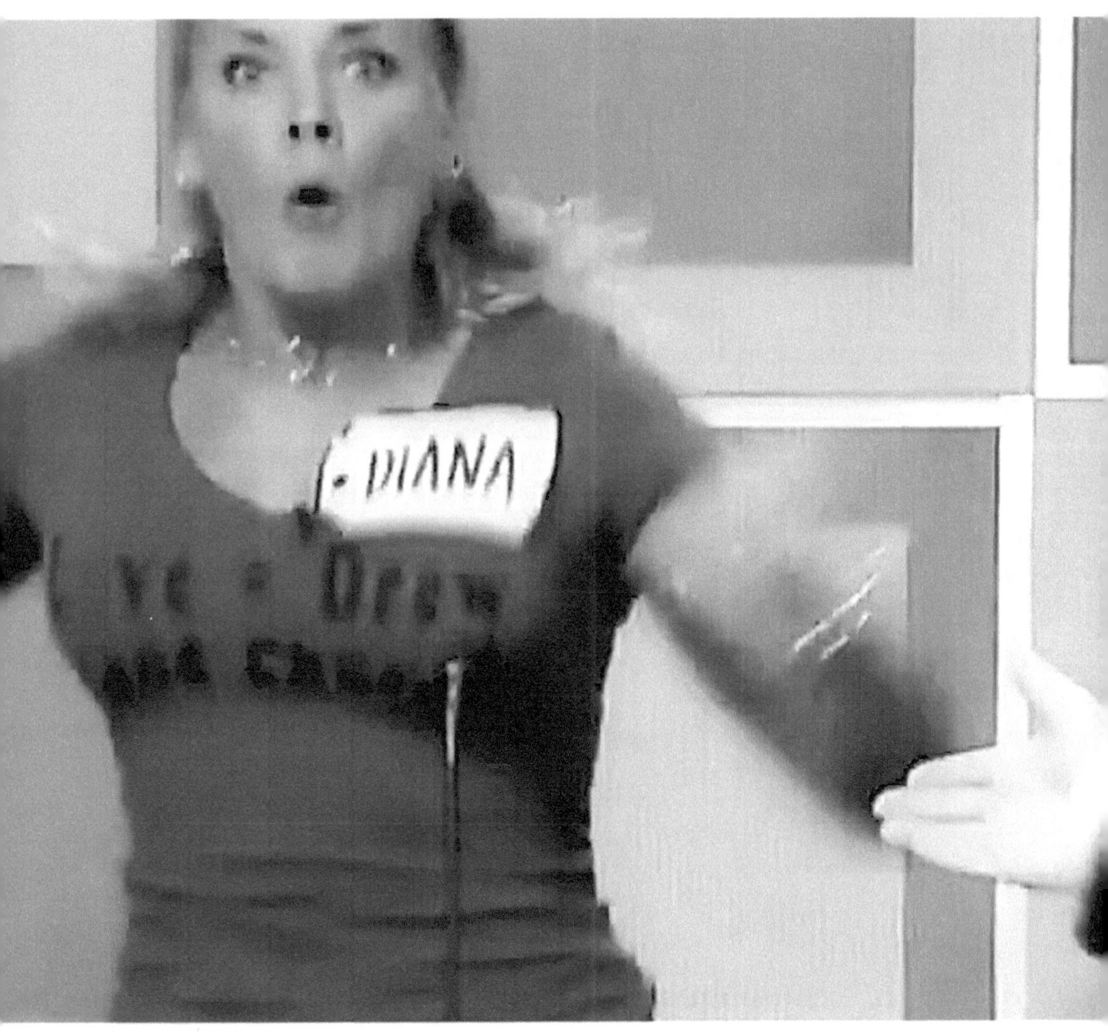

DIANA

Idaho

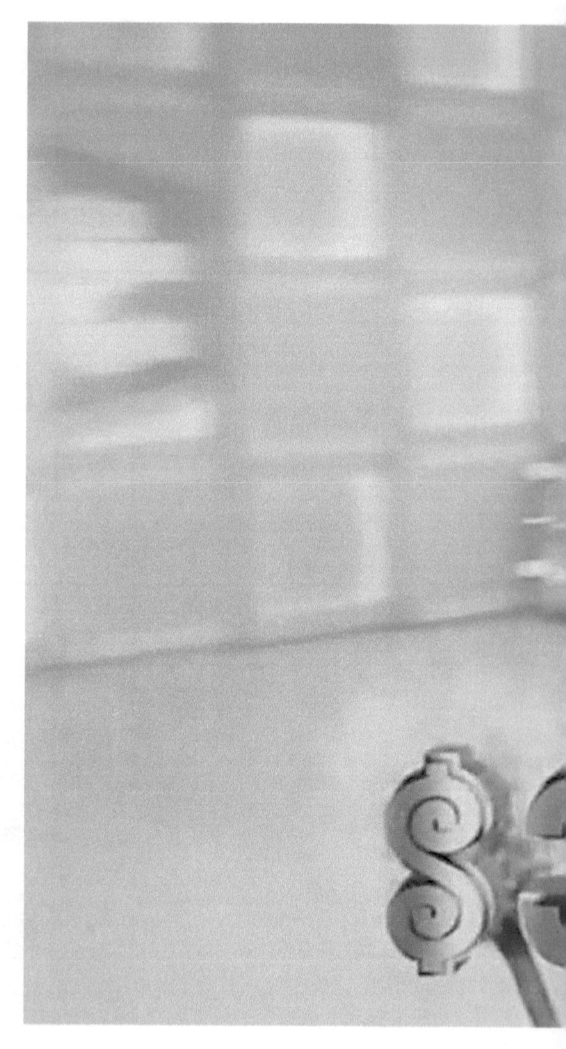

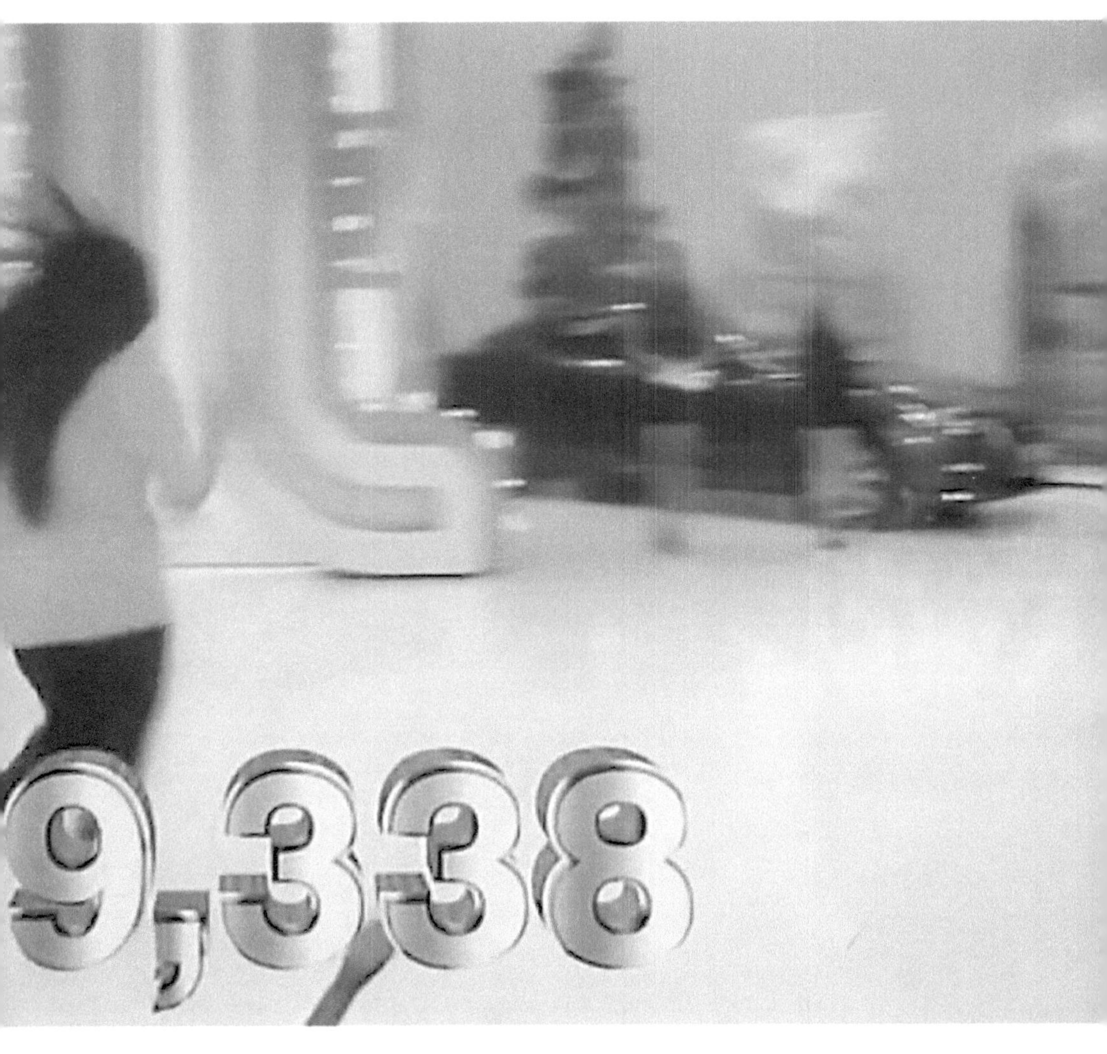
9,338

Italy

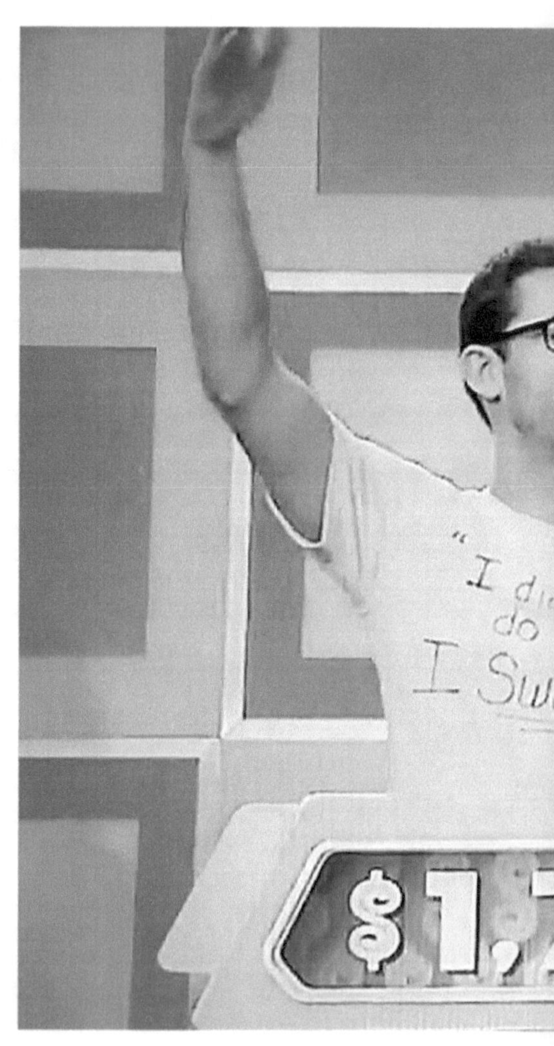

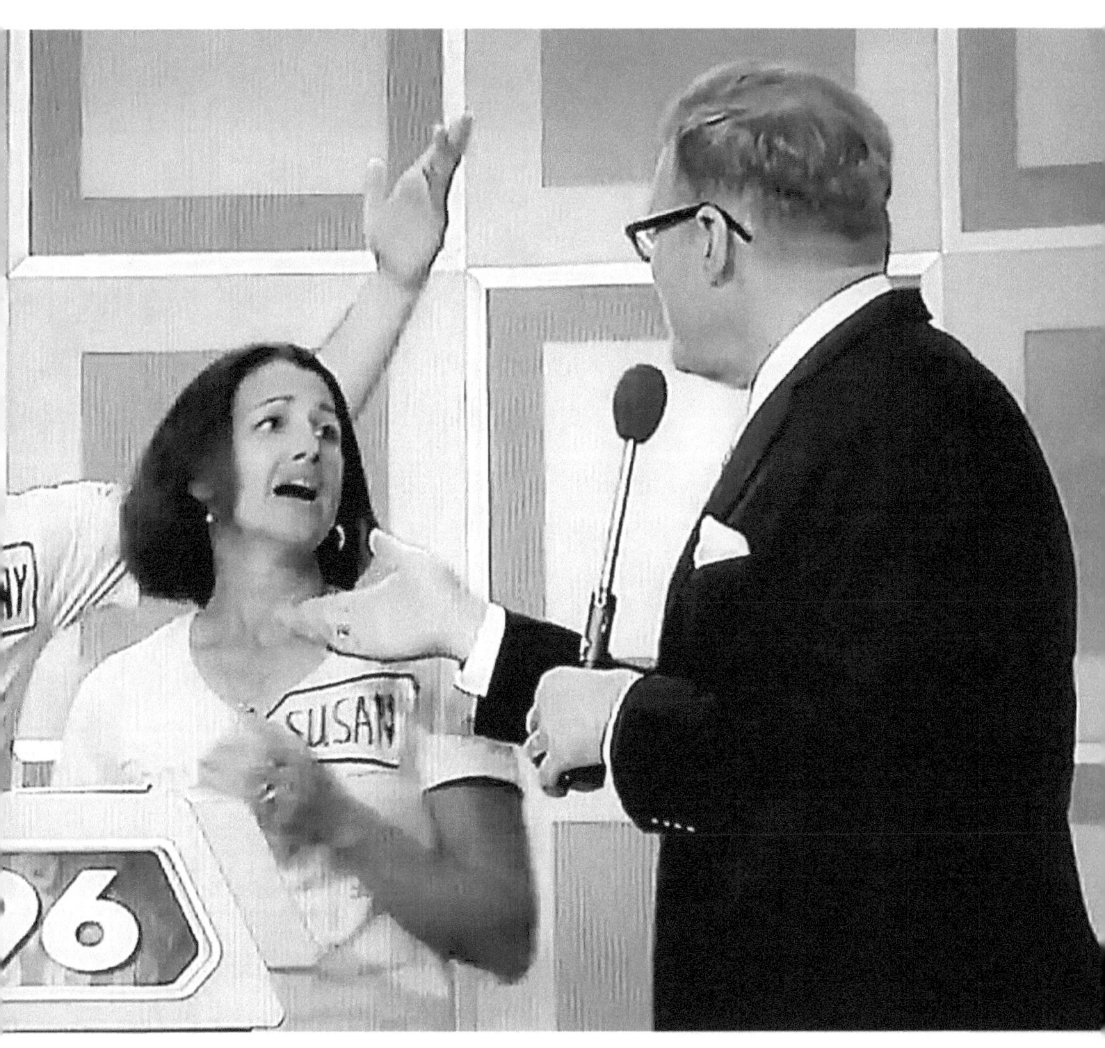

SUSAN
96

Ixtapa

the
PRICE
$5
AR
EDUCA KAKEN
NEED
FIELD TRIPS
TOO!
the
Price
is
Right
SHOWC

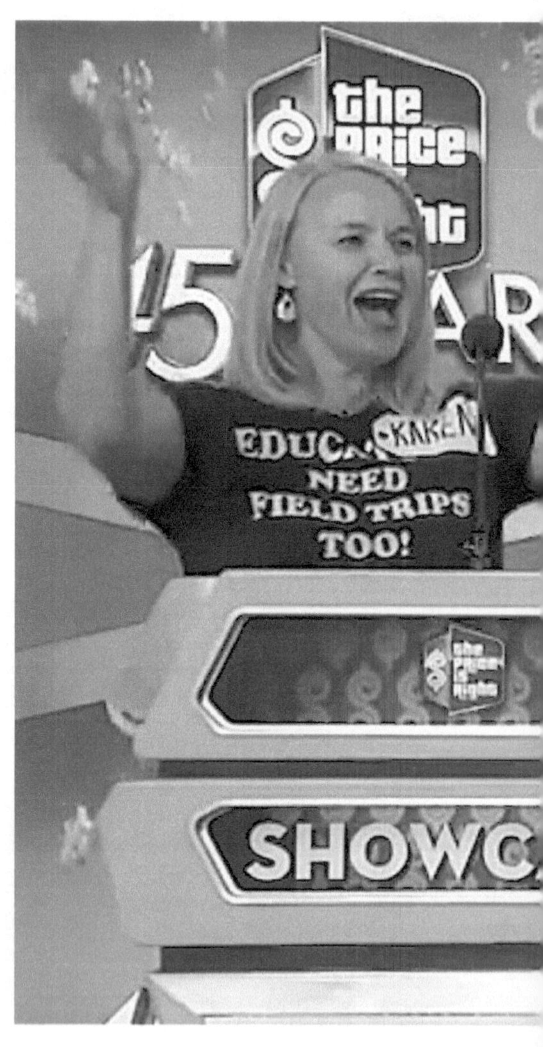

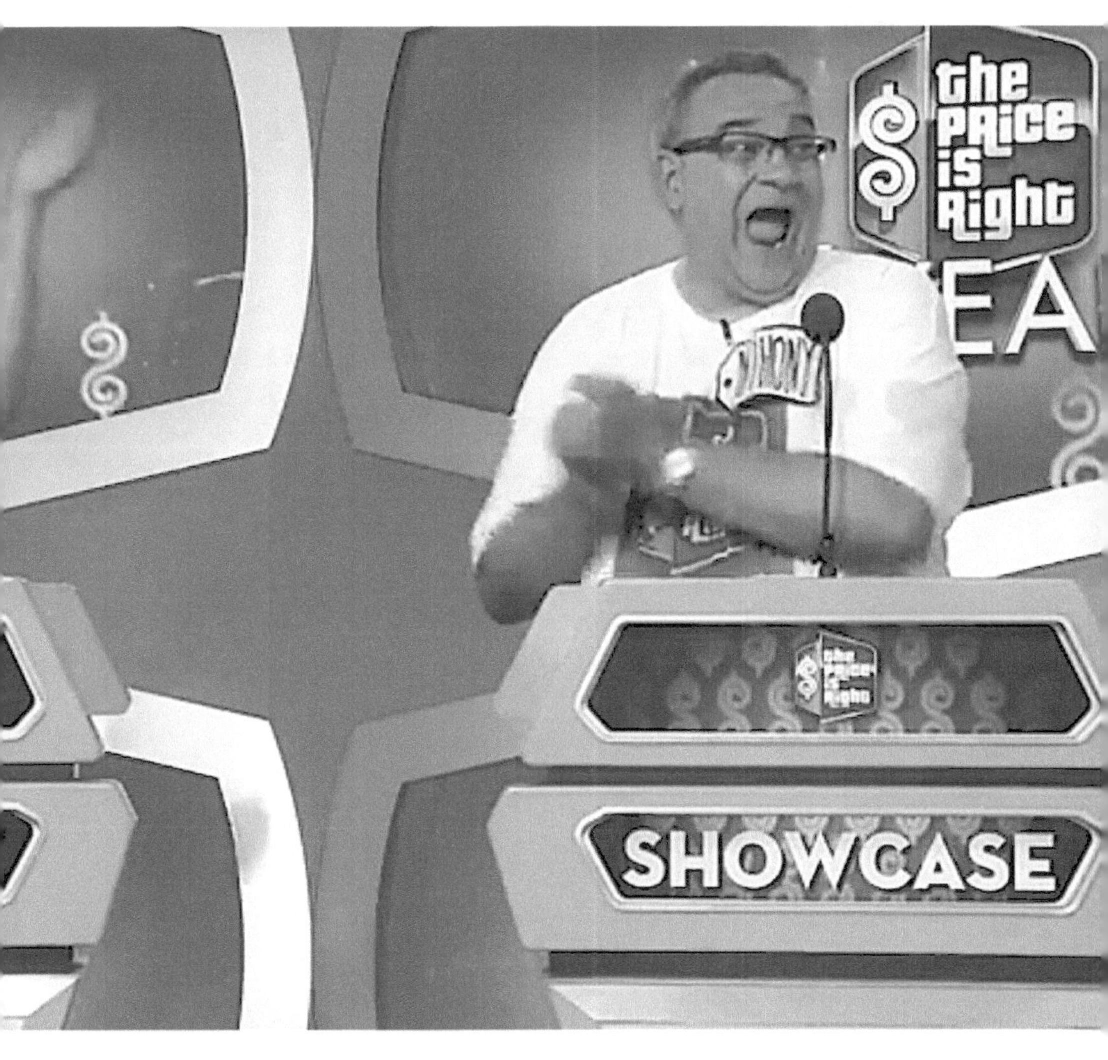

the PRICE is RIGHT
EA
SHOWCASE

Las Vegas

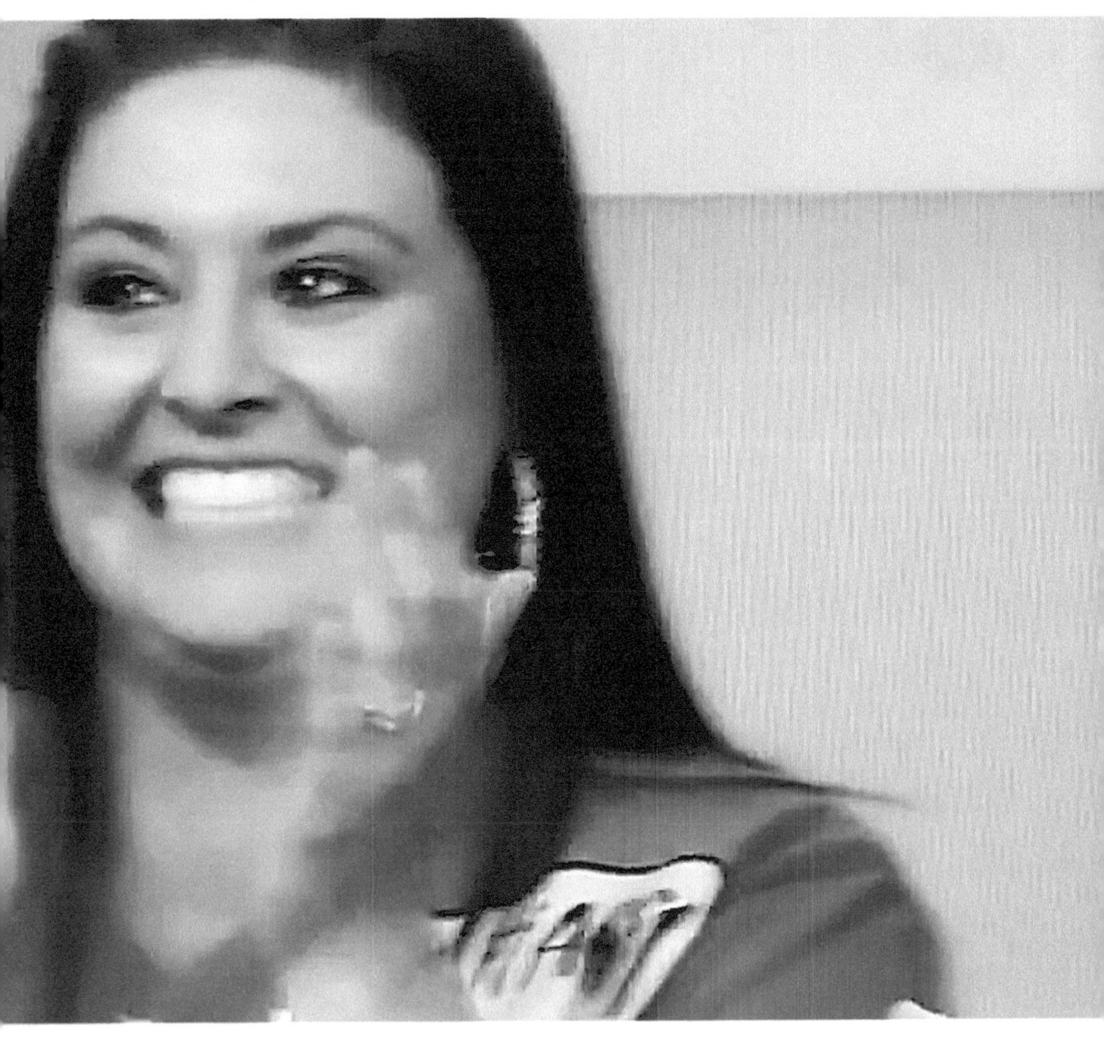

Las Ve-gas

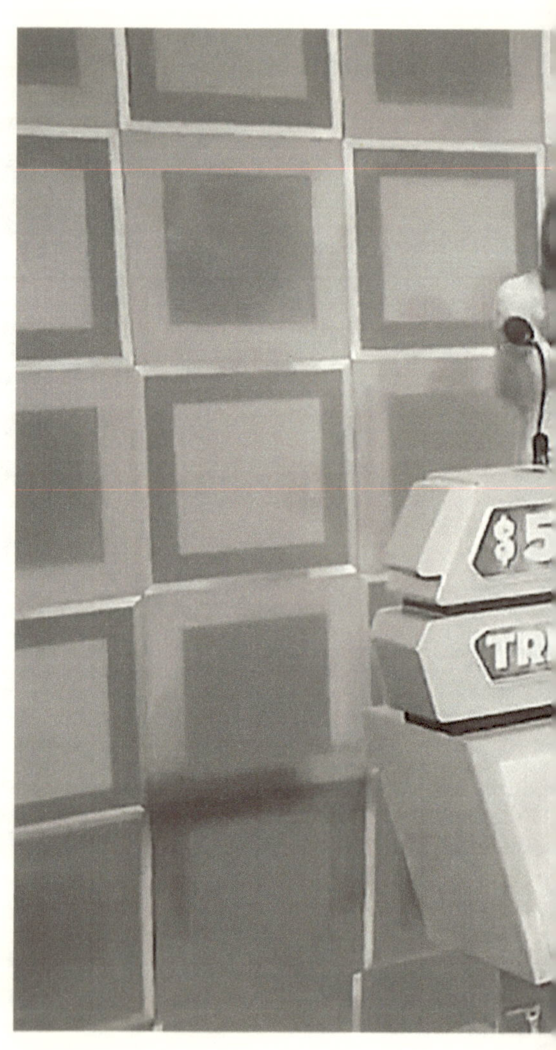

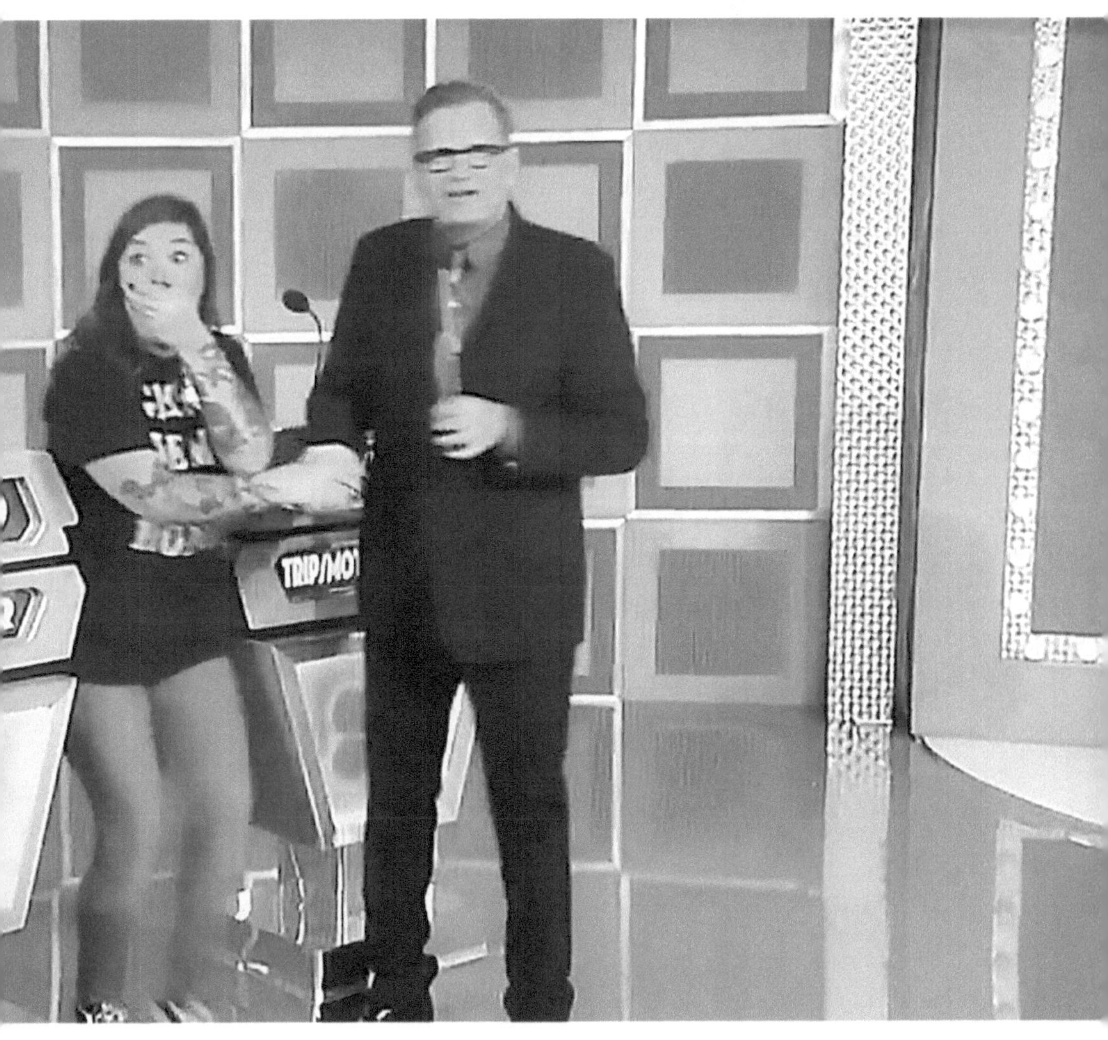

TRIP/MOT

Las Vegas

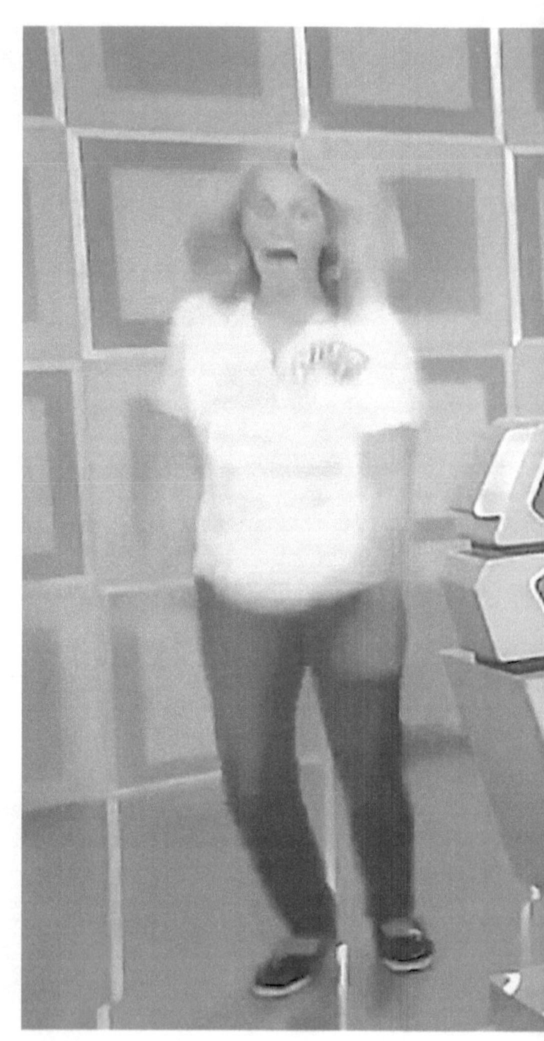

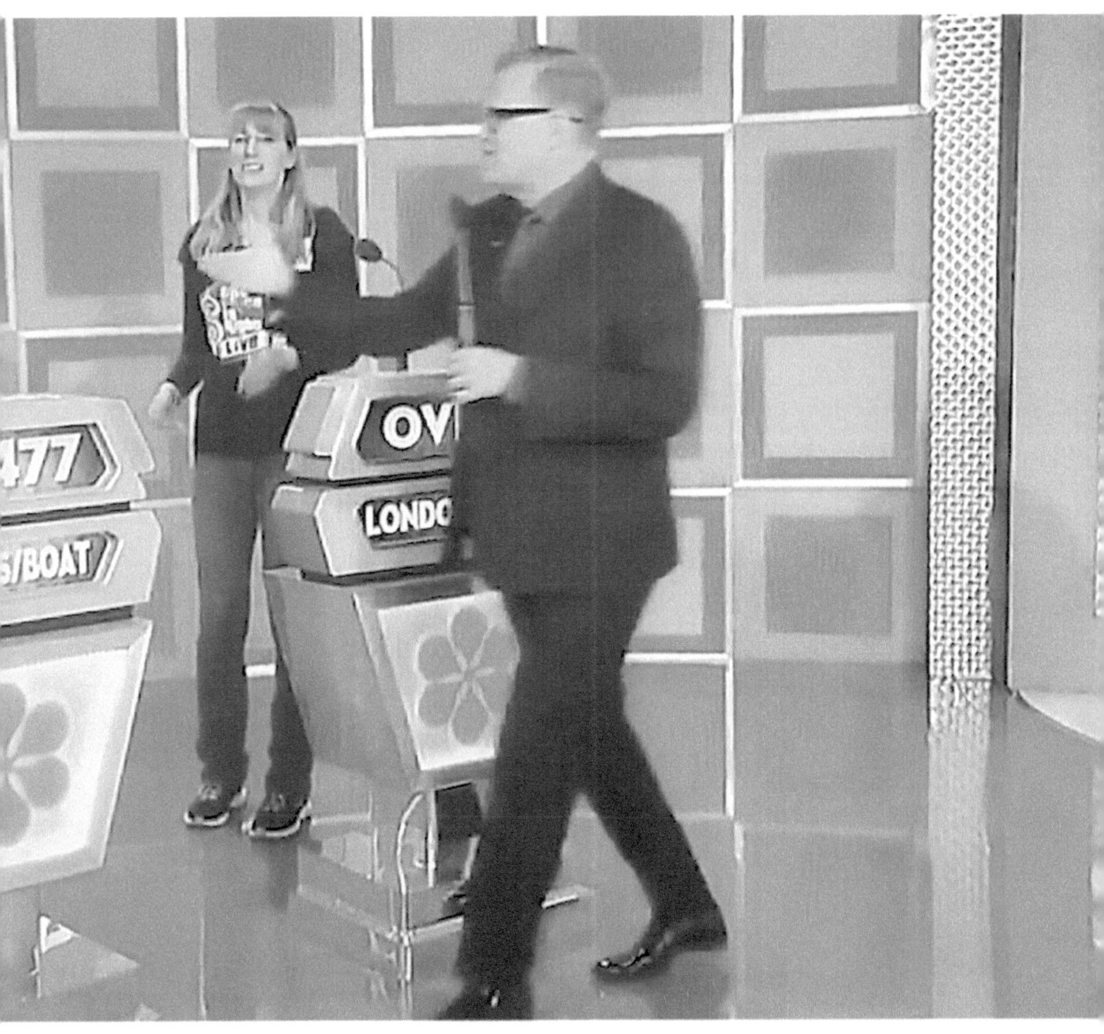

477
S/BOAT
OV
LONDO

Lisbon

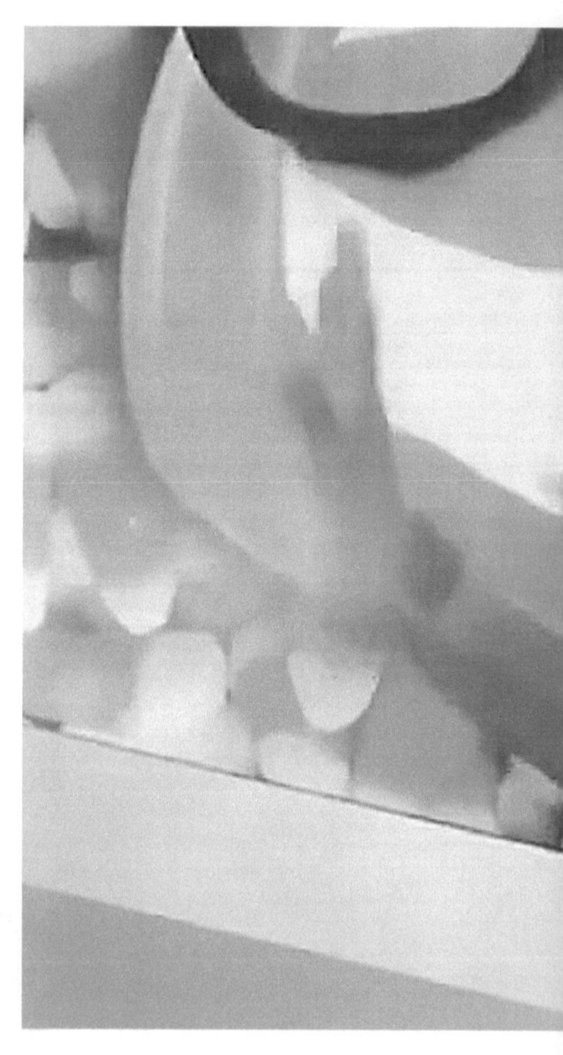

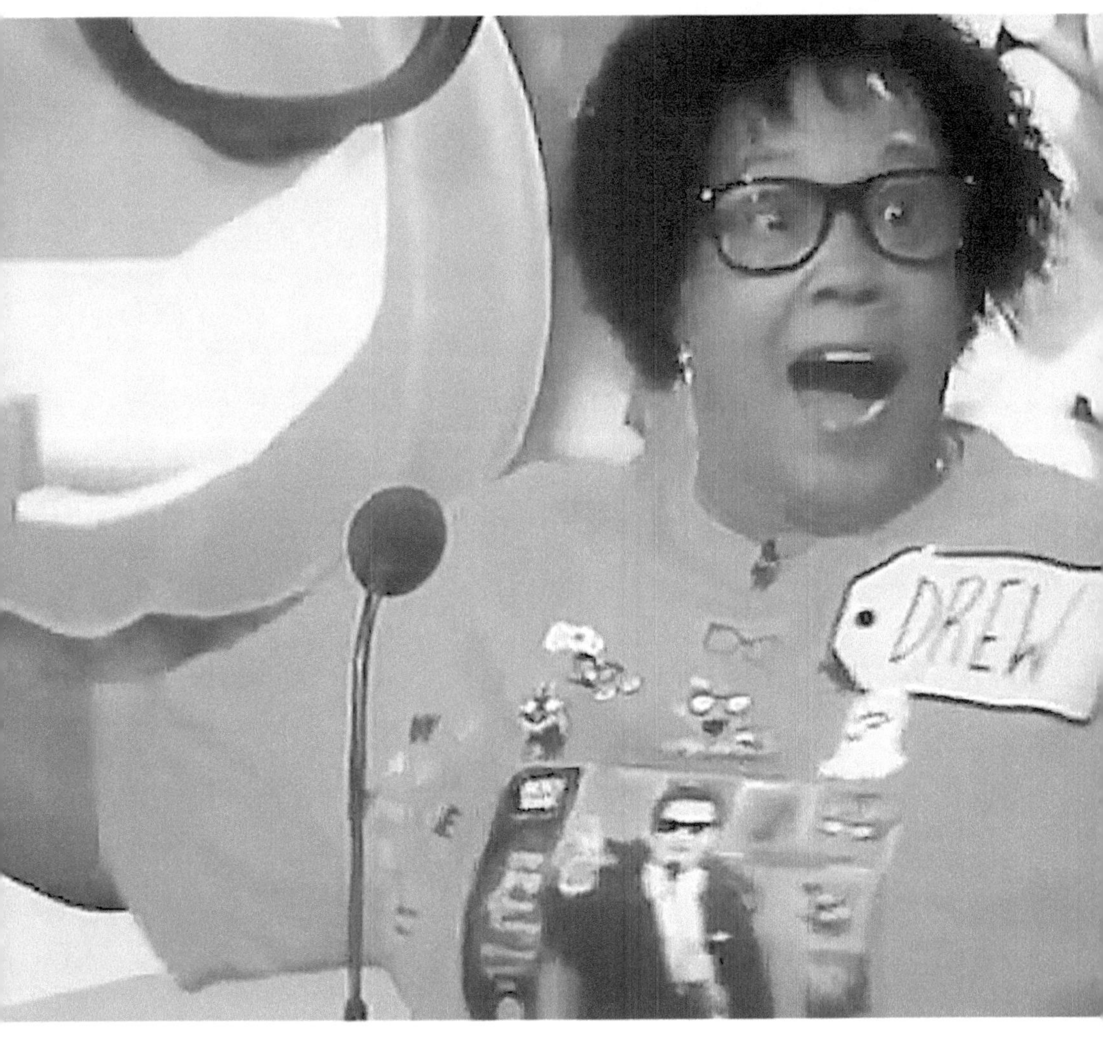
DREW

London

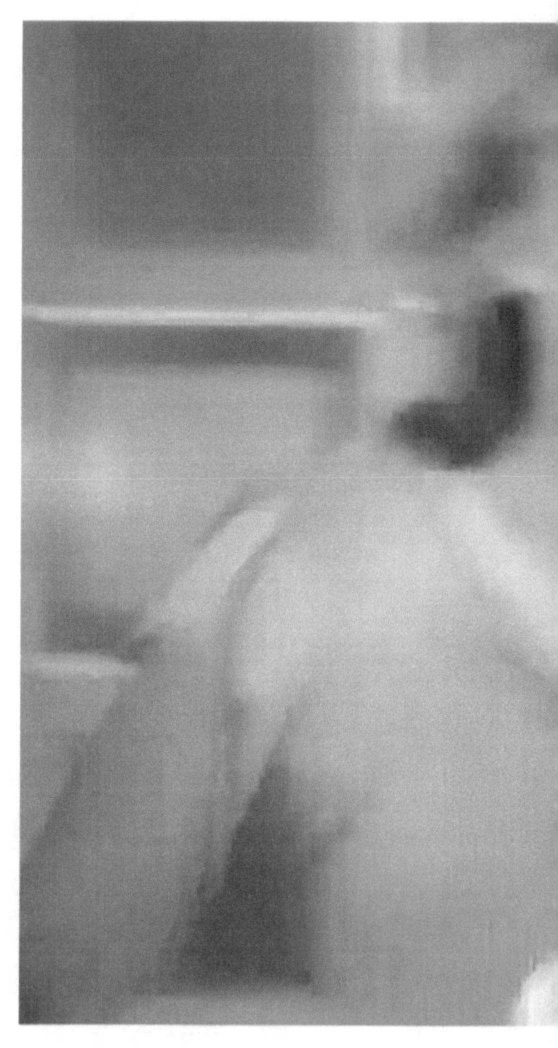

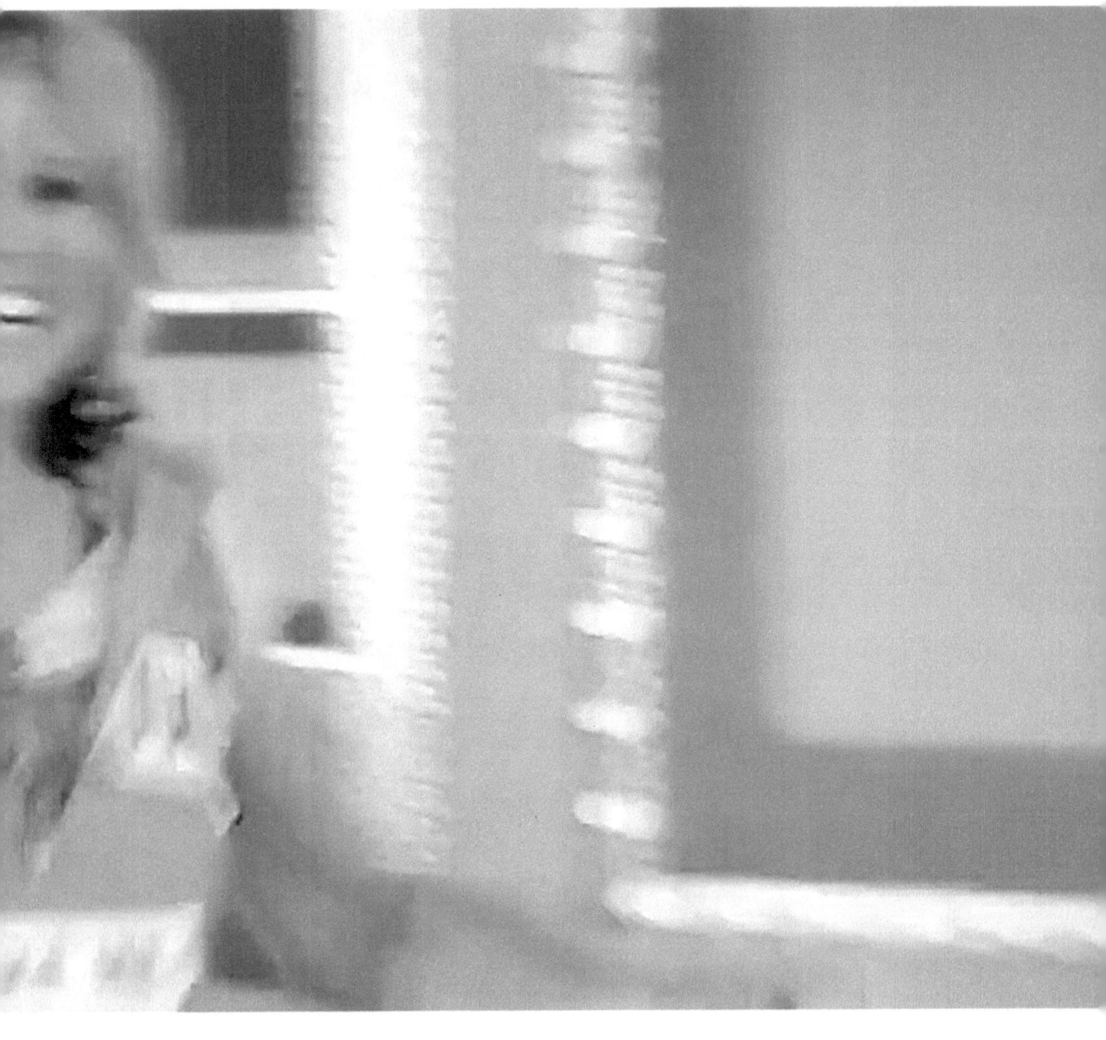

Lon- don

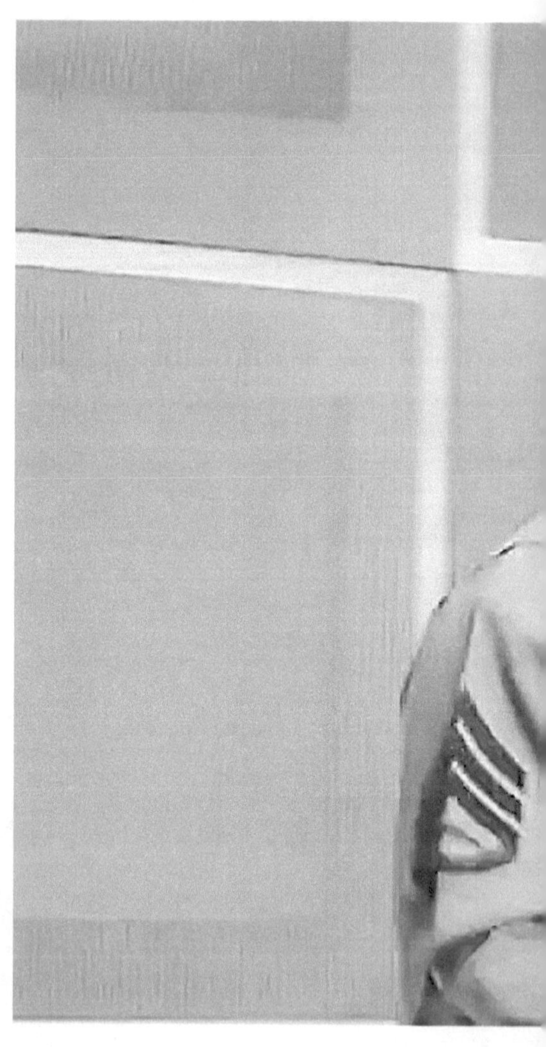

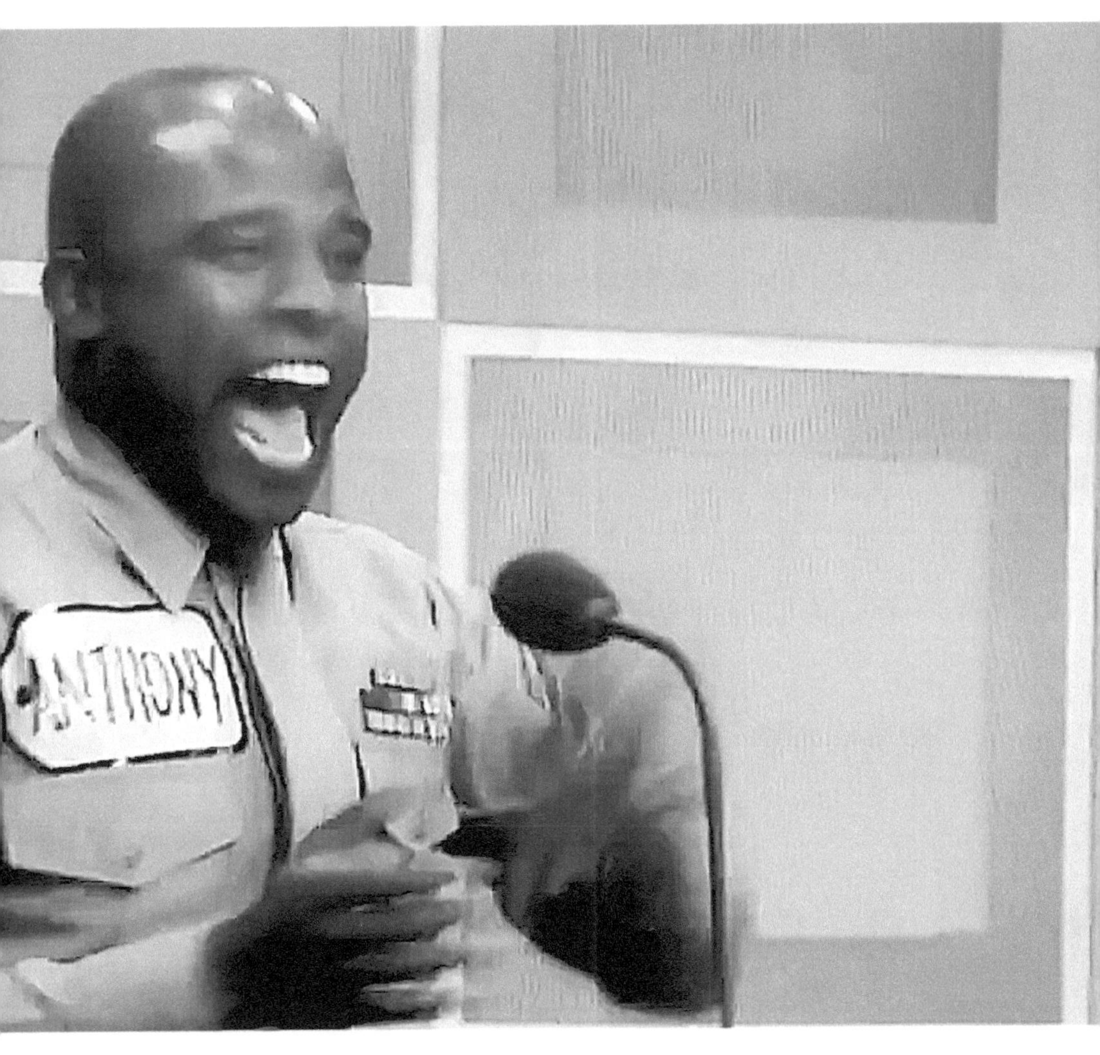
ANTHONY

Lon-
don

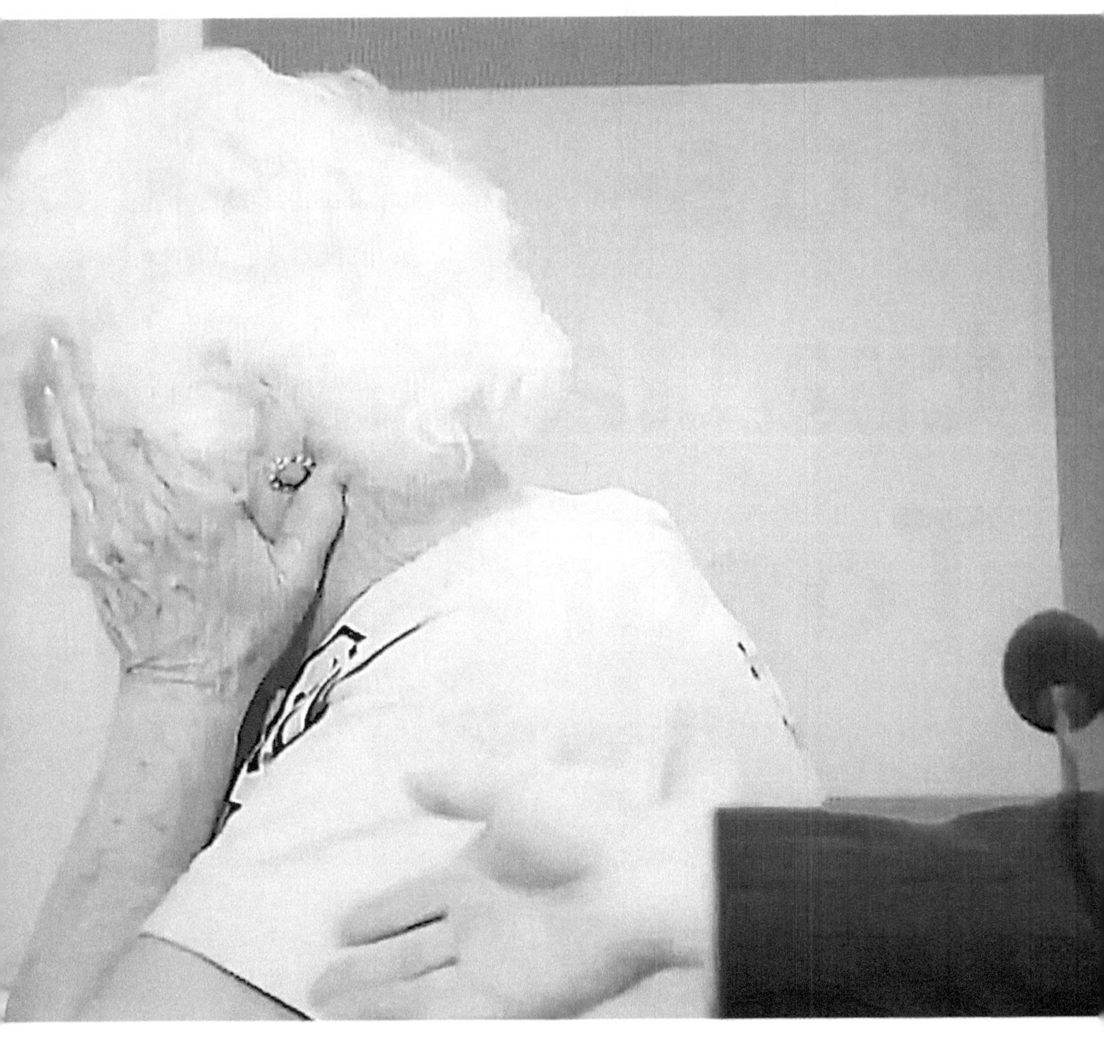

London/ Australia/ Toronto

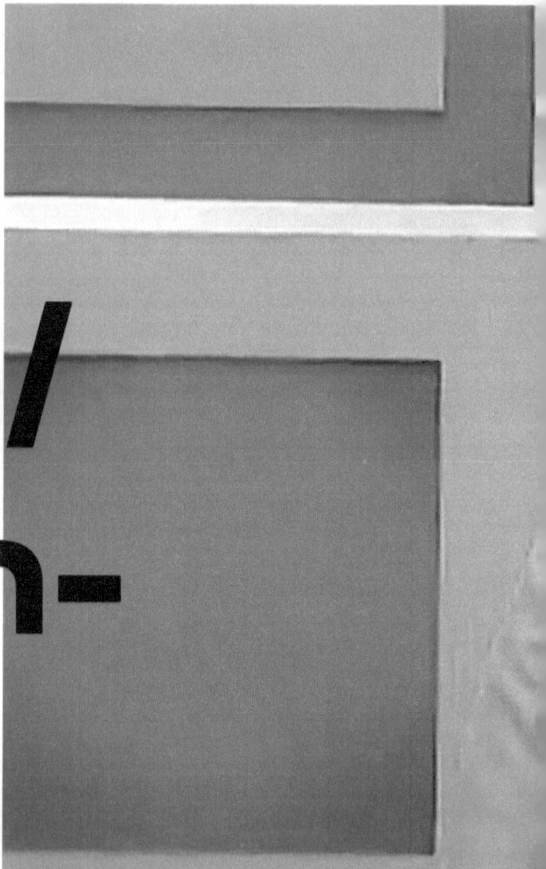

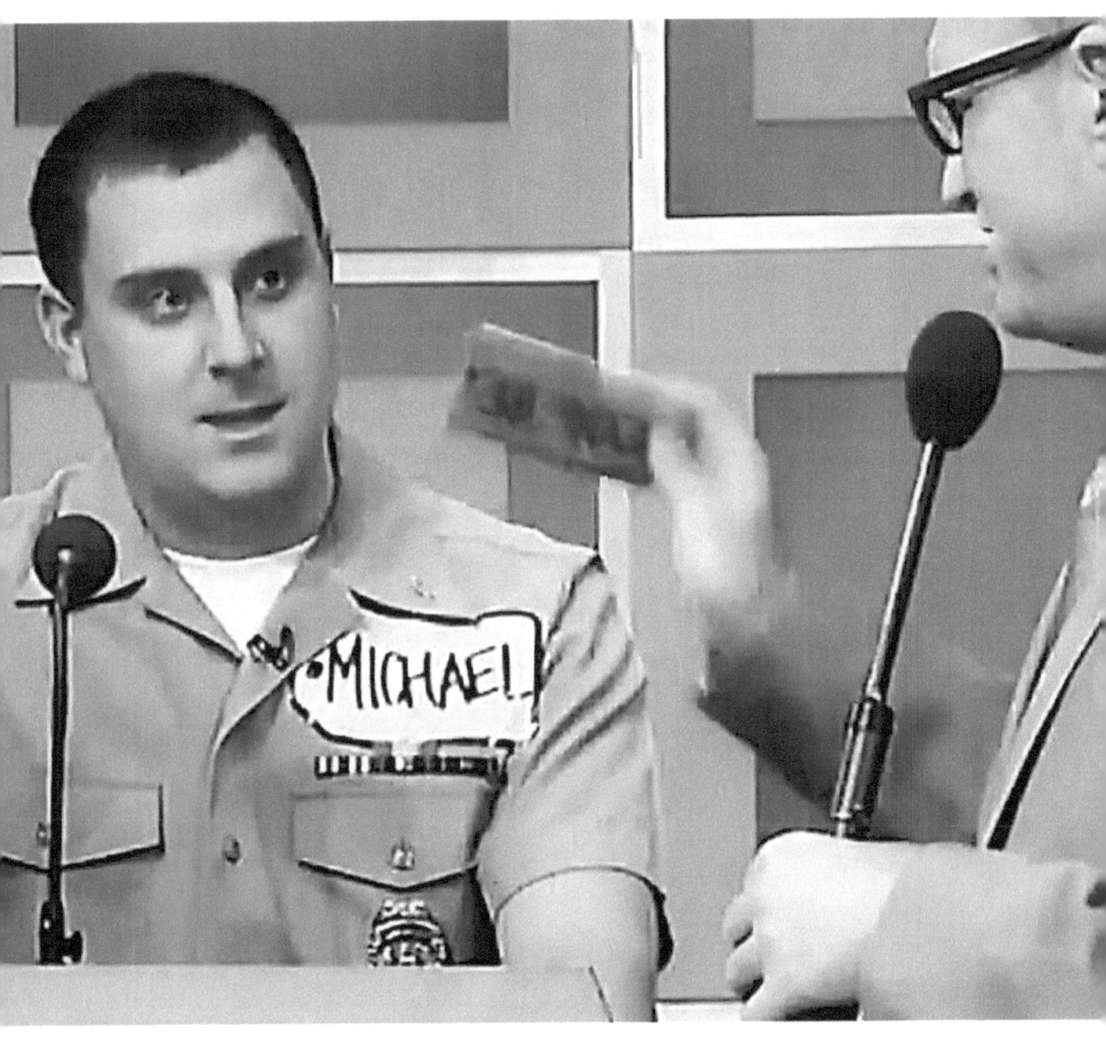

MICHAEL

Mal-
dives

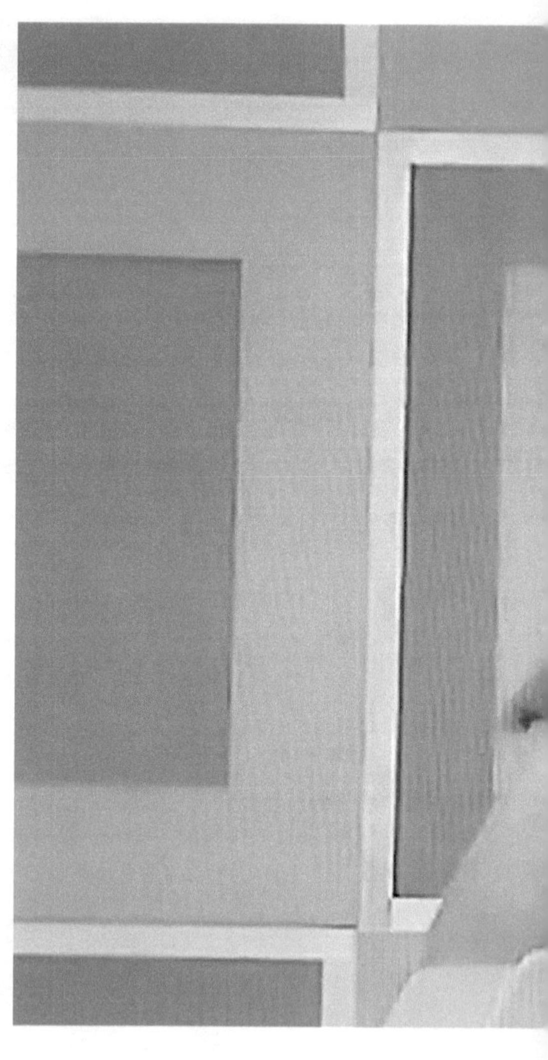

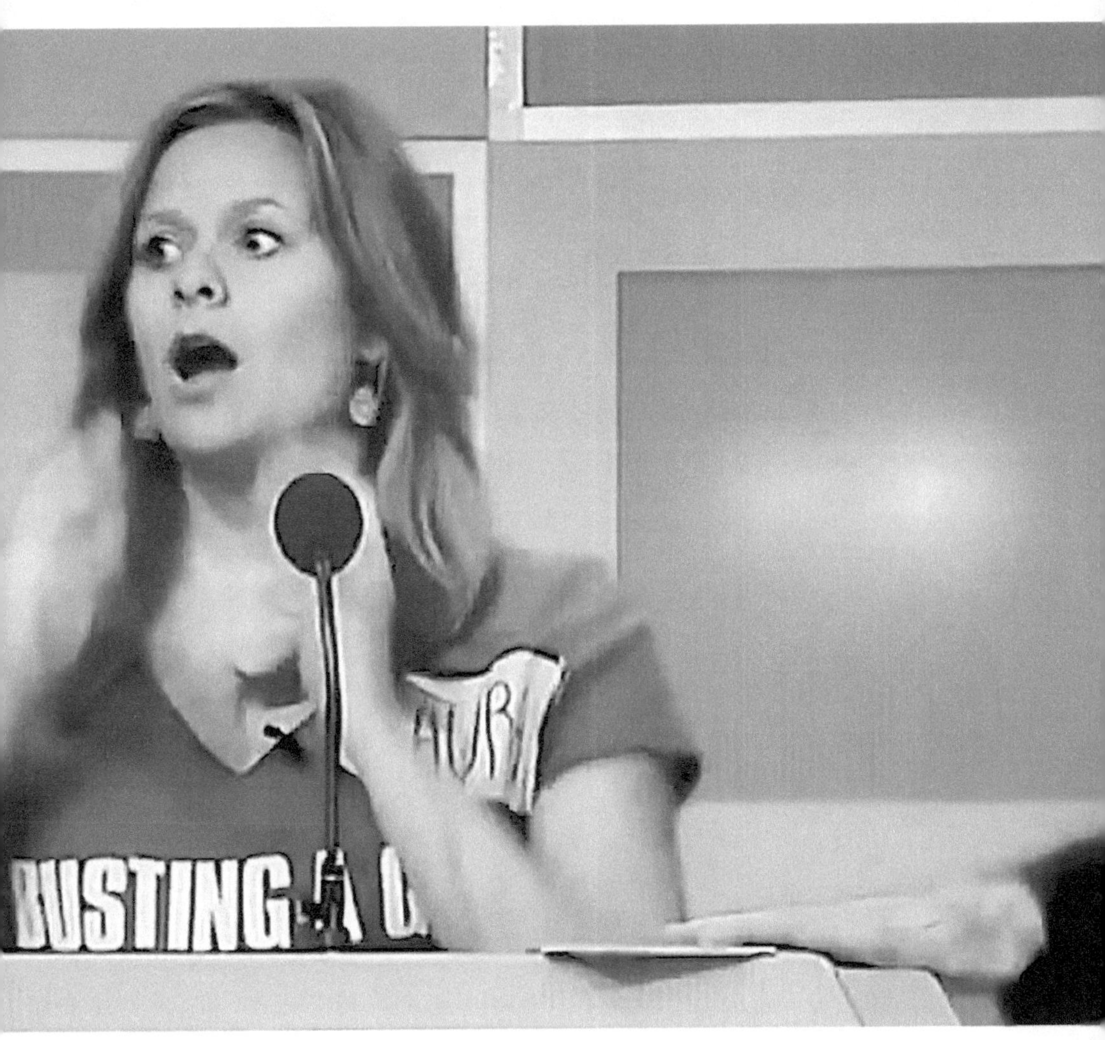
BUSTING A O

Paris/
New
York/
Sim-
fero-
pol/

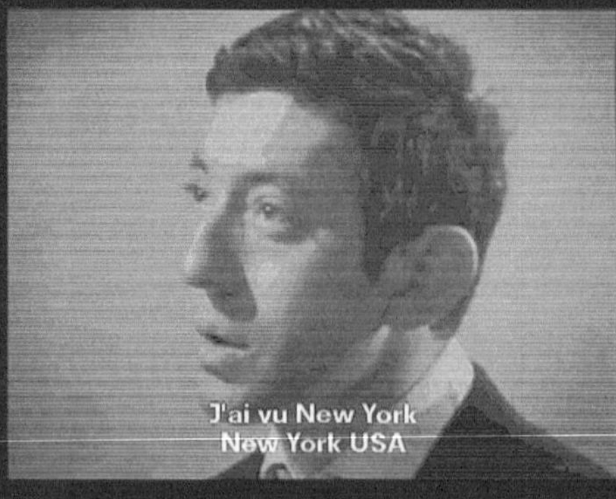

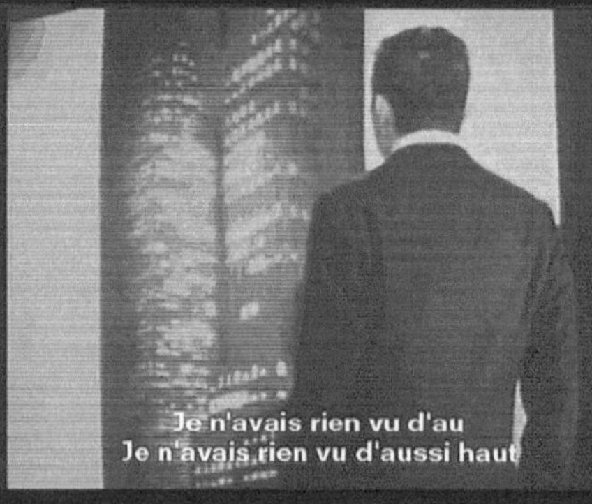

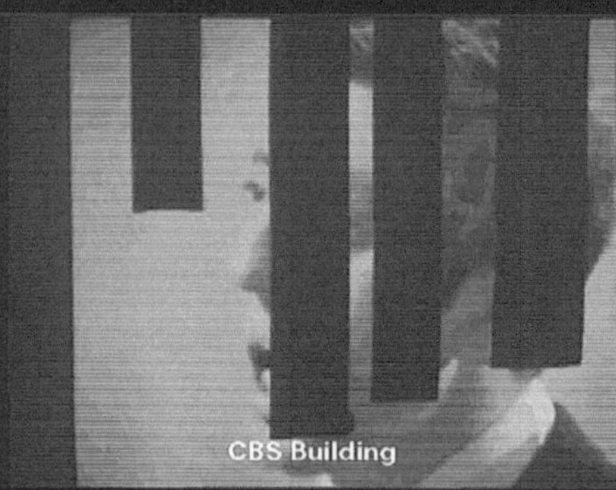

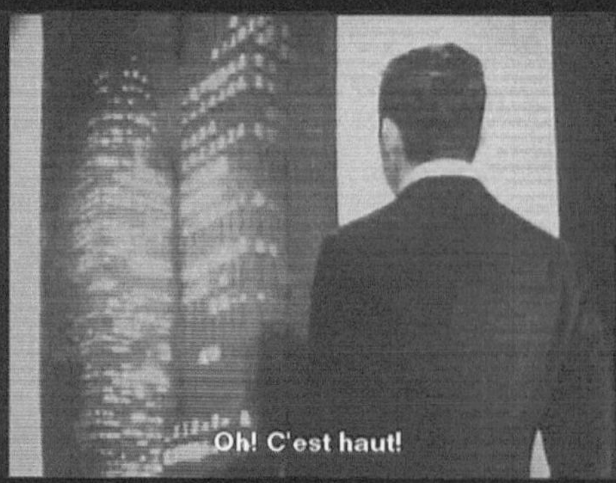

This is a excerpt from a transcript of a presentation about "How about to …" given 2011–2022.

In 1964 Serge Gainsbourg sang an ode to American architectural sublime simply titled "New York, USA." In the song, he lists a series of names of famous New York landmarks: Empire State Building, Astoria Waldorf, Rockefeller Center, Manhattan Bank. With each mention of a building, the backup singers respond with: "It is tall."

It is strange to hear the words: "First National City Bank" in the context of a pop song, but the song is a list — an itinerary of singer's journey at once in love with and terrified by the city. "I saw New York," Gainsbourg sings, "I've never seen anything so tall."

With each mention of the place name, the listener is transported to a new destination on this imaginary city tour; asked to imagine another wonder of American urbanism.

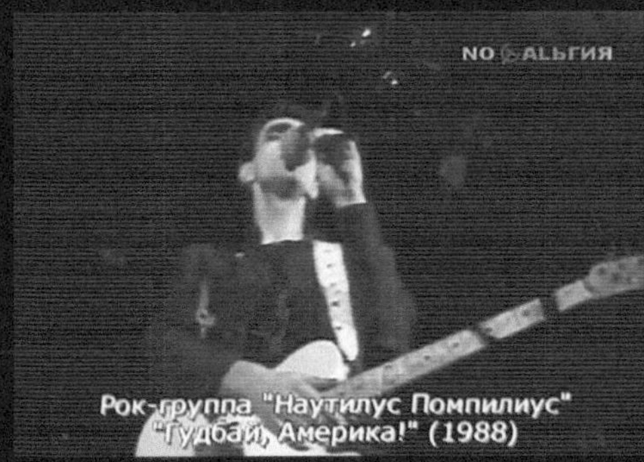

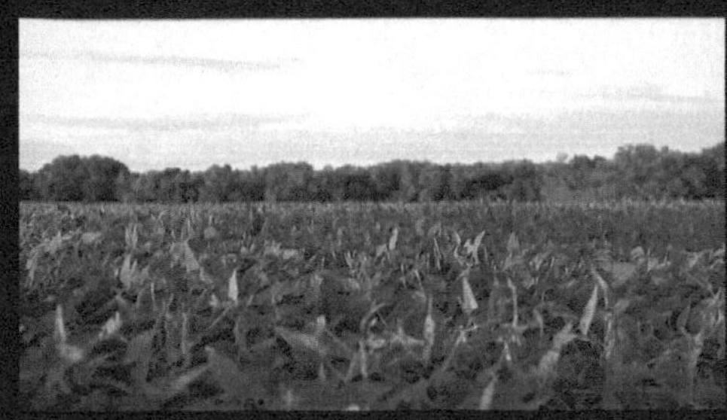

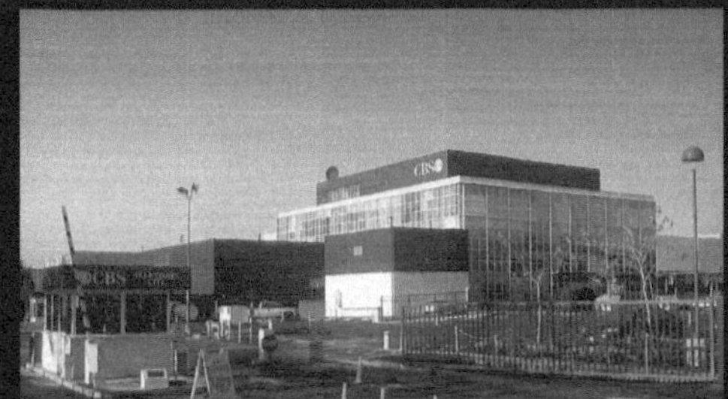

In 1989, on a tape loaned to me by my aunt, I discovered the music of Nautilus Pompilius—a Perestroika-era Soviet rock band, and their song Farewell Letter (Goodbye, America). Unlike Gainsbourg's narrator, who has seen New York and is overwhelmed by the height of the buildings, the narrator of the Soviet song is saying goodbye to an America where he has never seen—a country of "faded blue jeans and banjos." At the time, I did not know that I would be living in there in two years.

Living in Urbana, Illinois, and going to high school among corn and soybean fields, I dreamt of American metropolises as well, but of a different kind.

This is CBS Television City, California, where my favorite show as a twelve-year-old, the "Price Is Right," was filmed. I would watch it on CBS and the soap opera, "The Young and the Restless," that followed, every day the summer of moving to the US, learning English in the process.

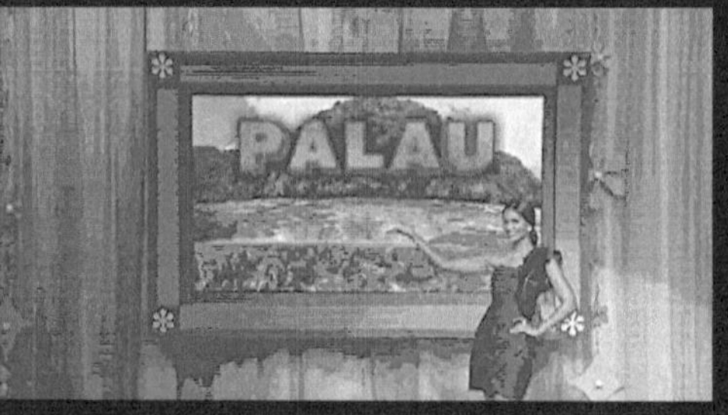

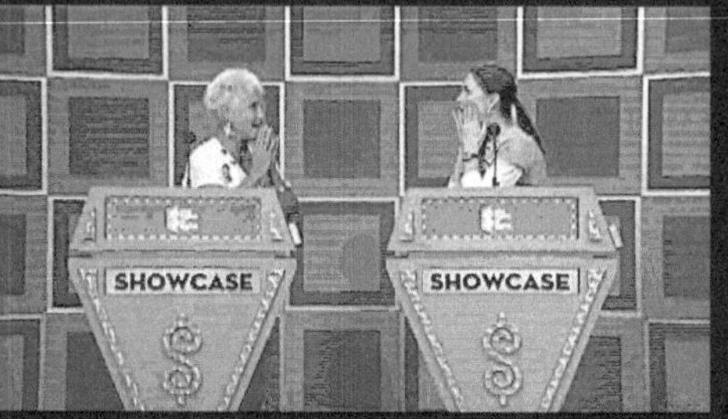

In the show—besides competing to win household appliances, cars and cash—the contestants are given a chance to win trips. "How about a trip to…" captures the reaction of contestants on the "Price Is Right" at the moment that it is announced where they might be going if they win this round. For a split second, their faces become *images of instant imaginary journeys* as they imagine themselves at that new destination; somewhere across the oceans, or just a few states over.

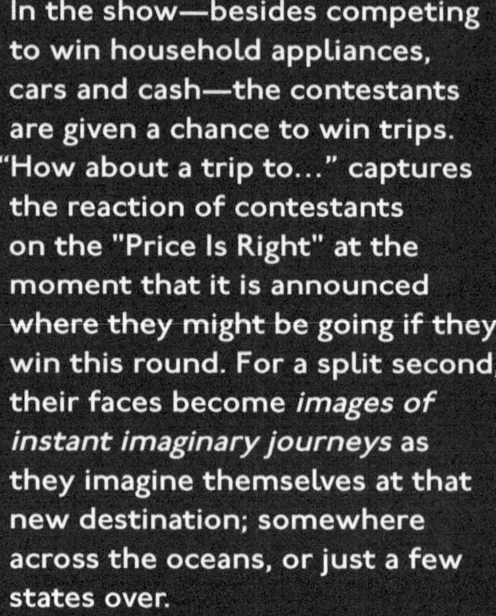

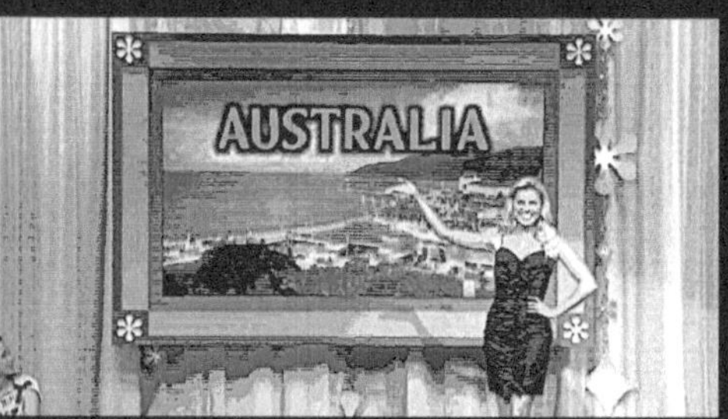

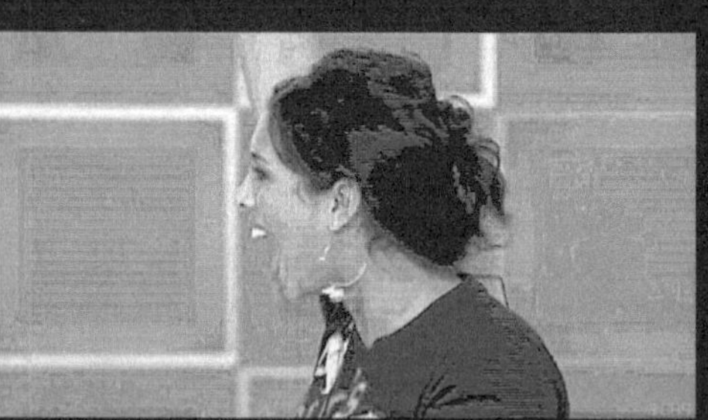

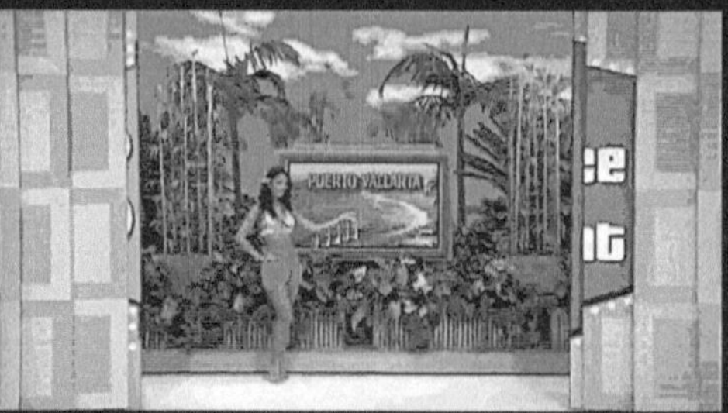

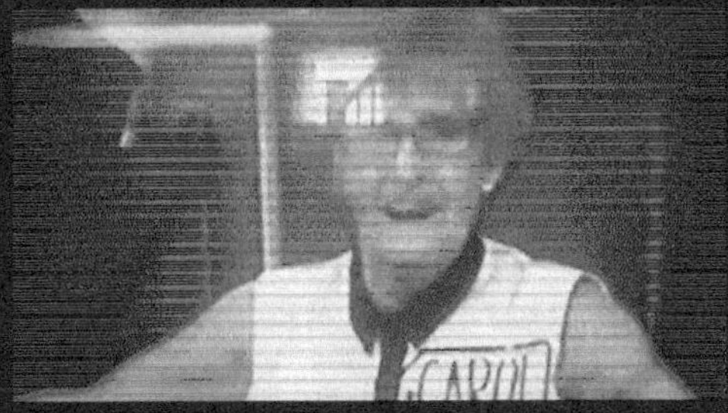

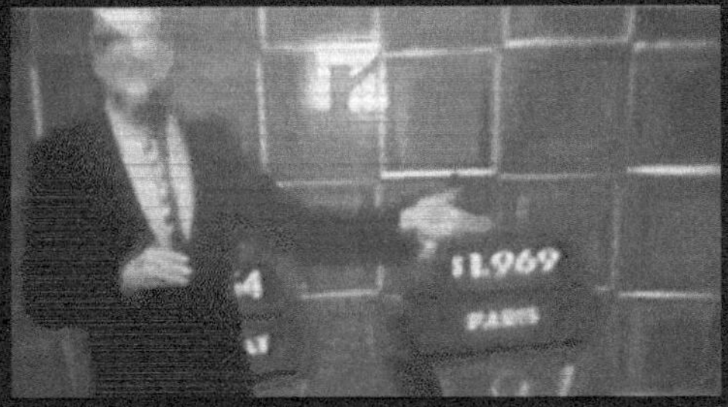

And while searching YouTube for new clips of the show, I recently came across an iPhone video of a contestant, Carol, who had just learned that she won a trip to Paris, imagining herself across the Atlantic, traveling to the city where over 50 years ago Serge Gainsbourg stood in awe of New York and sang to a photograph of the city mounted on a soundstage.

Ur-bana/ Los Ange-les/ Paris

Maui

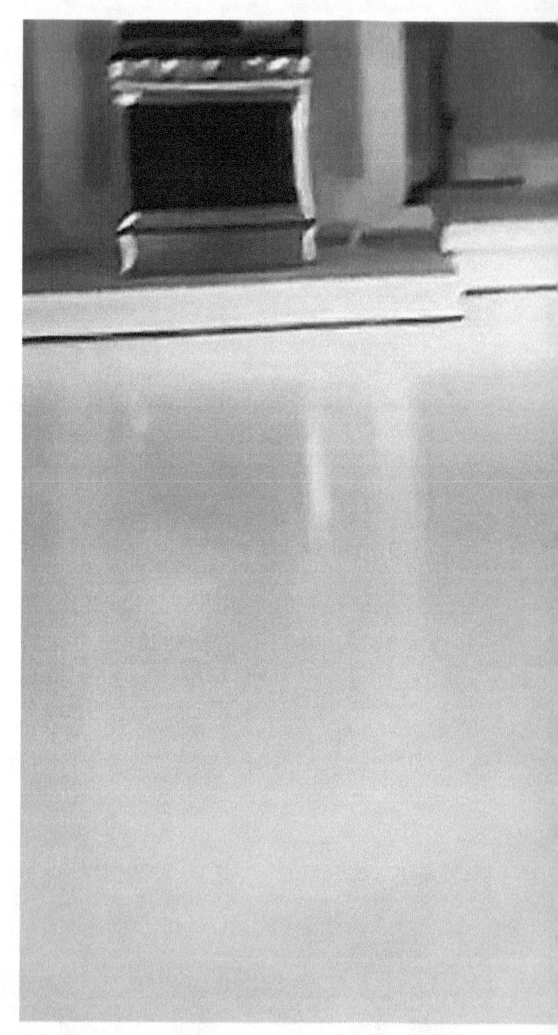

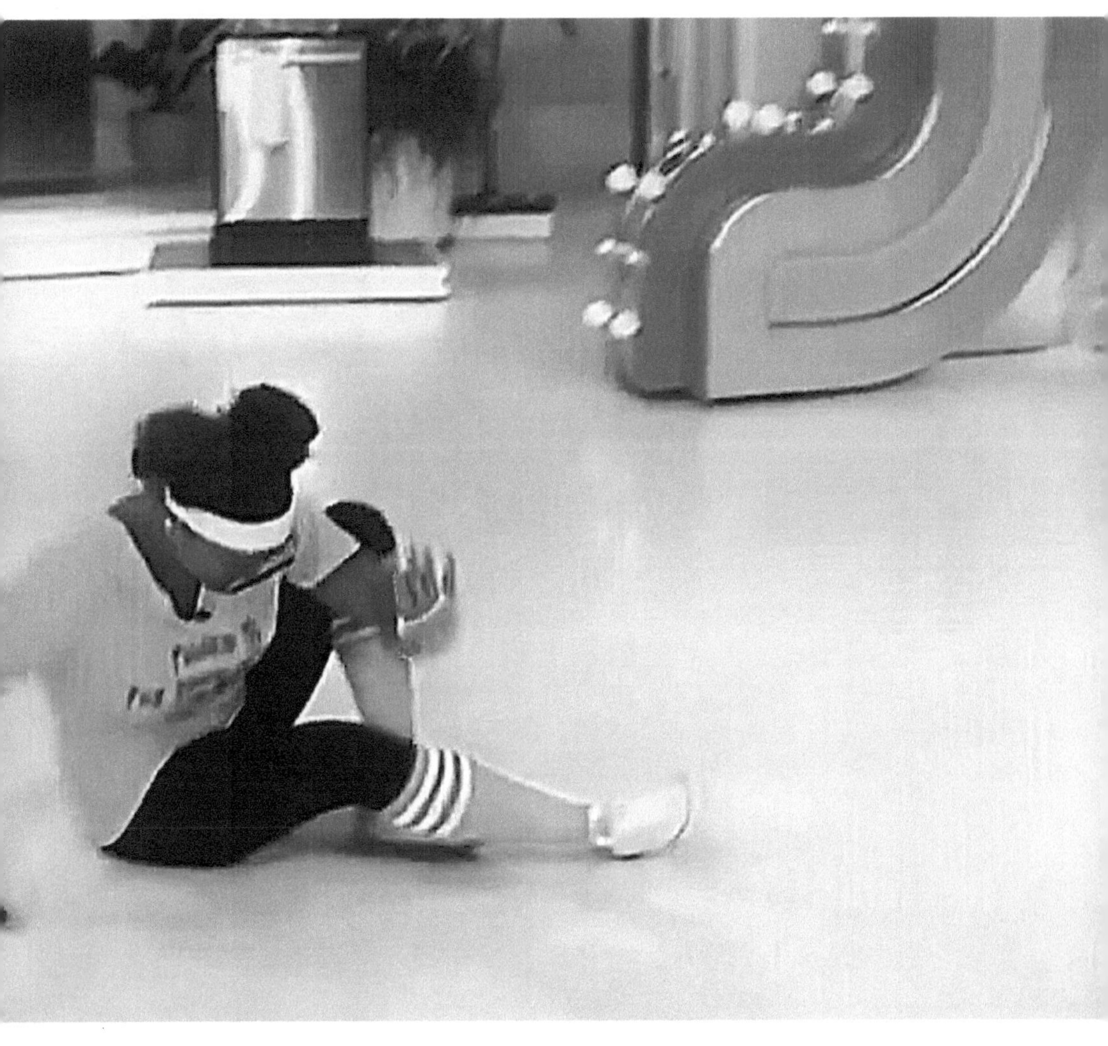

Maui

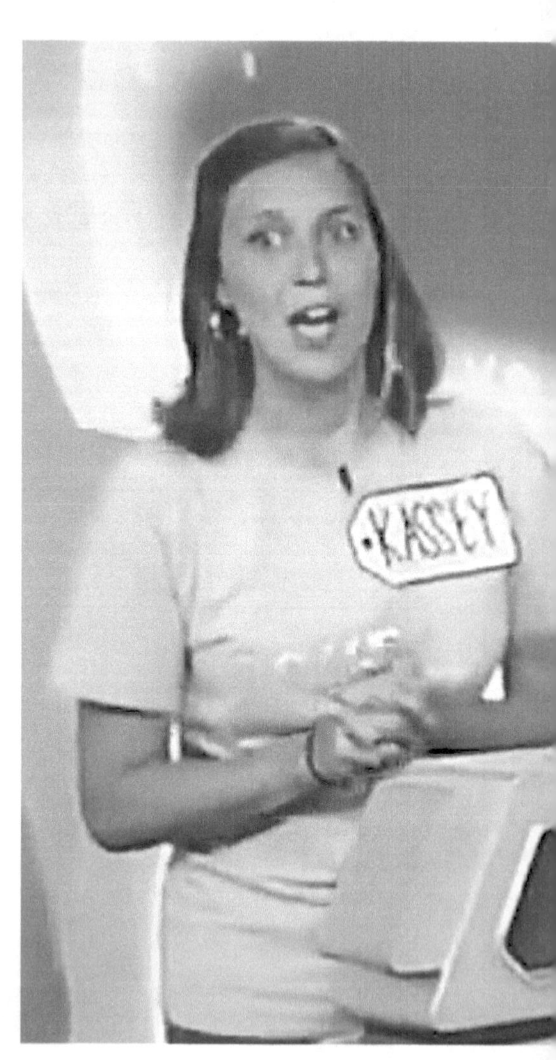

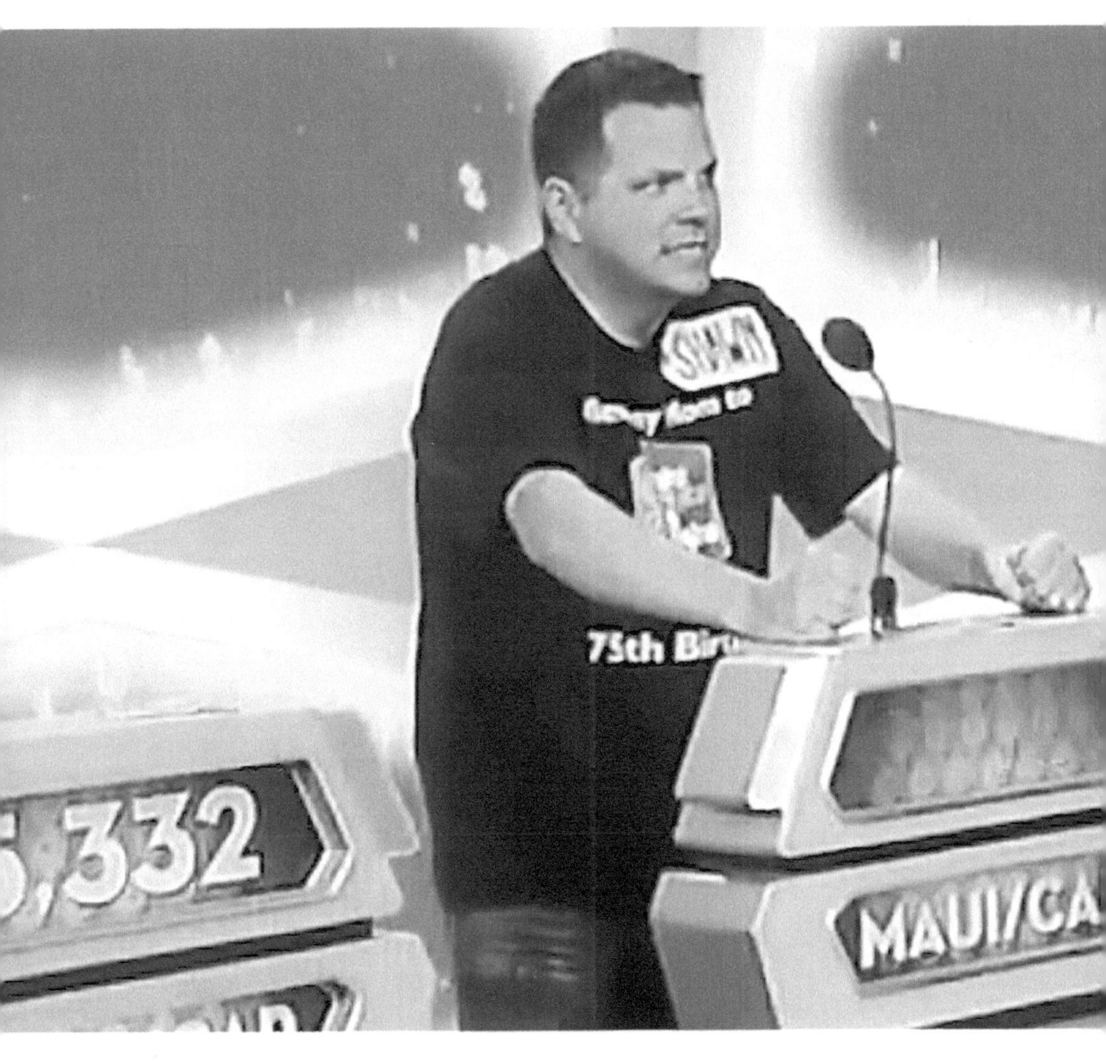
5,332
MAUI/CA
75th Bir

Mauri-
tius

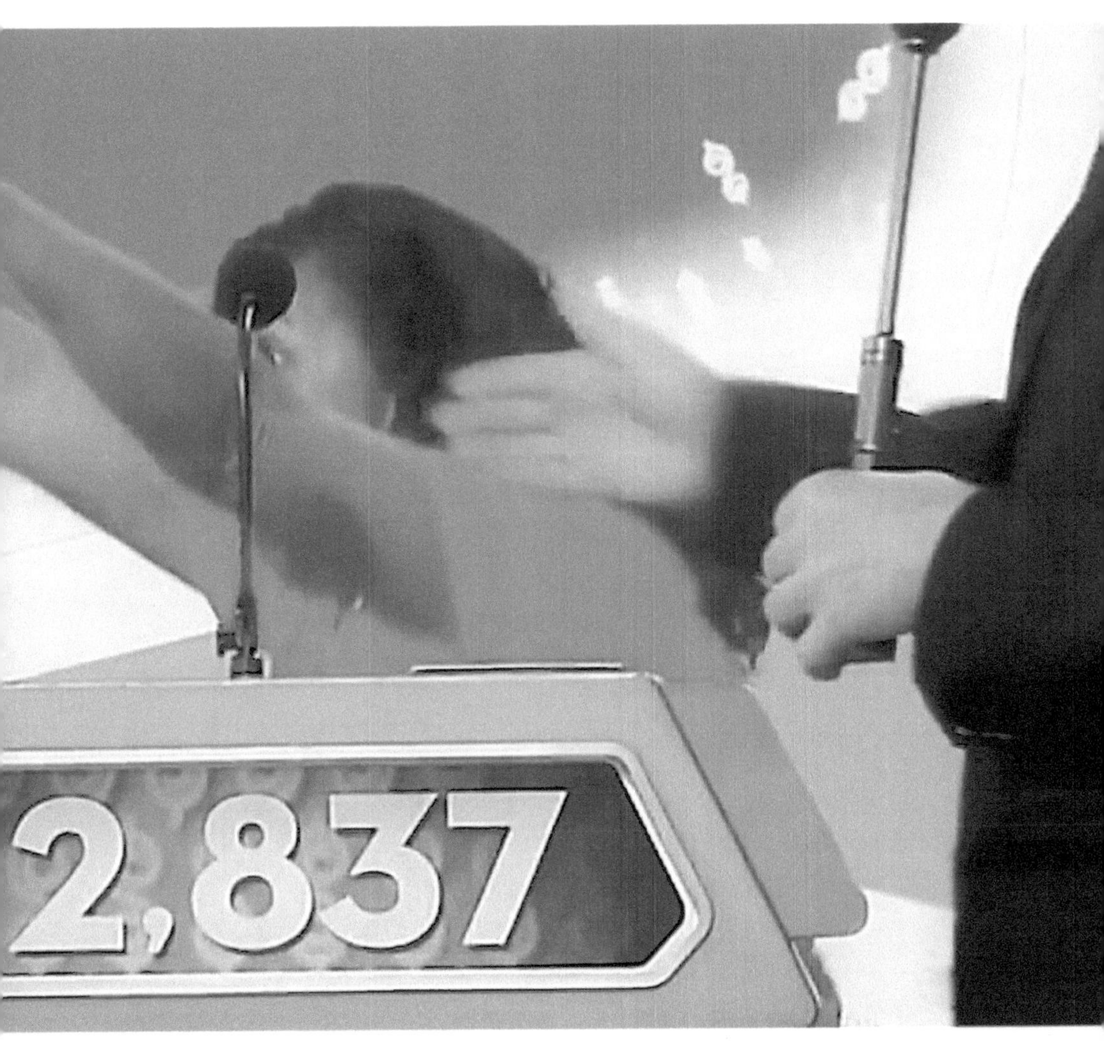
2,837

Miami

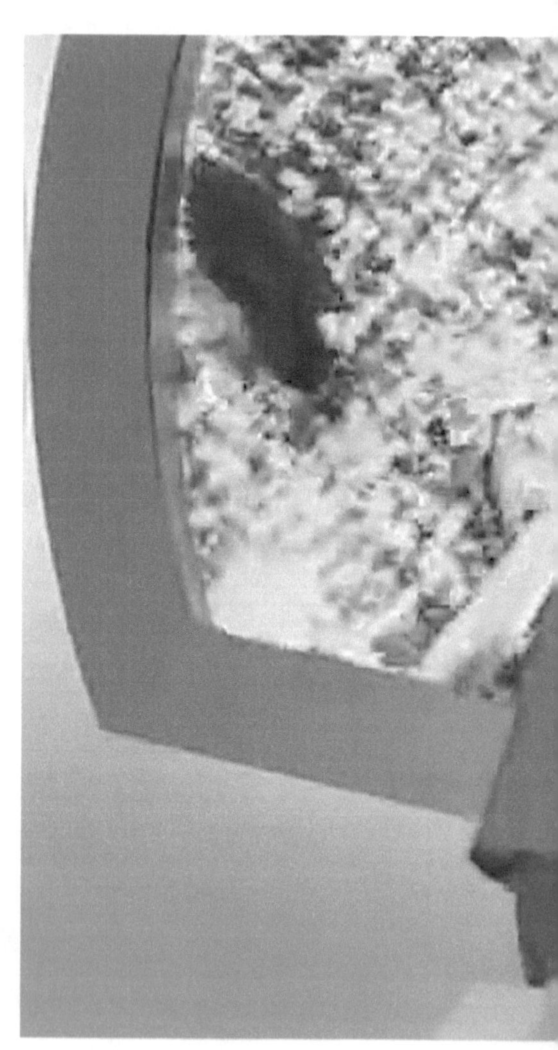

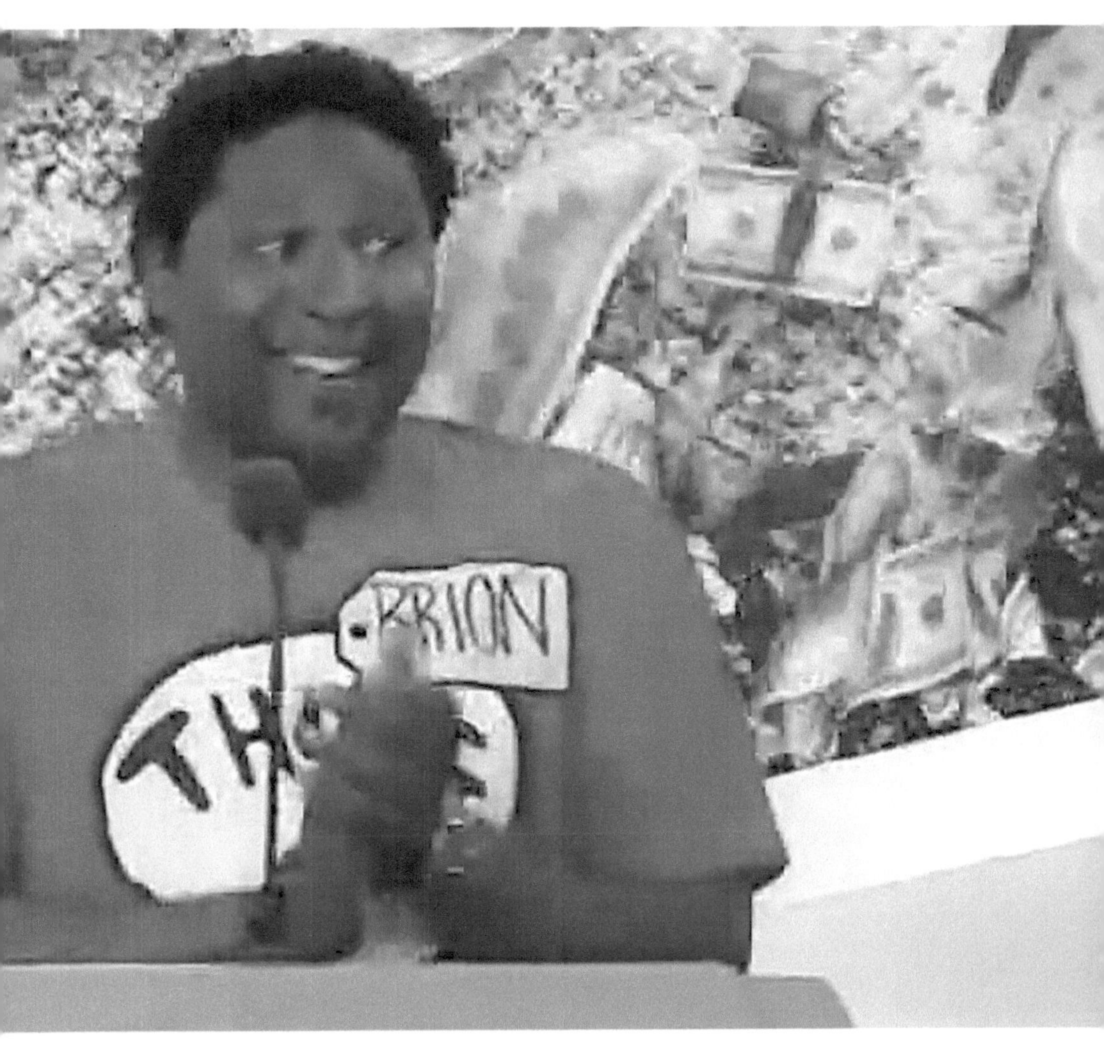
PRION
TH

Milan

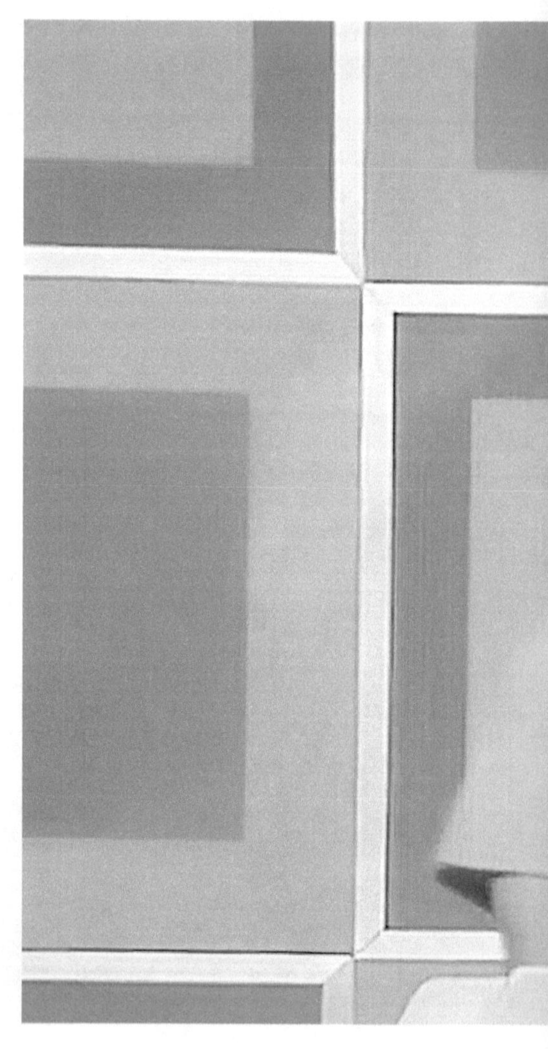

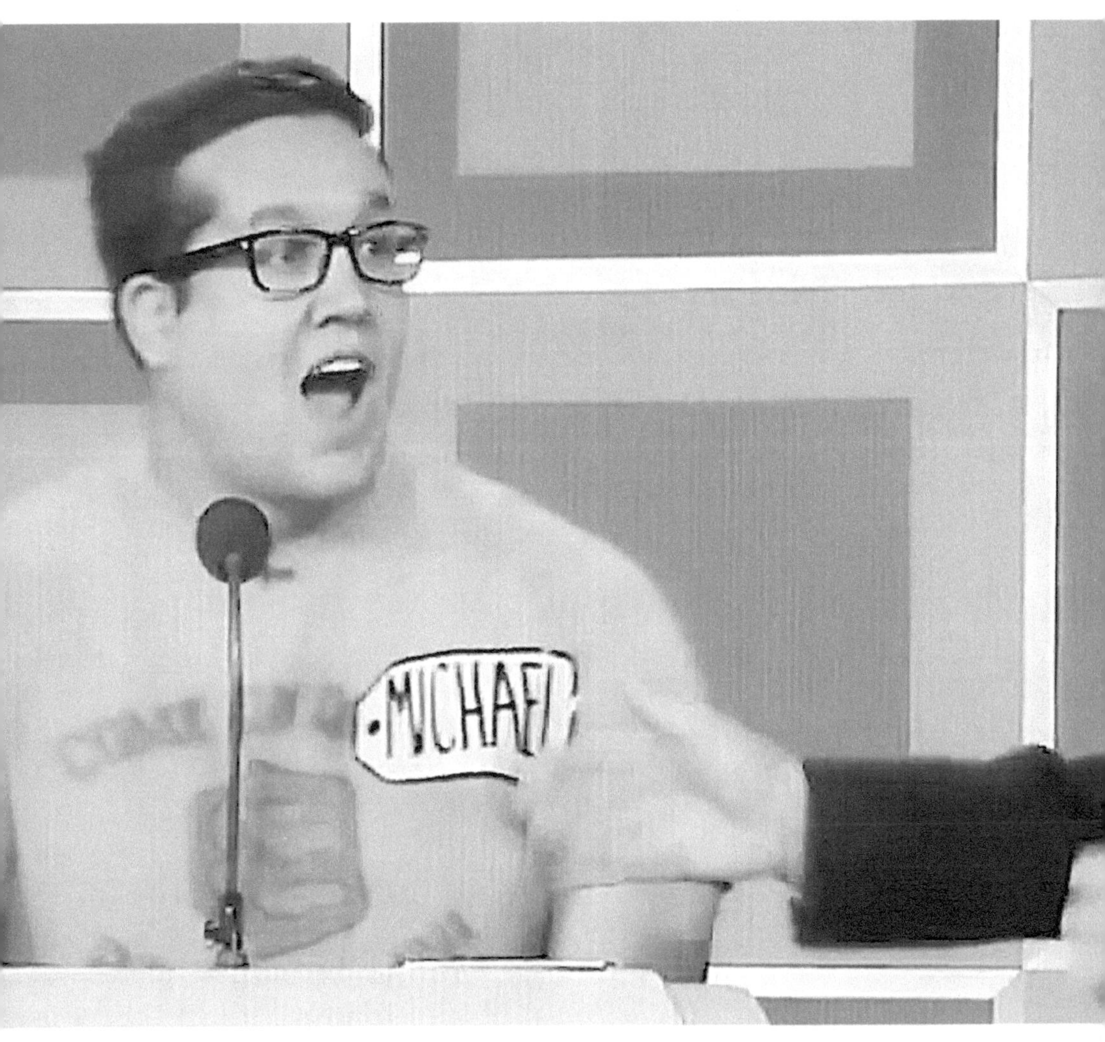

MICHAEL

Mon-
tana

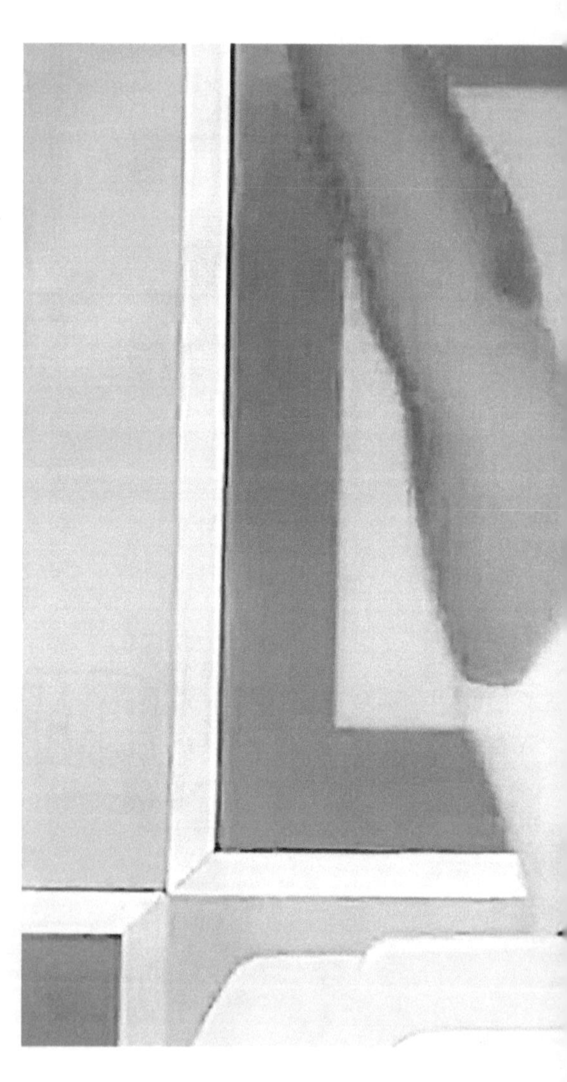

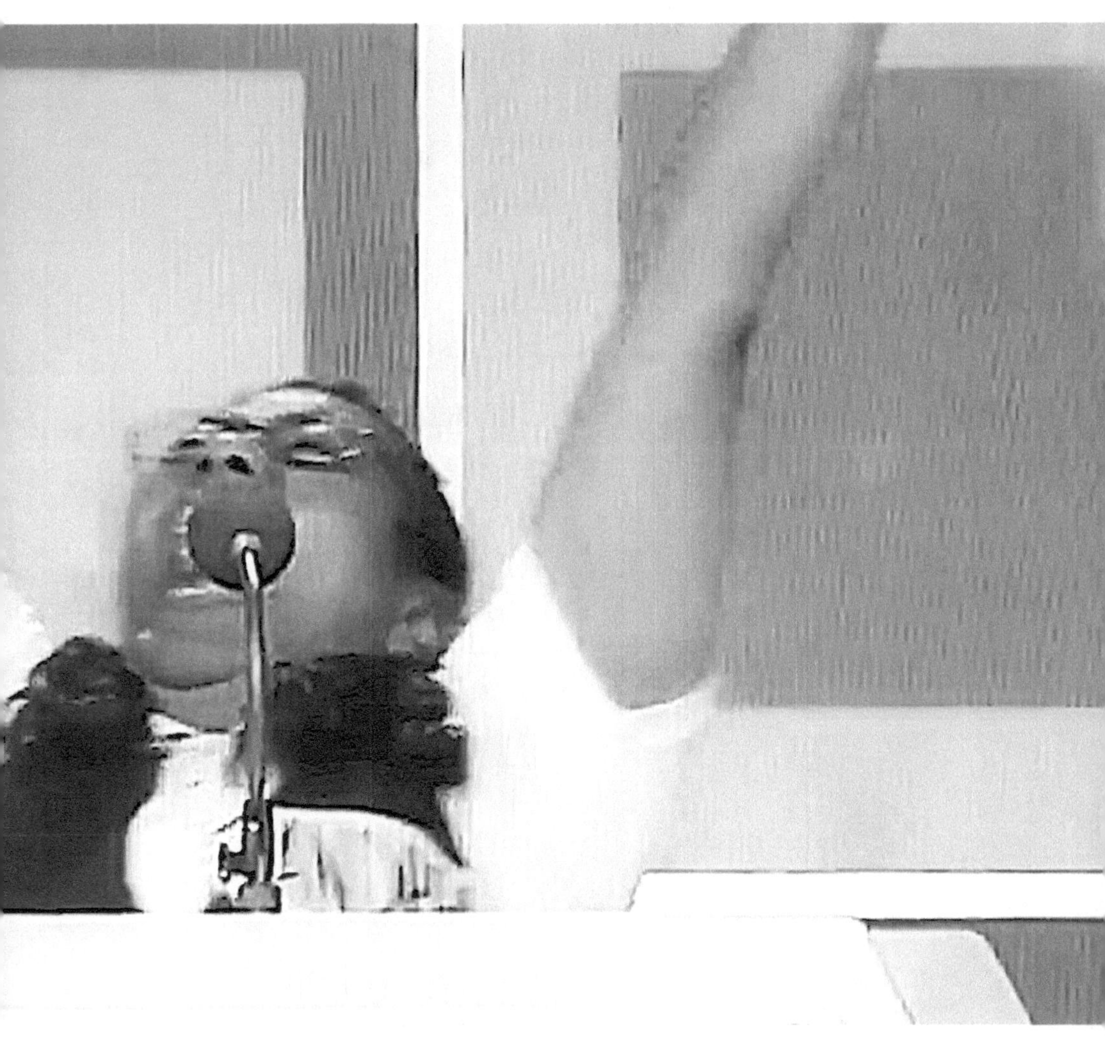

Mon-
tene-
gro

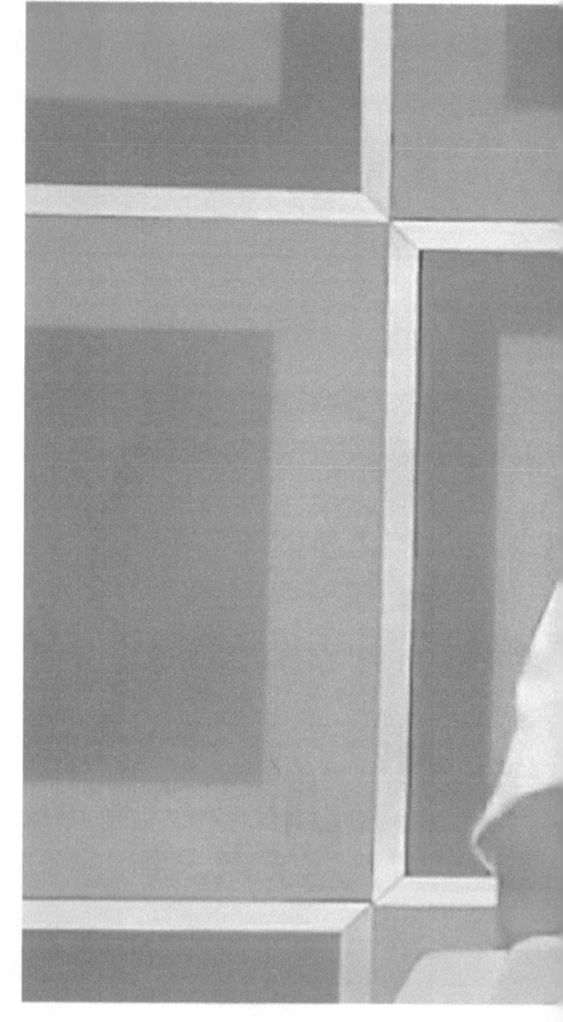

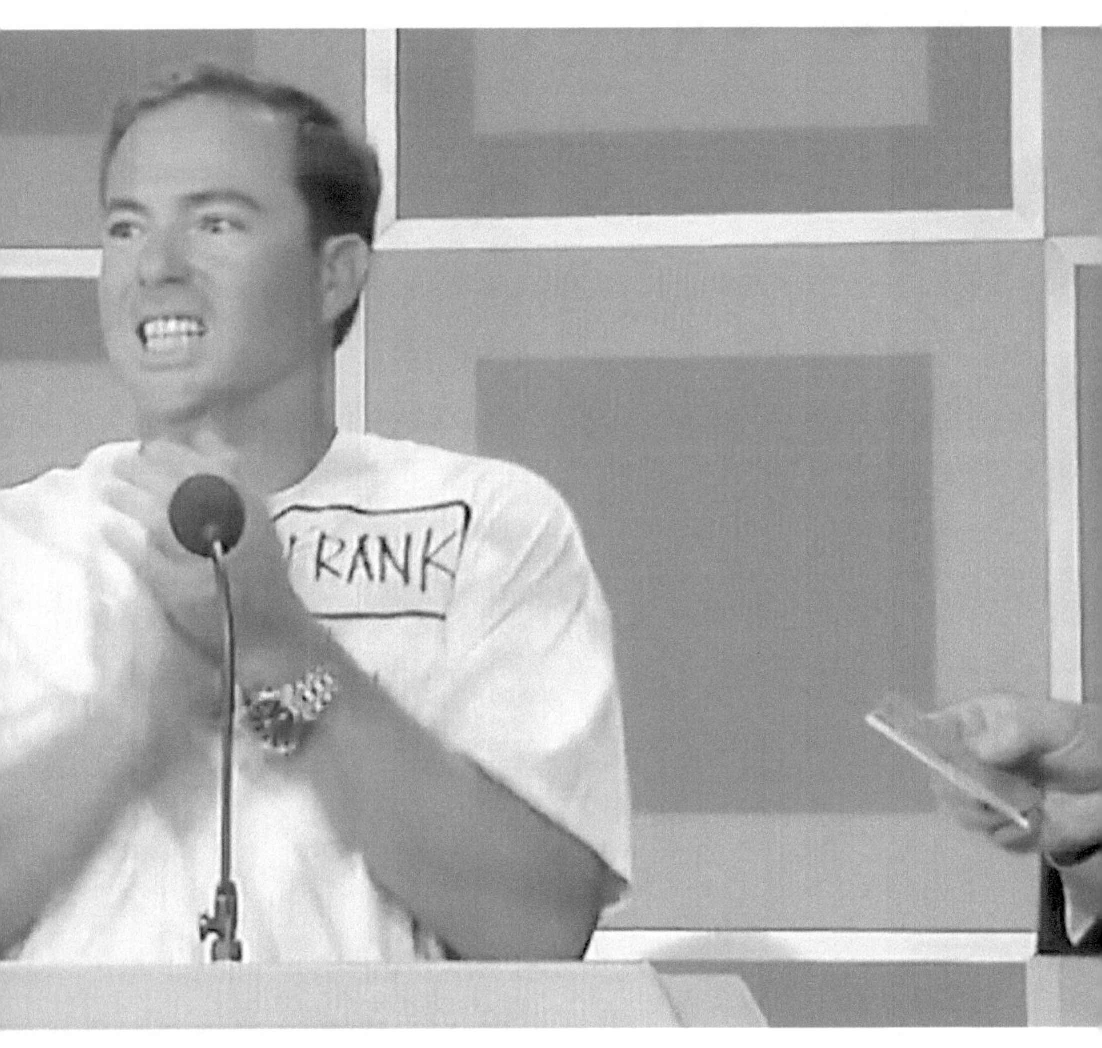
RANK

Mos-cow

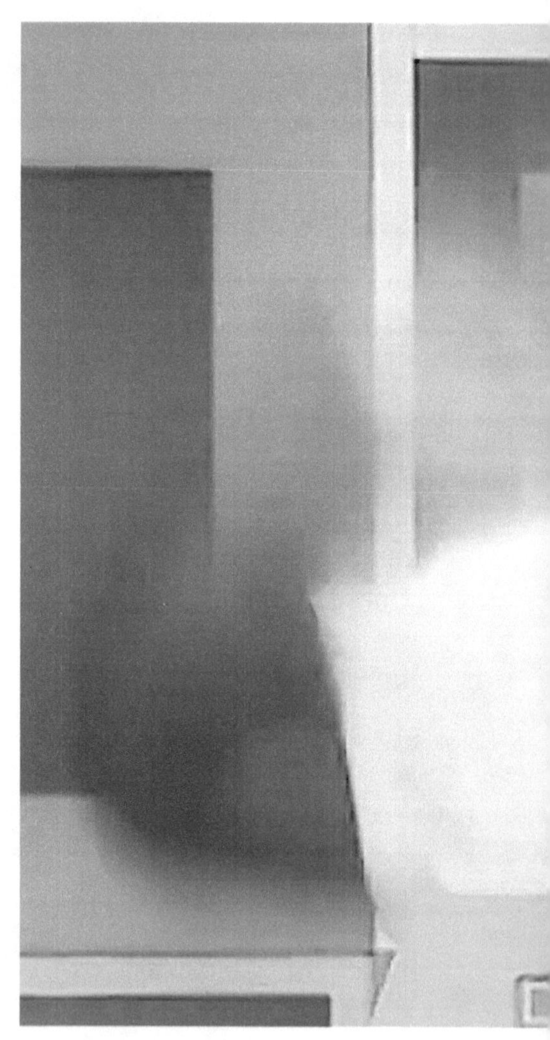

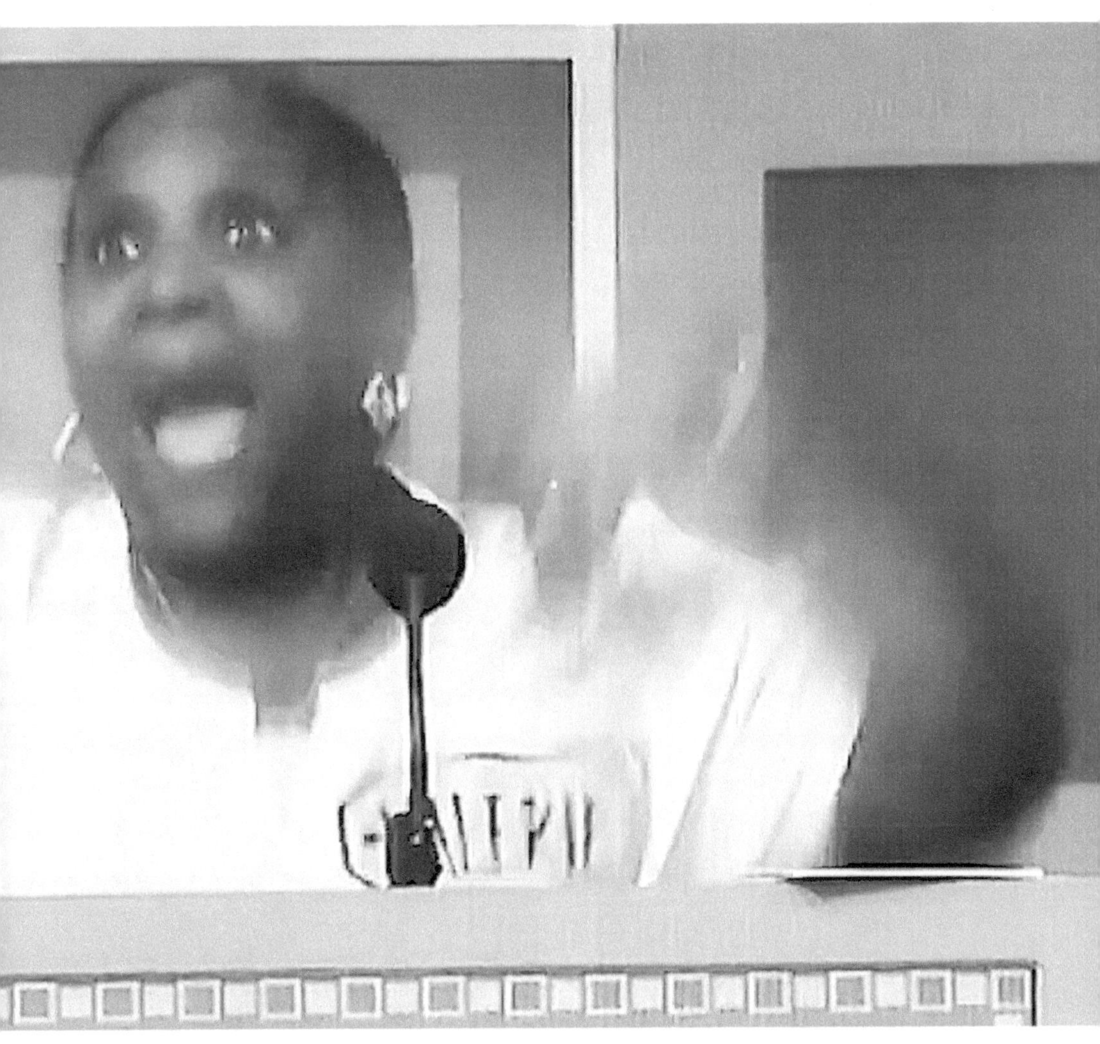

Napa Val
ley

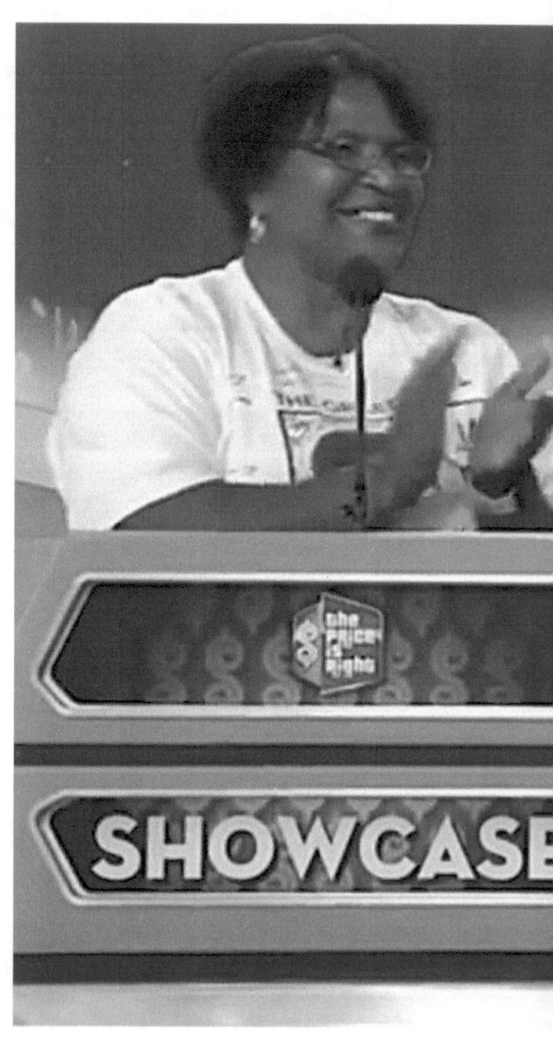

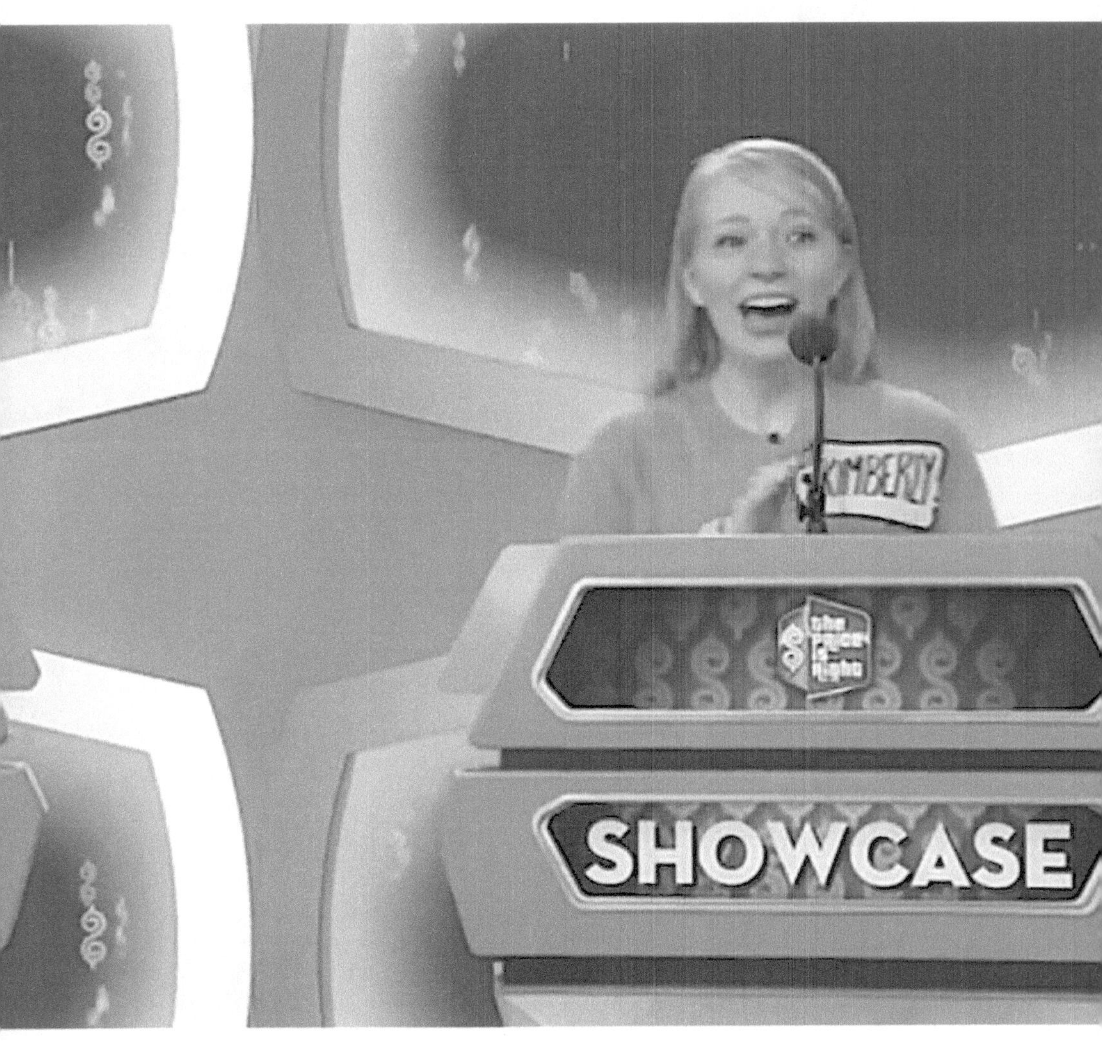

SHOWCASE

Napa Valley / England

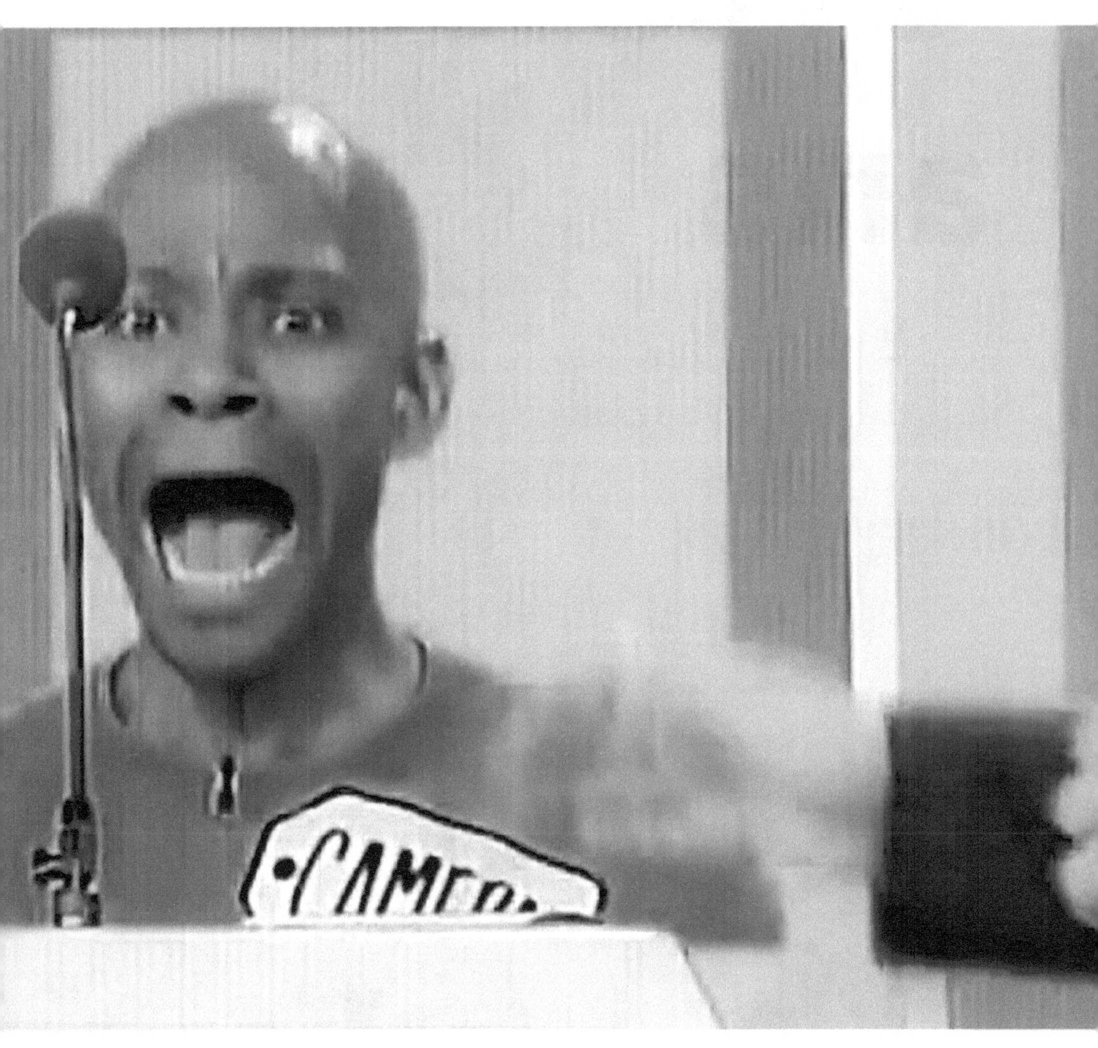
CAMER

New Orleans

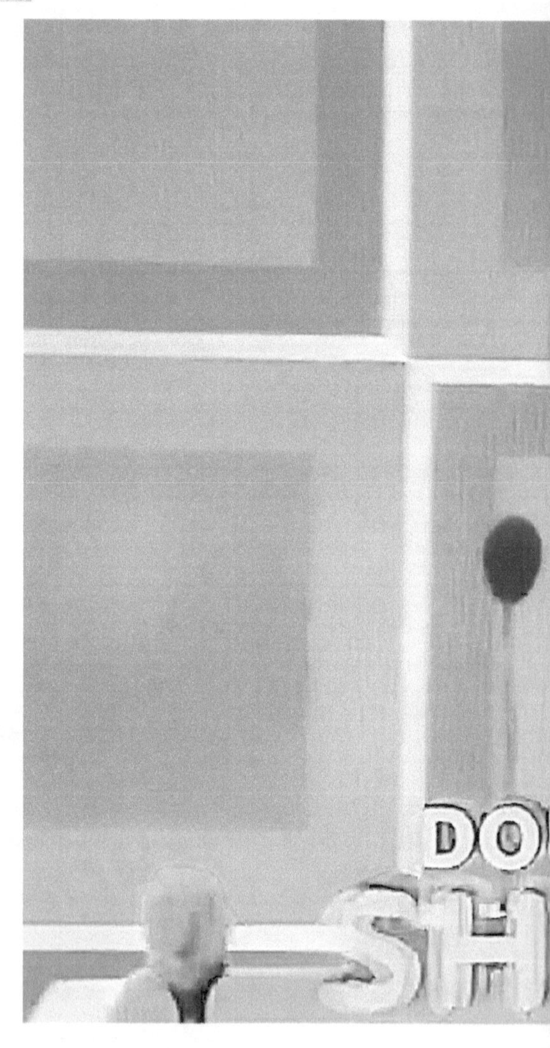

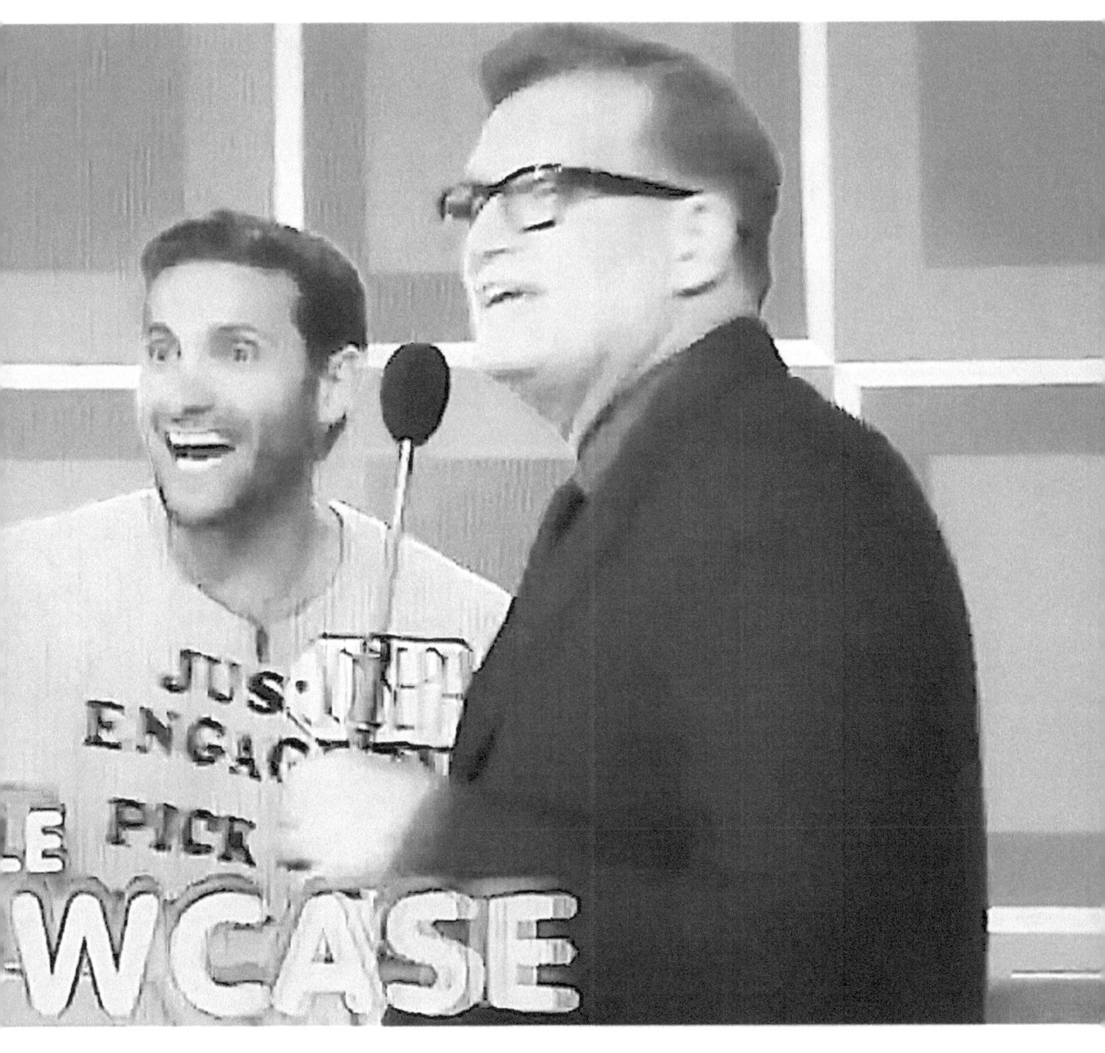
JUS...
ENGAG...
LE PICK
WCASE

New Orleans

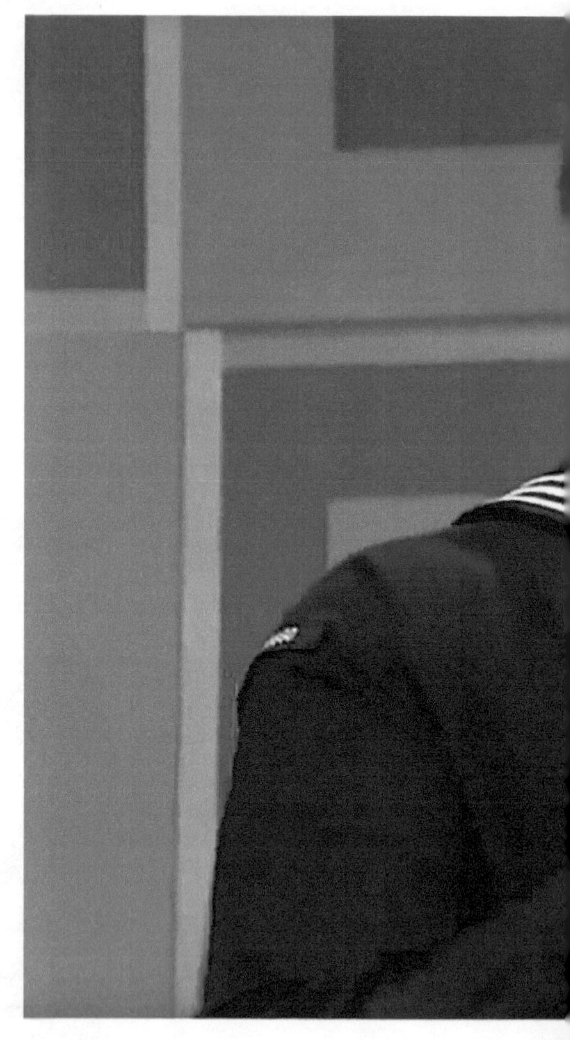

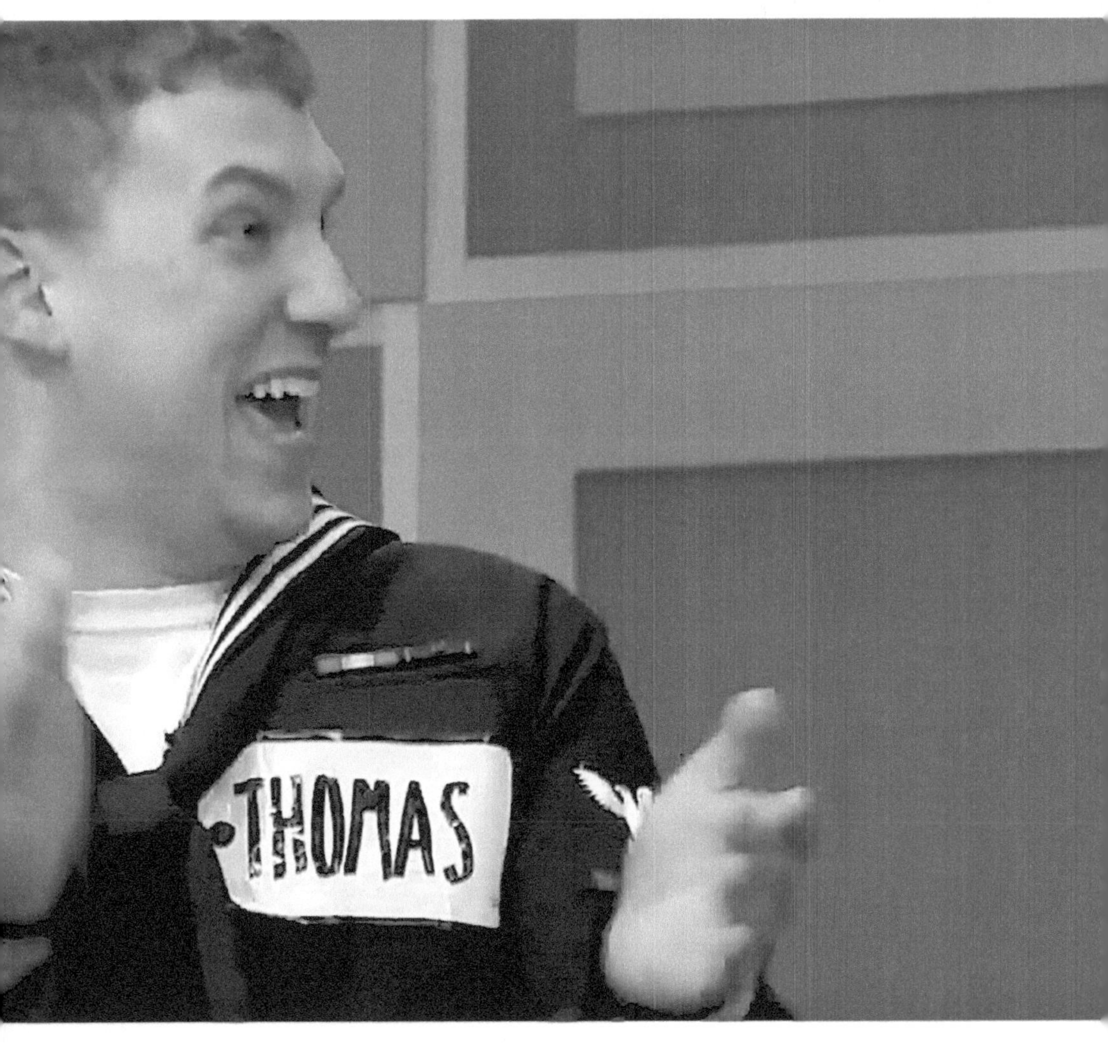

·THOMAS

Newport Beach/ Japan

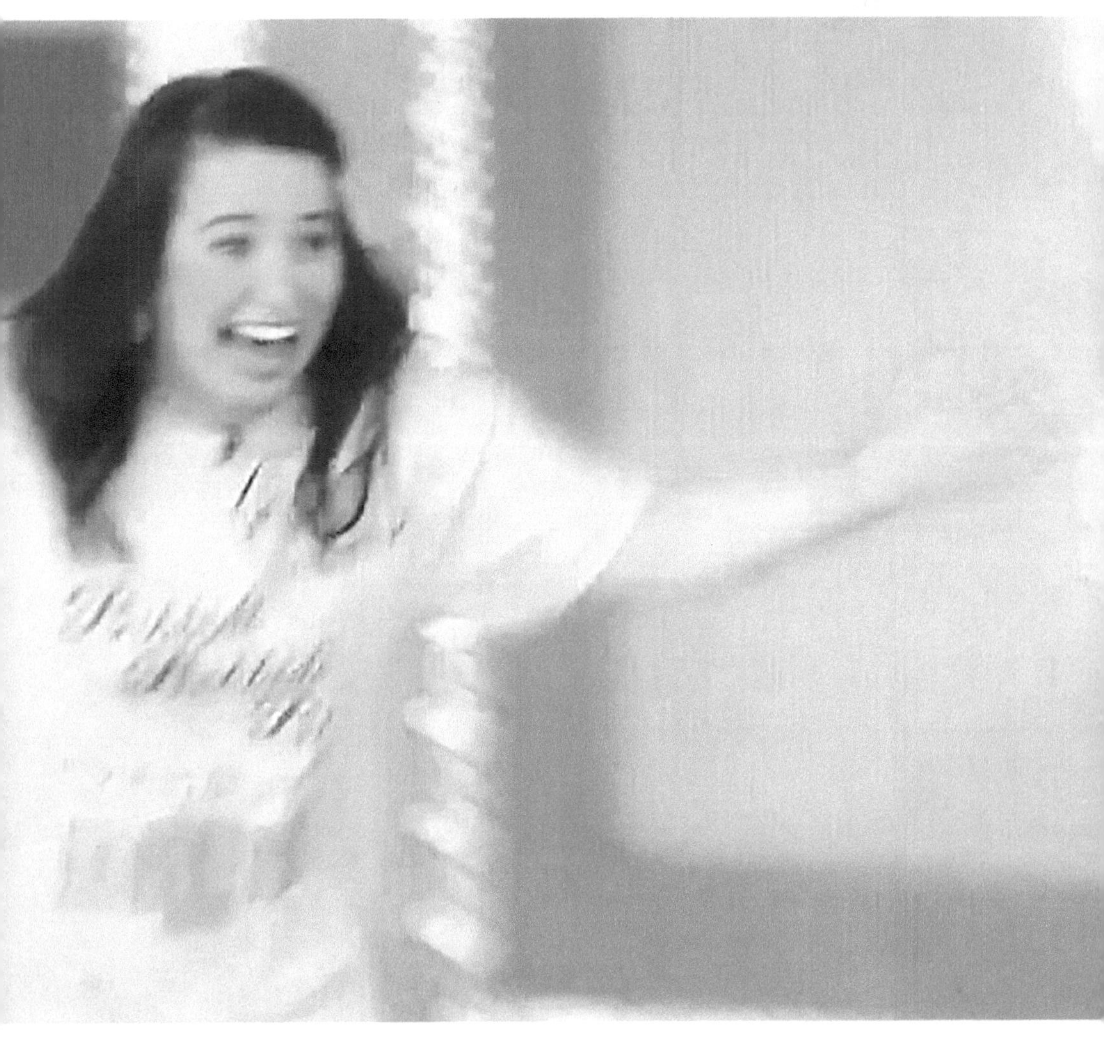

New York

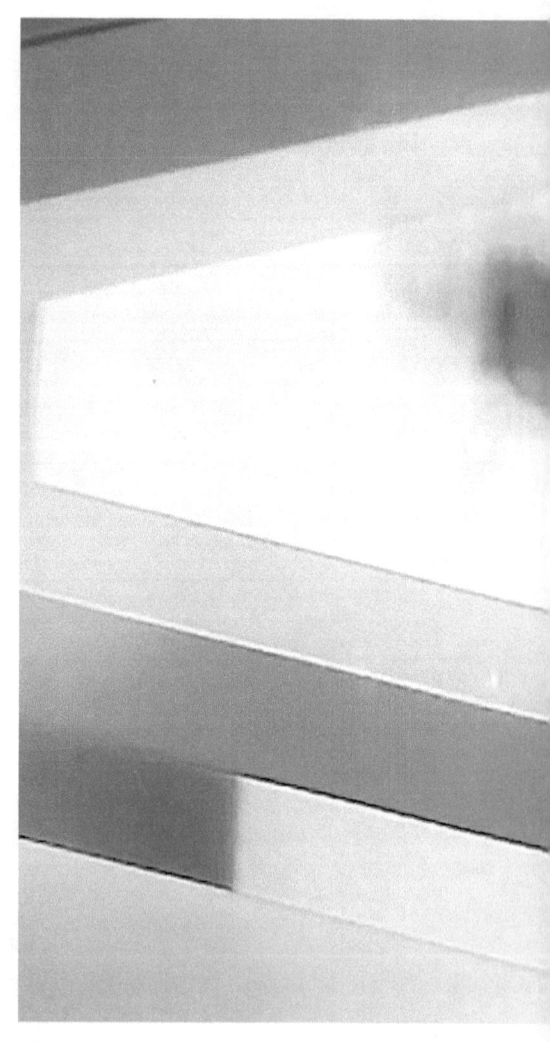

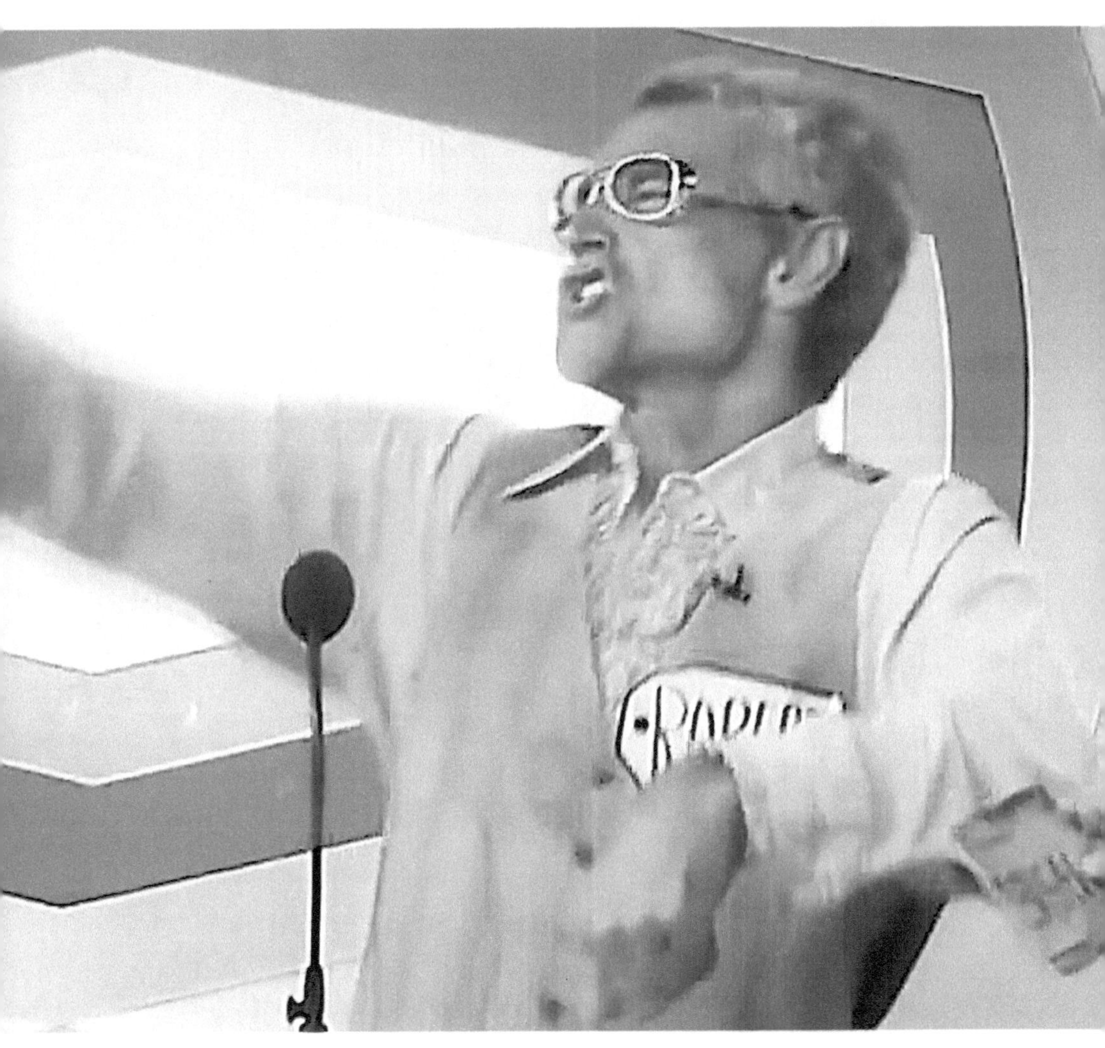

New York

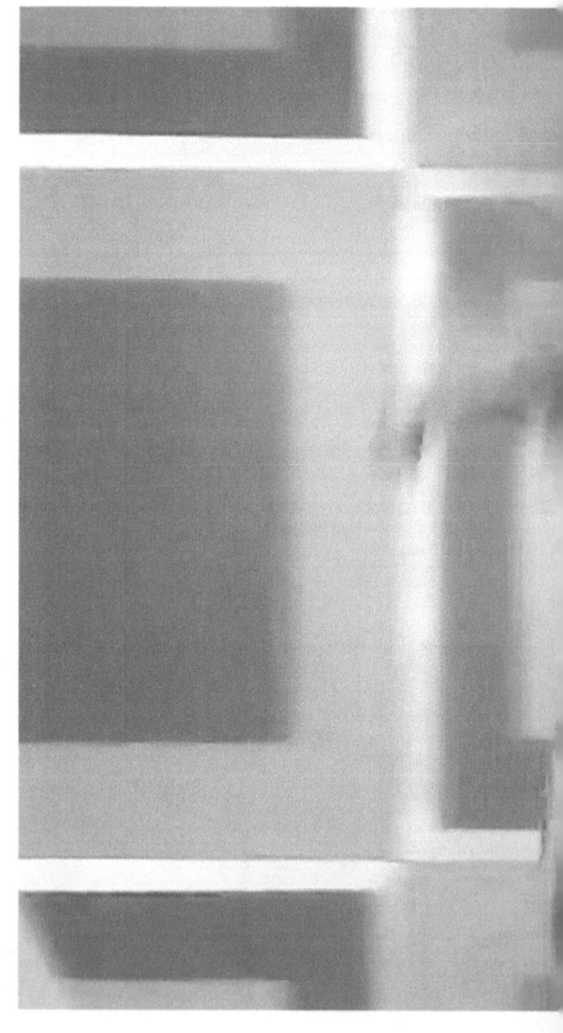

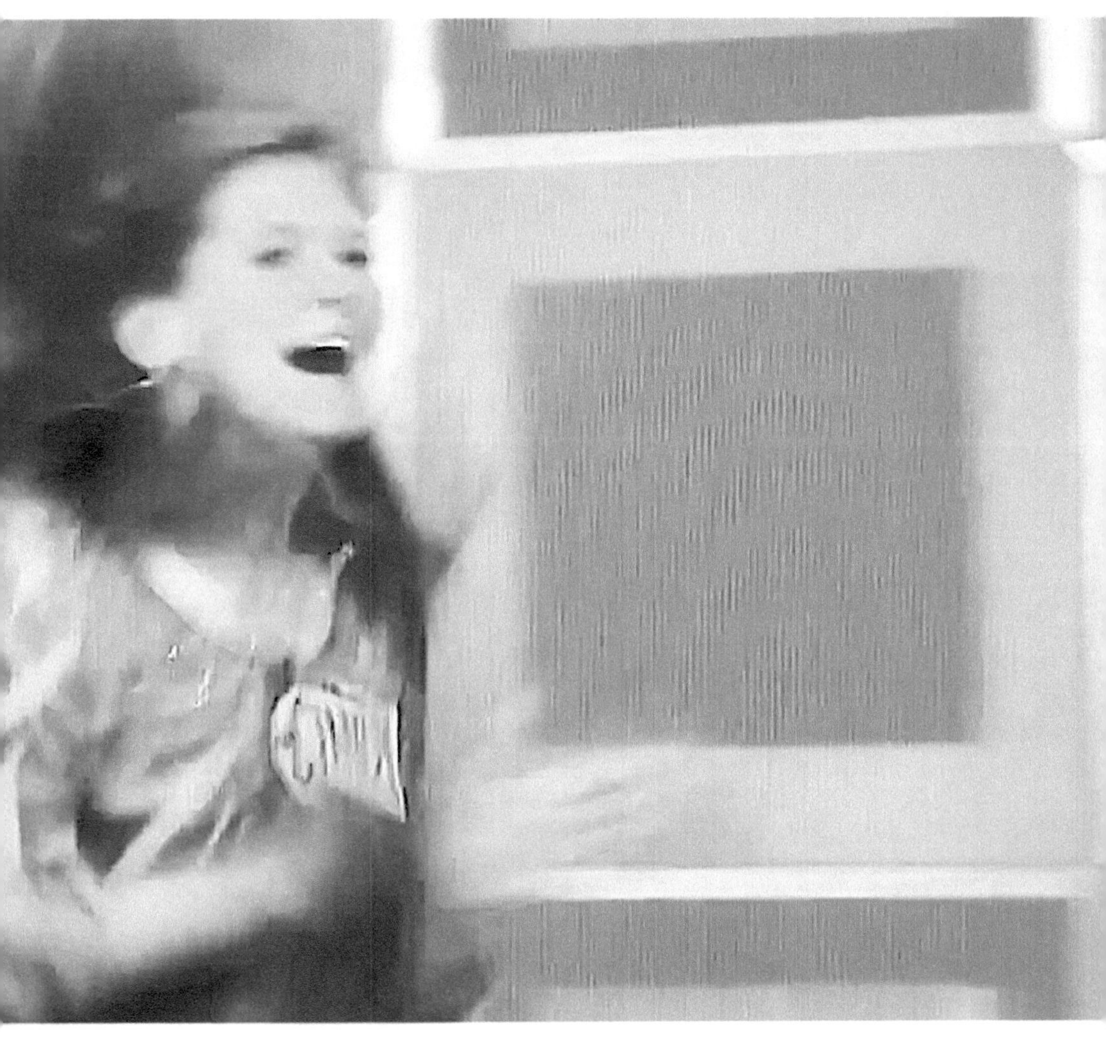

New York

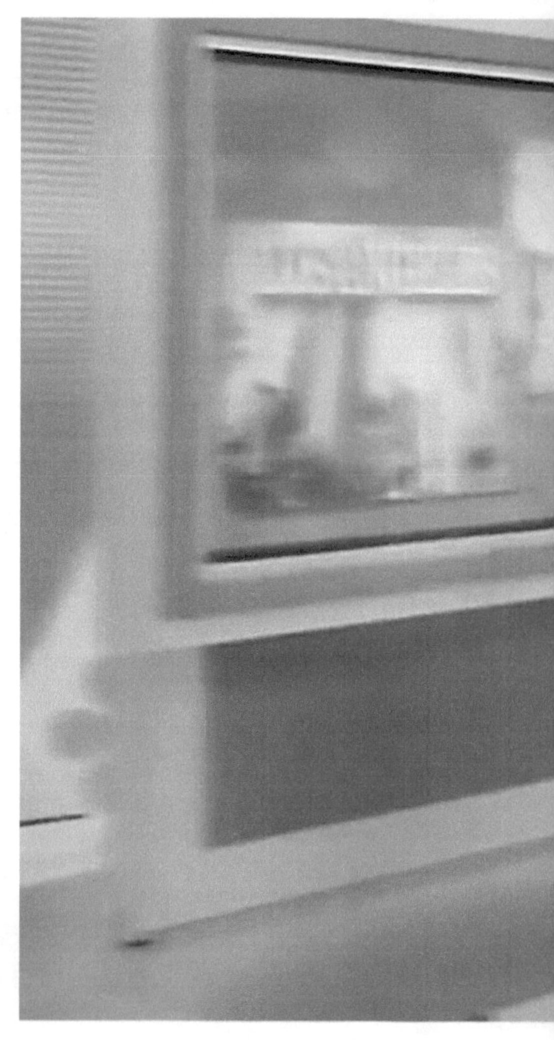

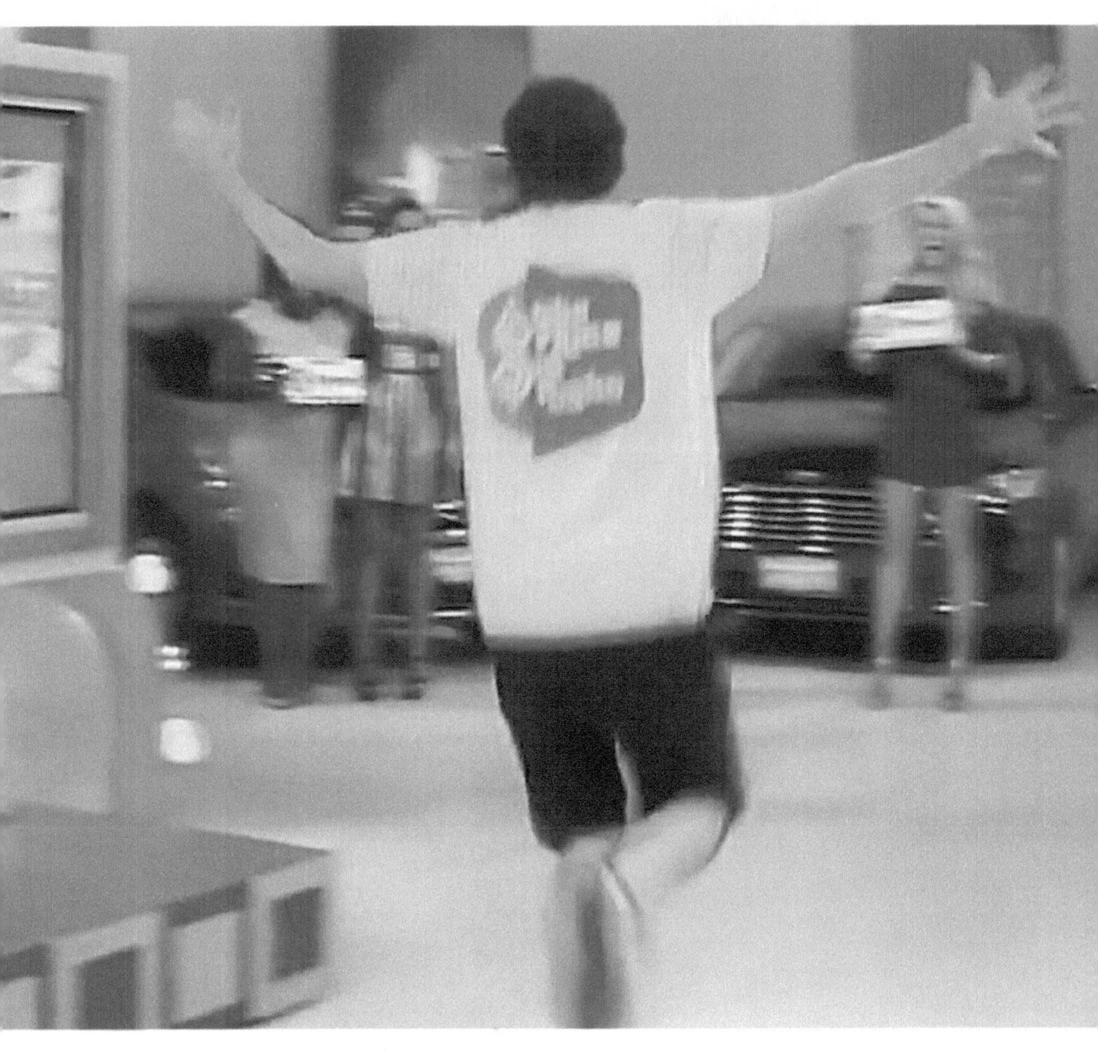

Nicara-gua

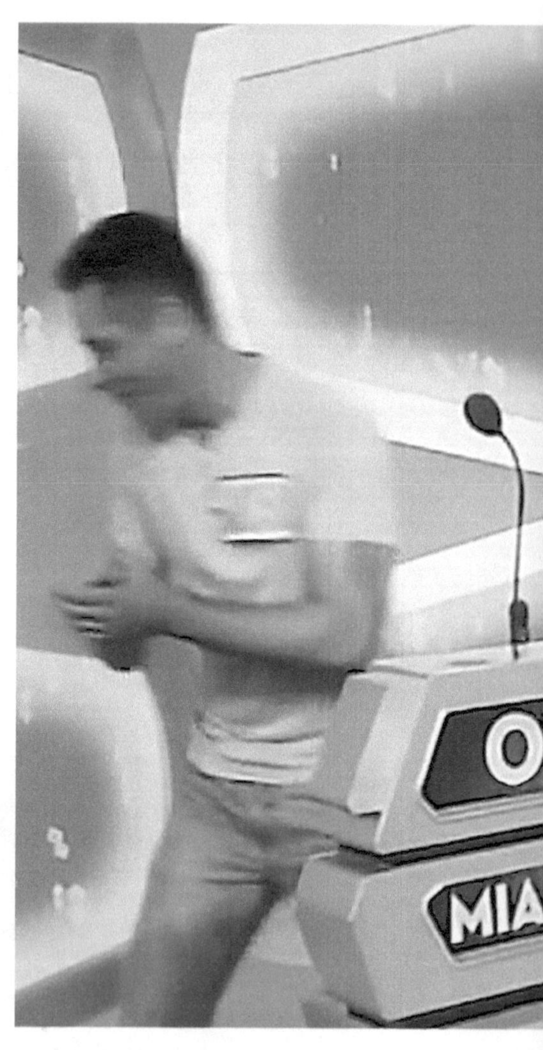

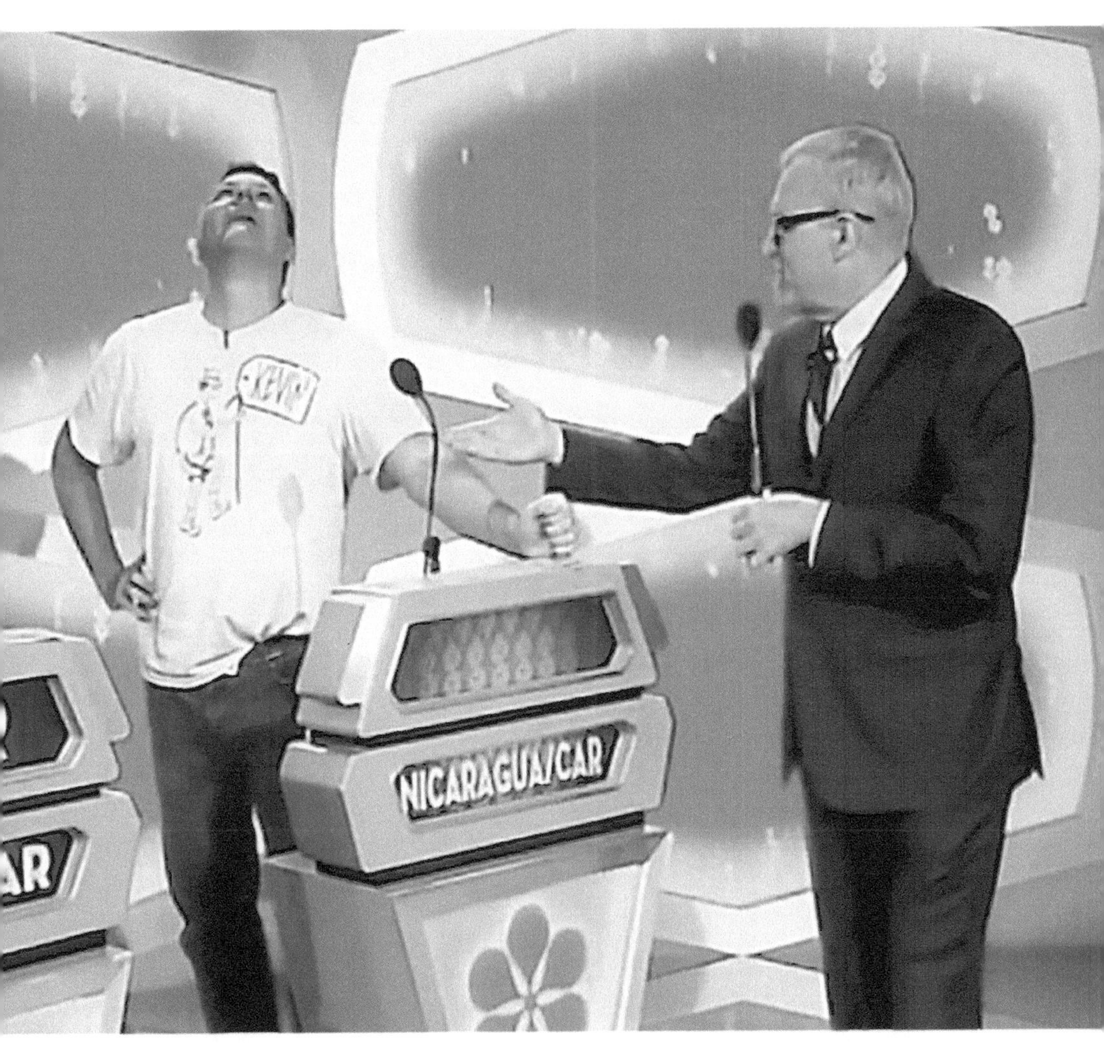

NICARAGUA/CAR

Ojai

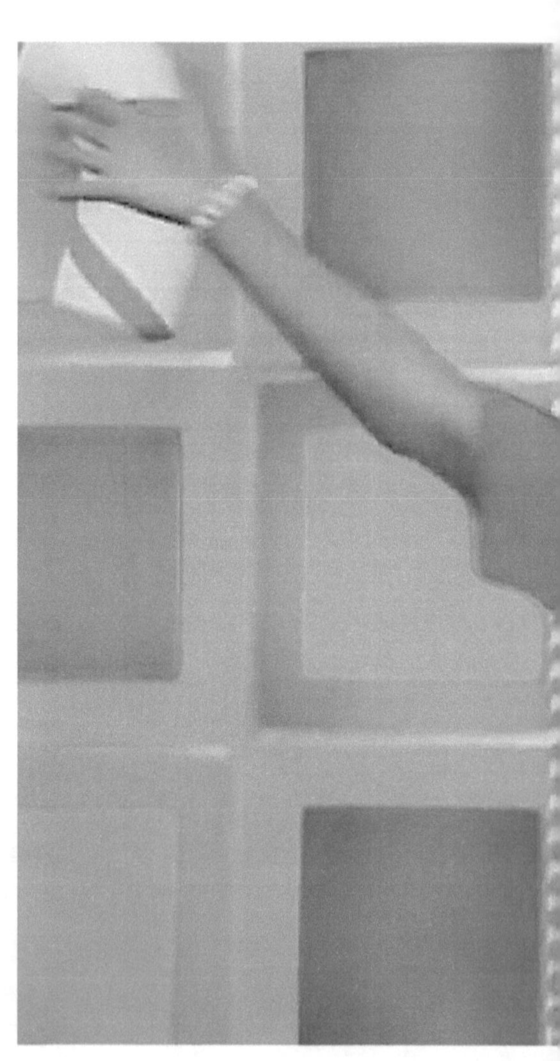

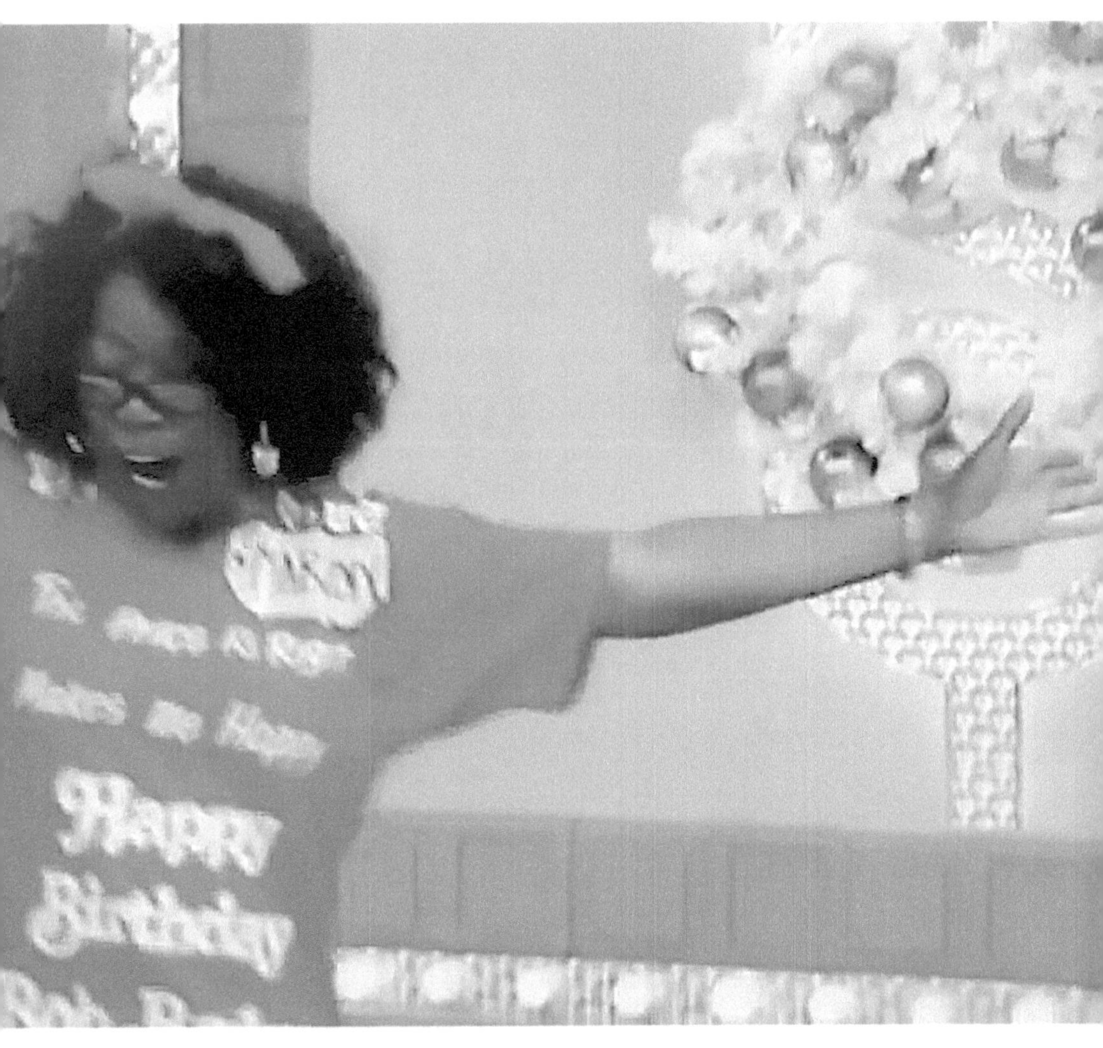

Orlan-
do

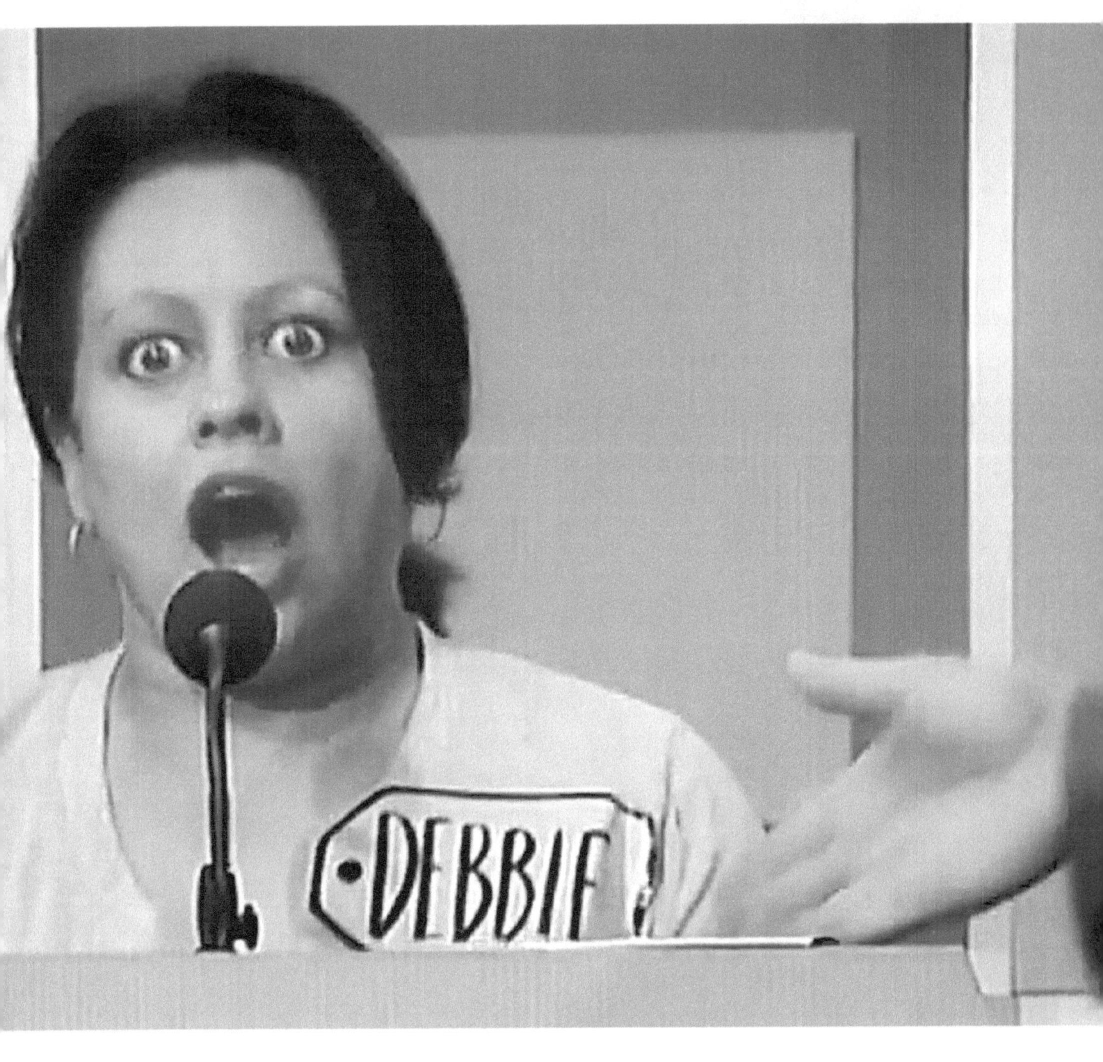

·DEBBIE

Orlan-
do

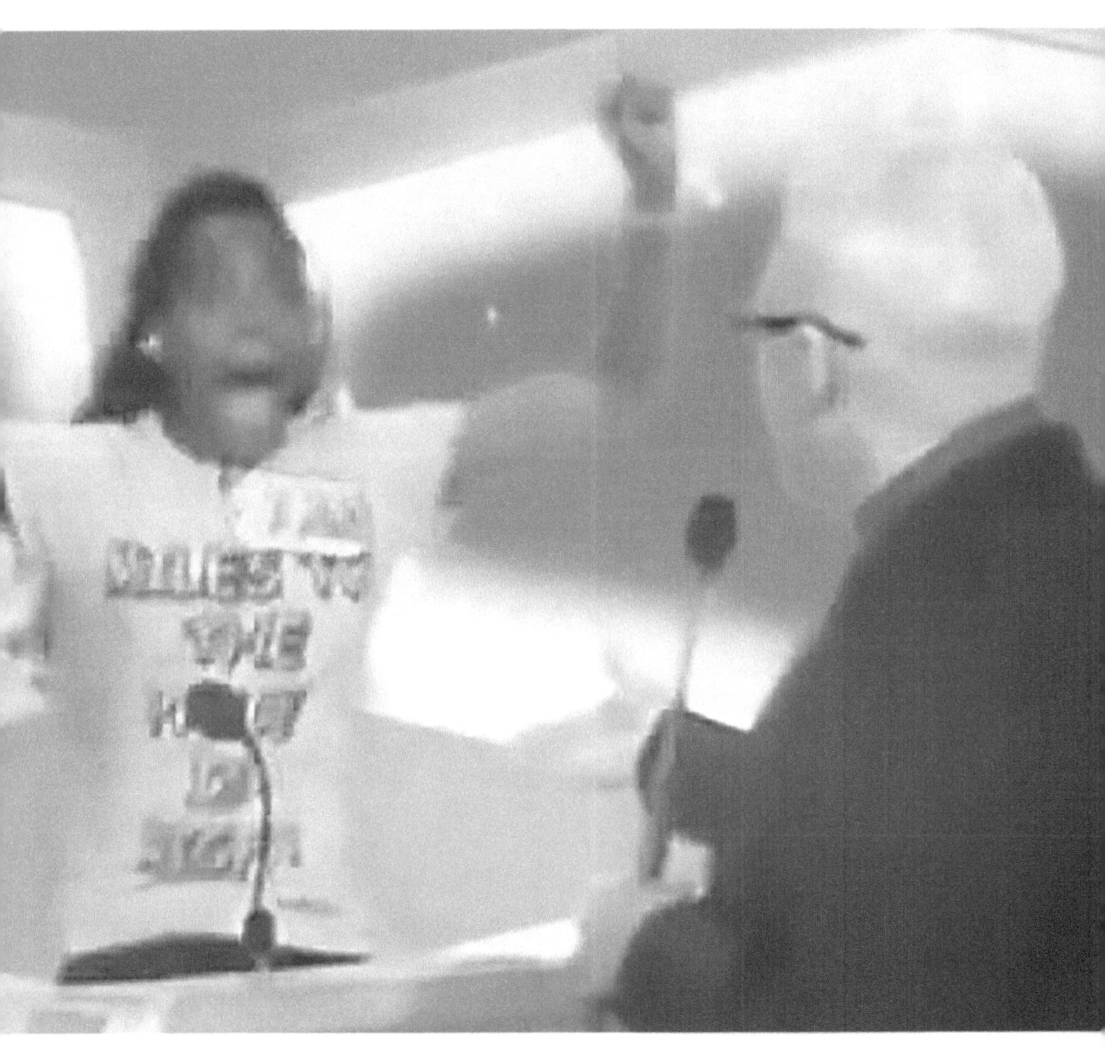

Paris

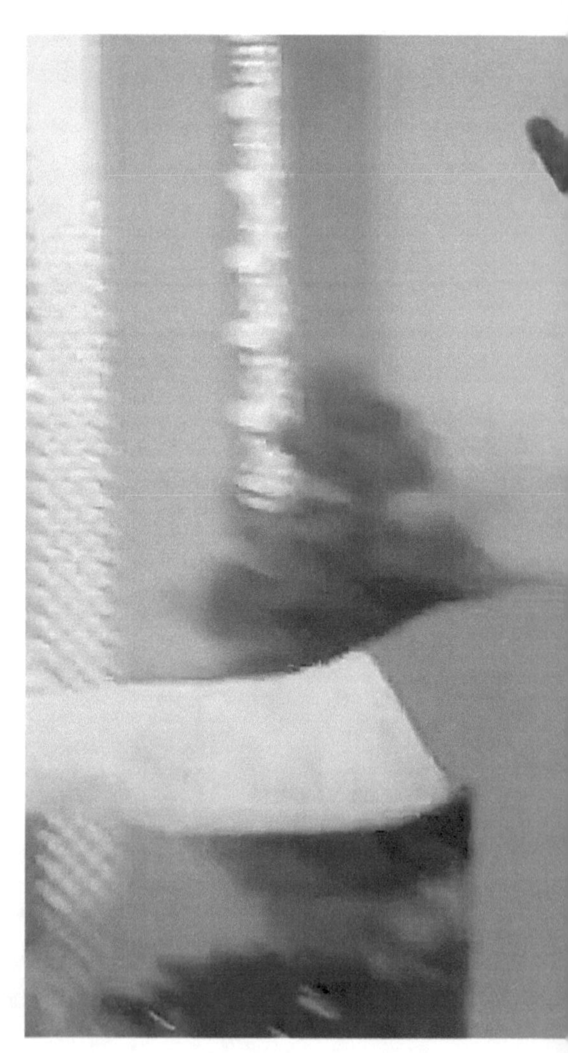

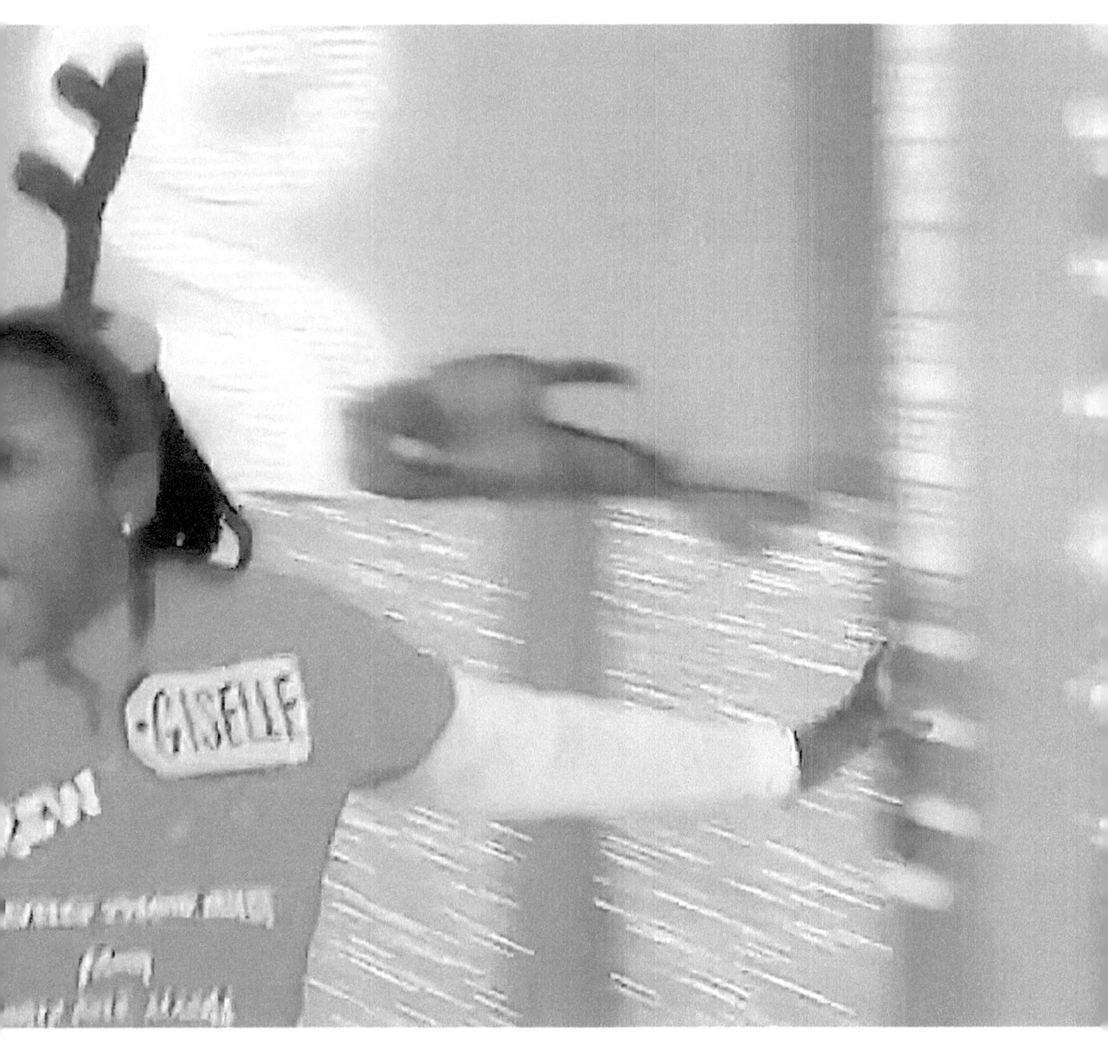

Paris/Florence

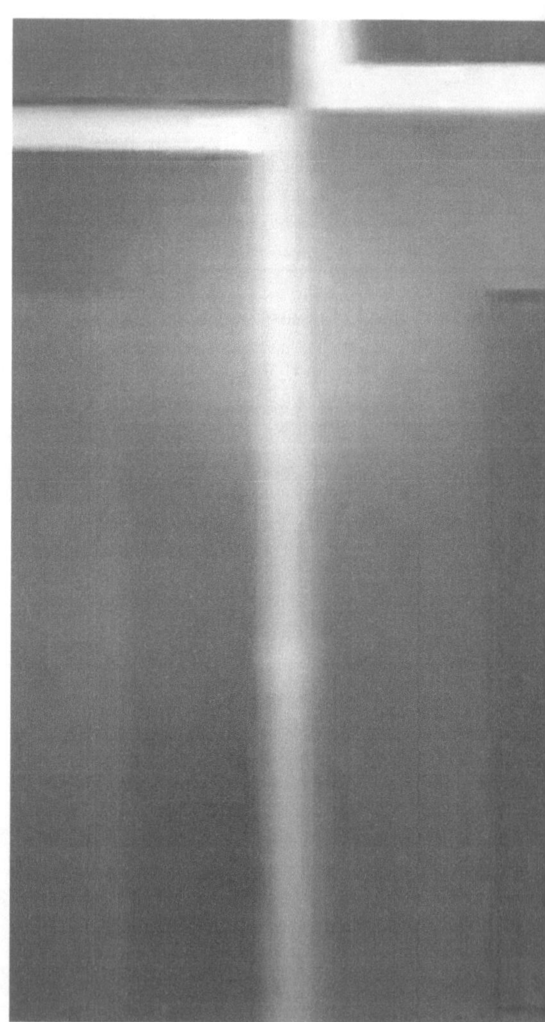

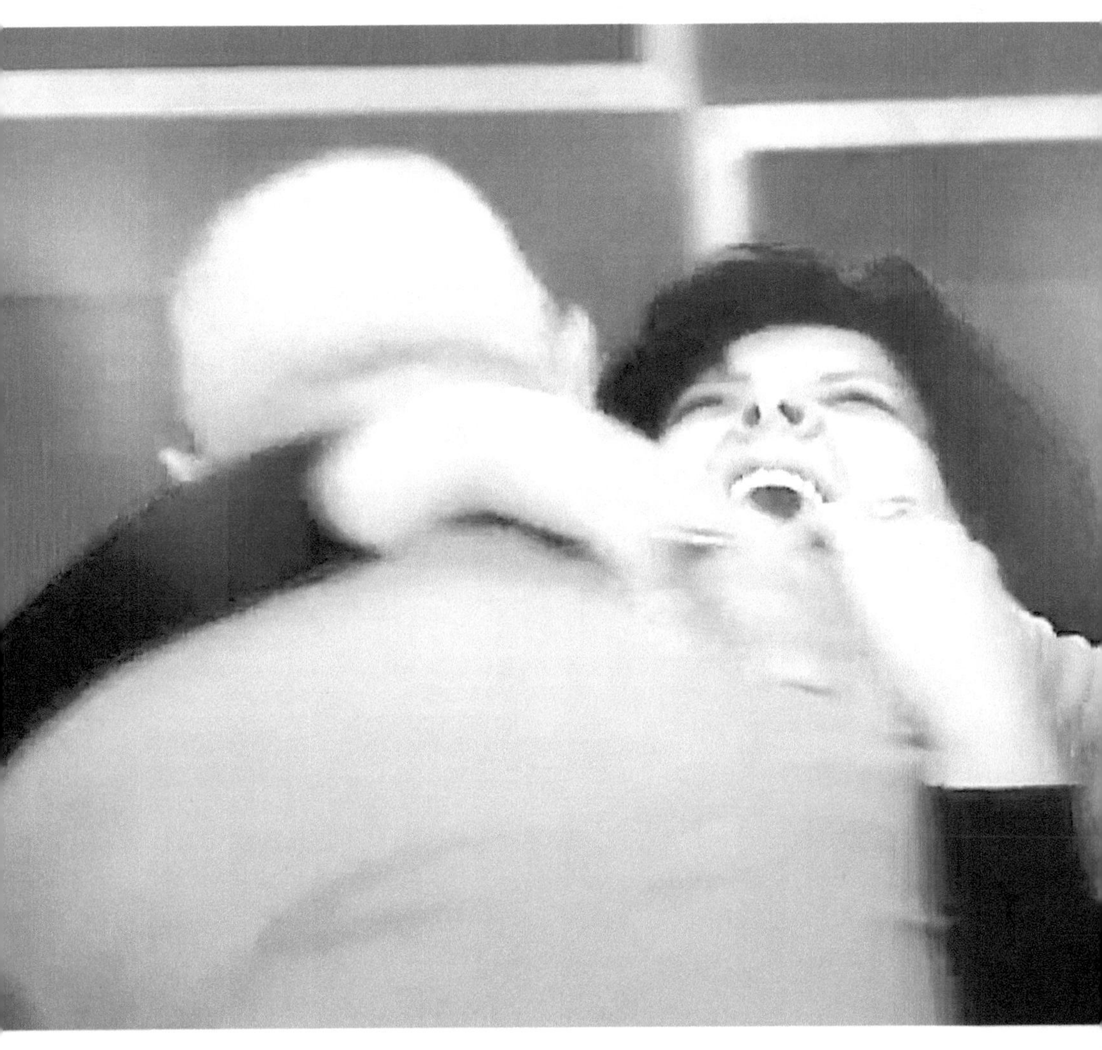

Paris/ New York

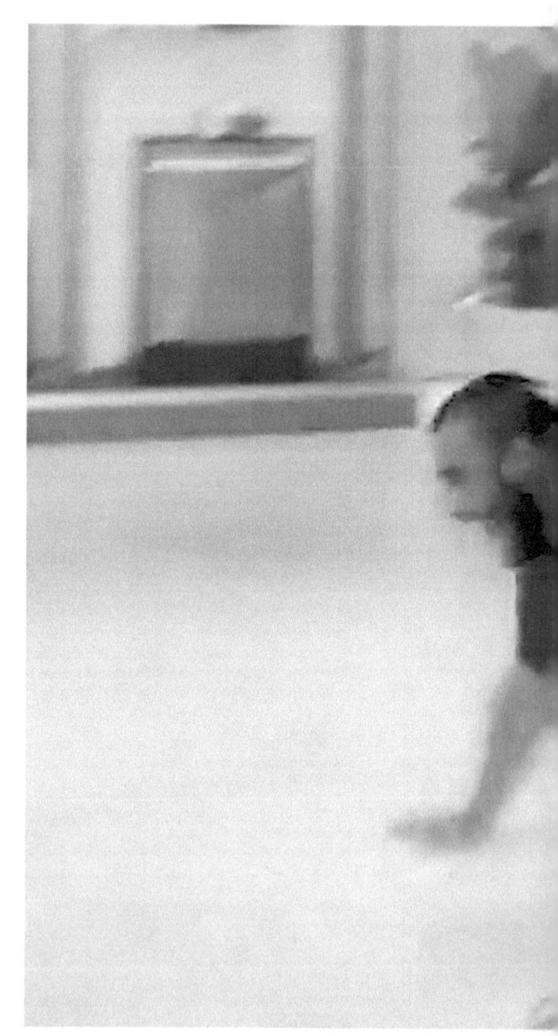

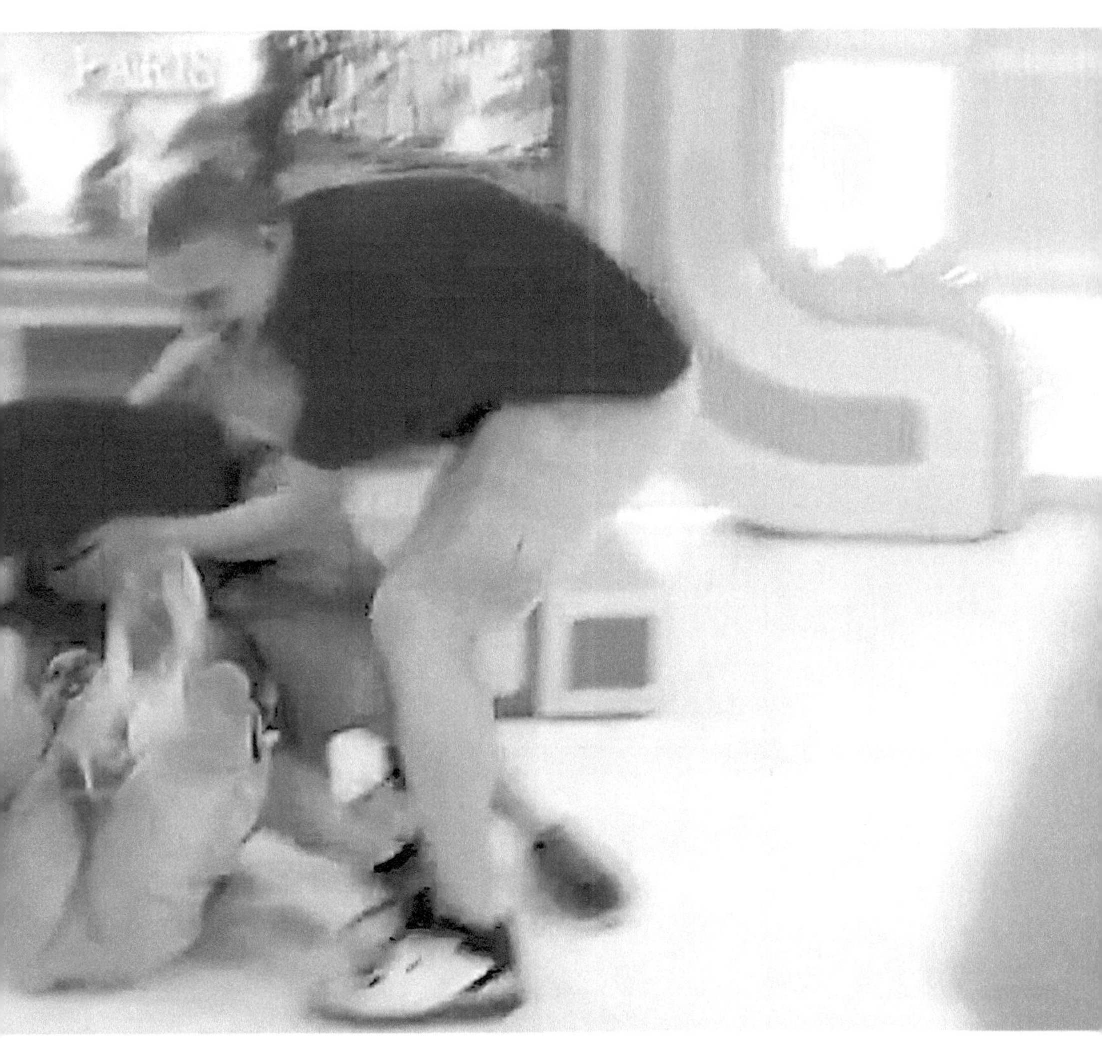

Pom-
peii

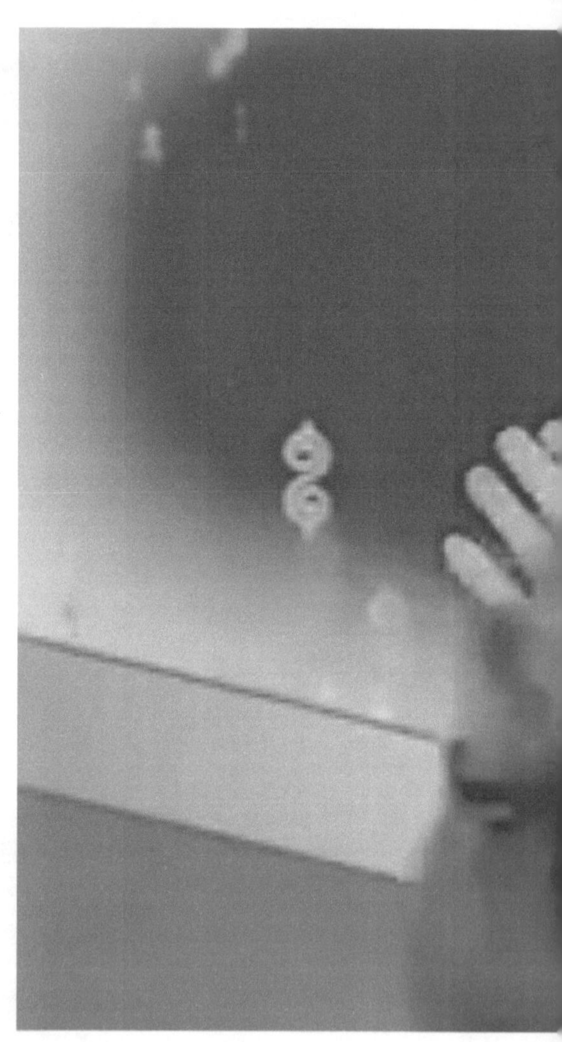

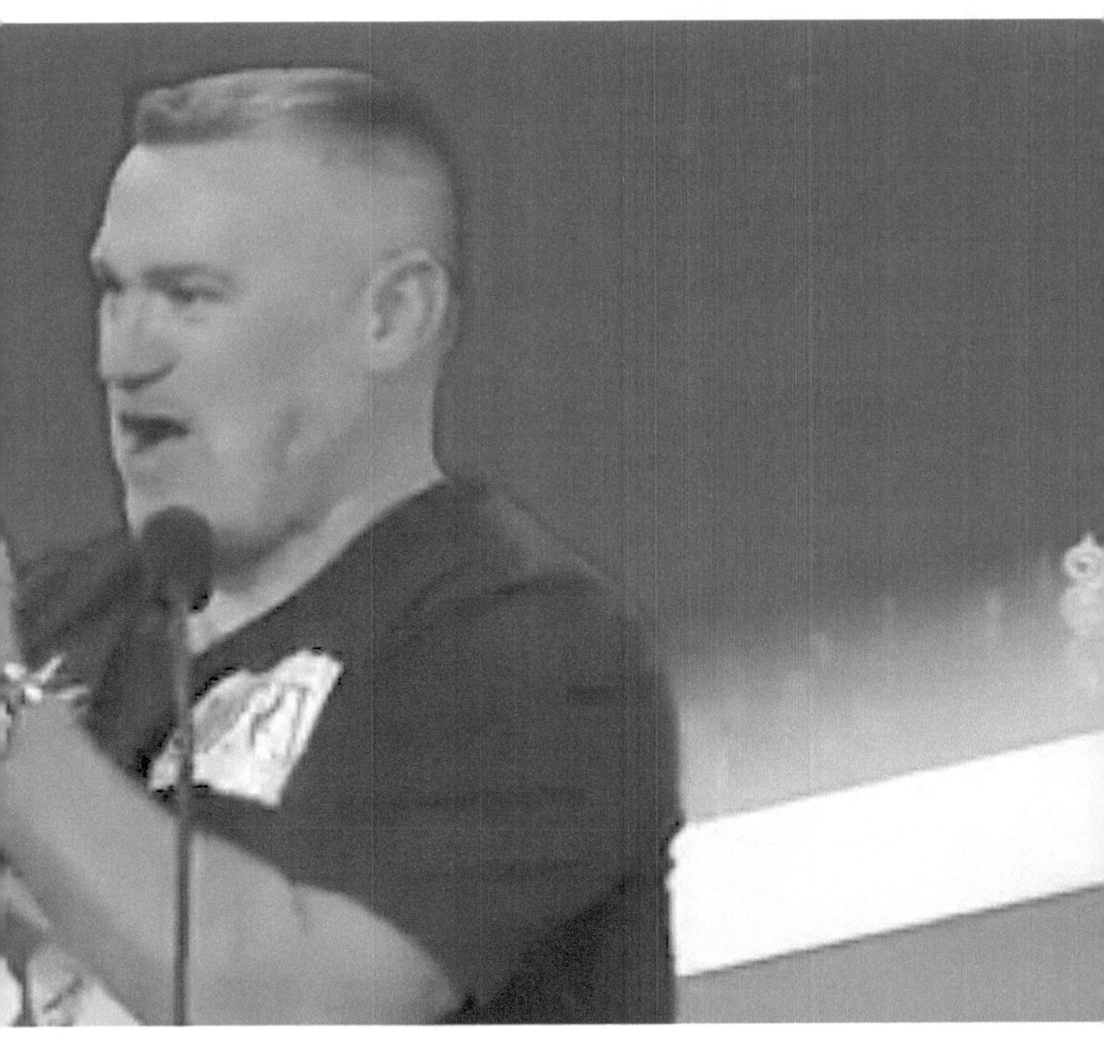

Puerto Rico

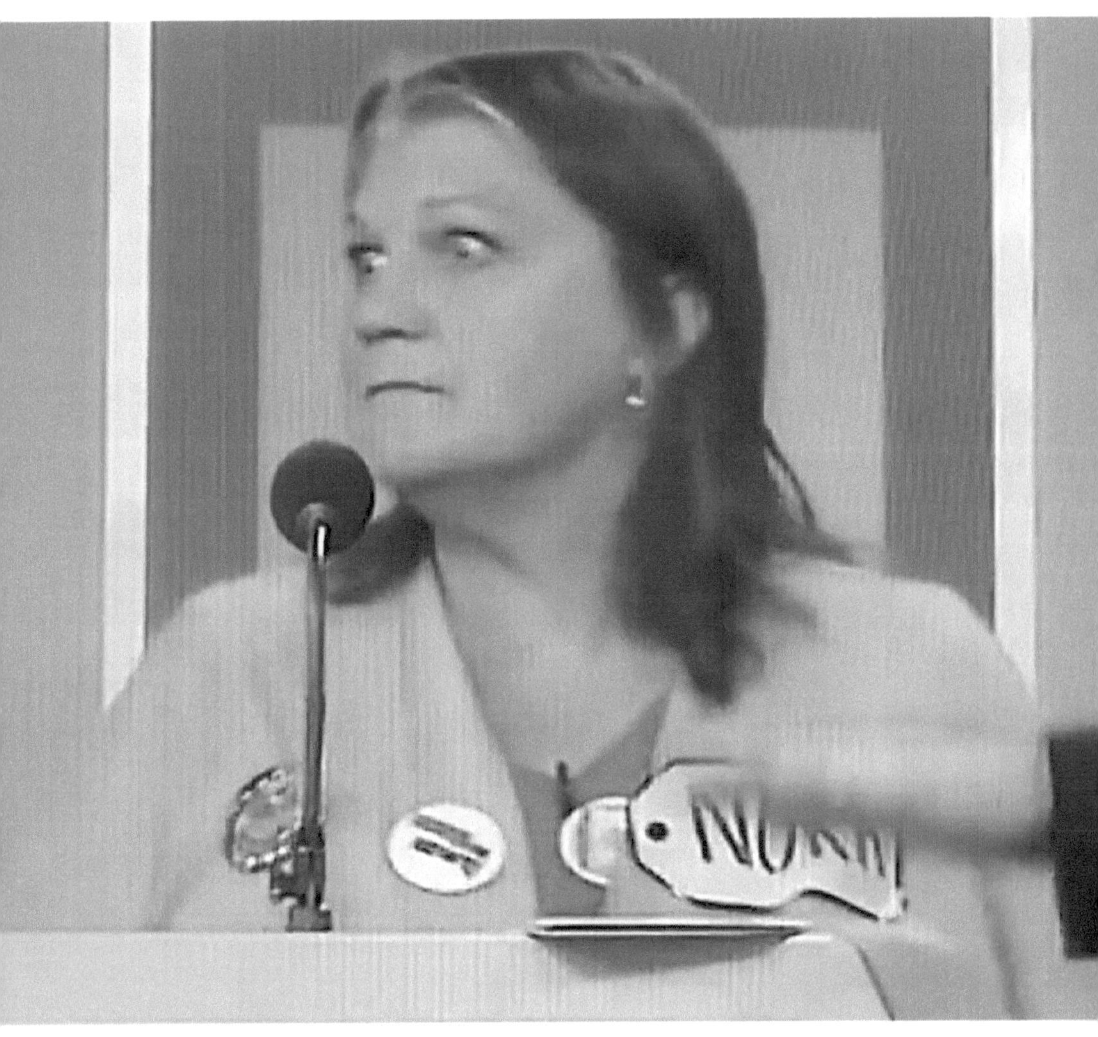
NUNN

Rome

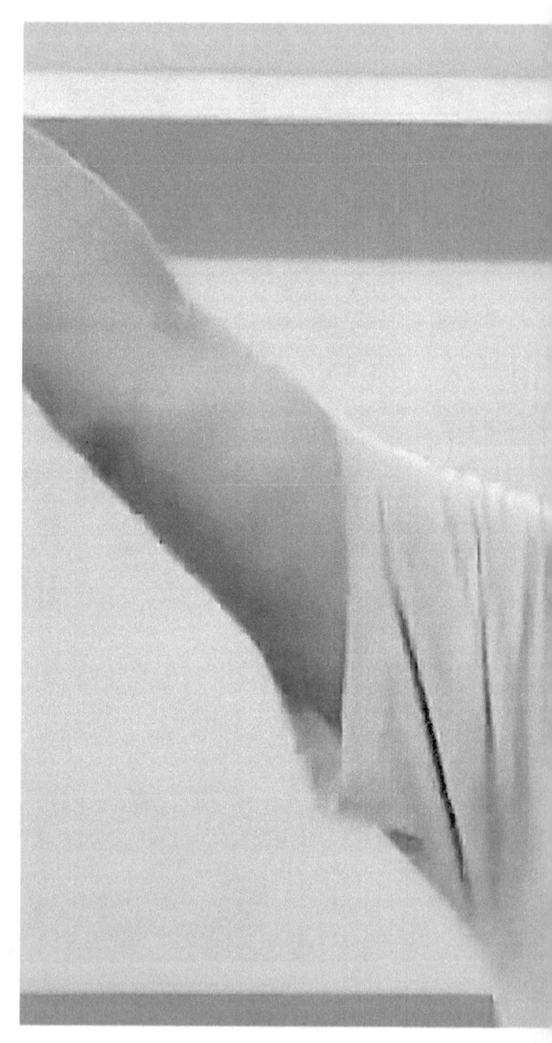

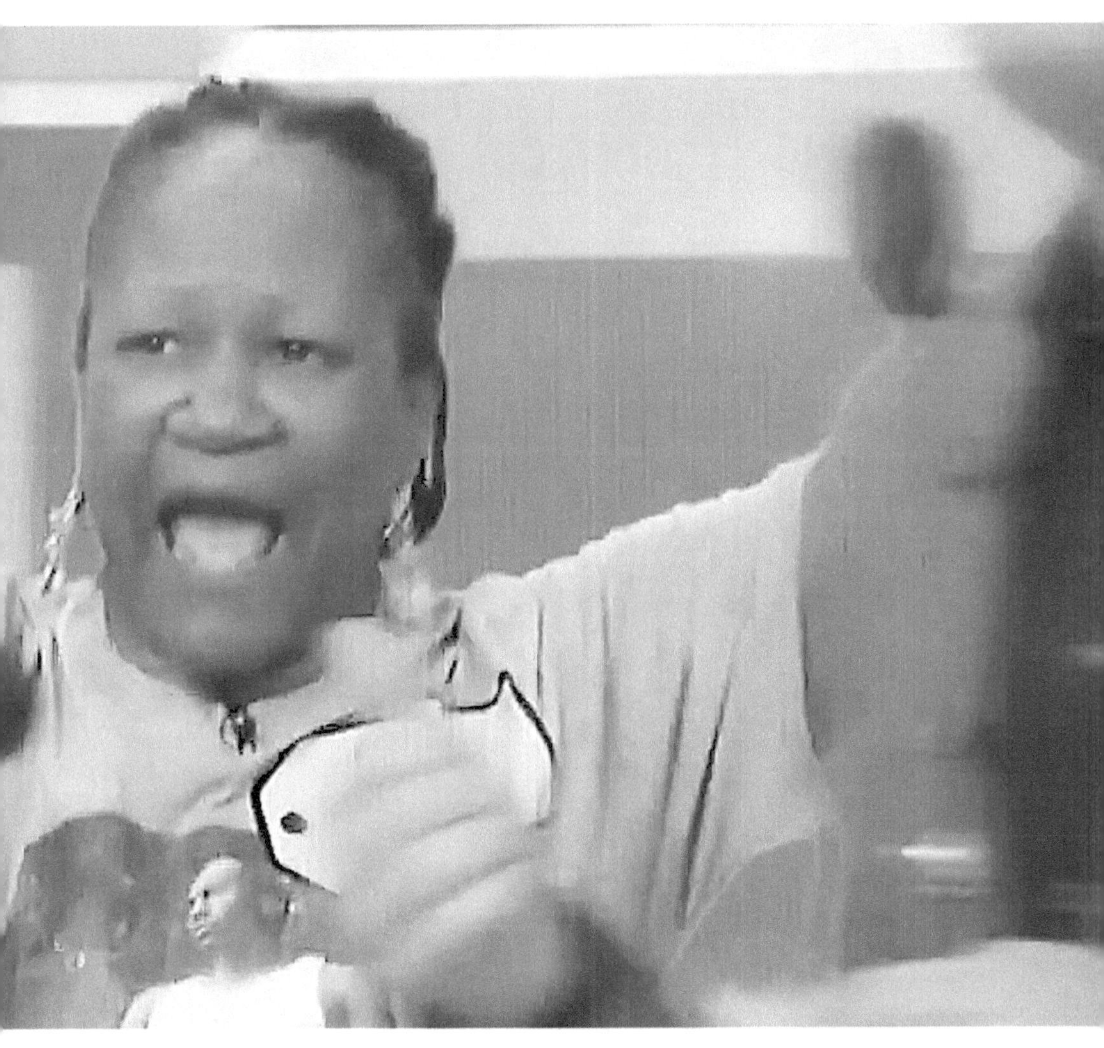

San Di-
ego

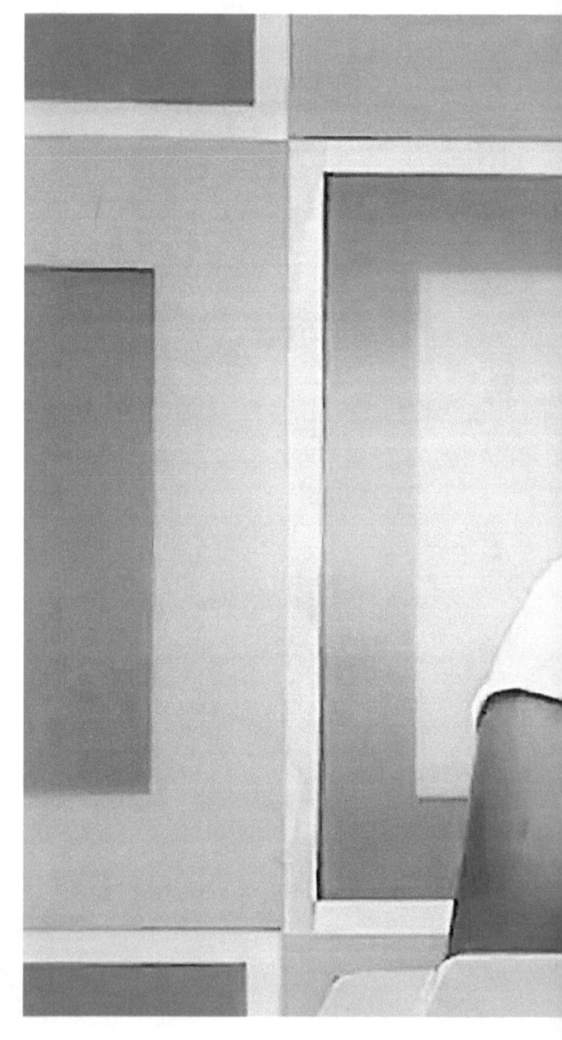

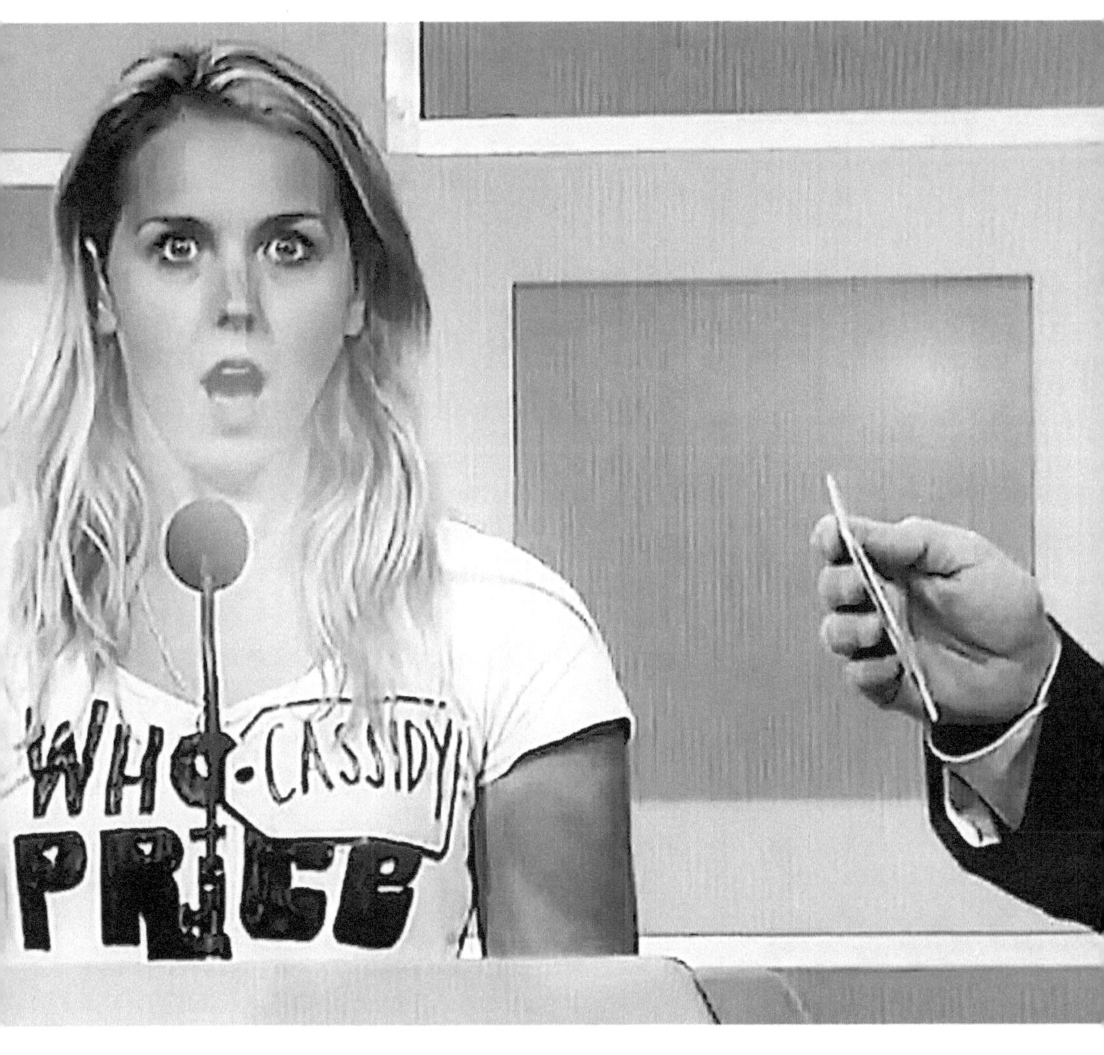
WHO · CASSIDY
PRICE

Seattle

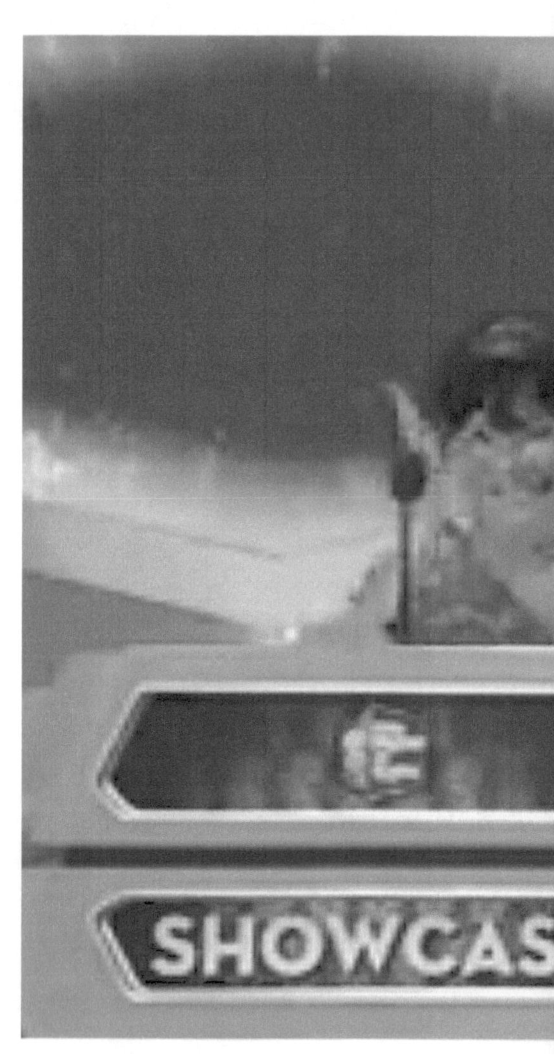

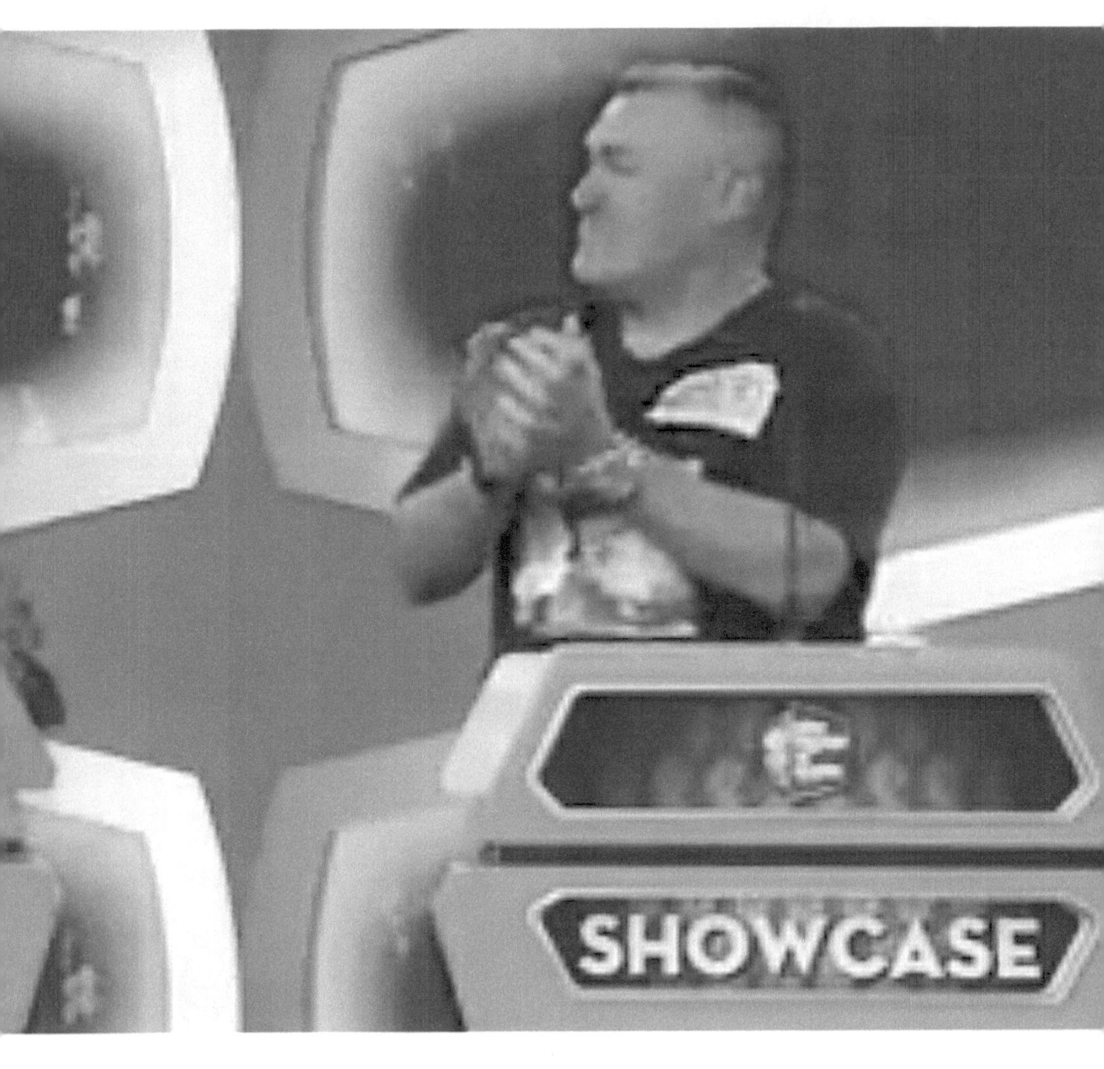

SHOWCASE

Seat-
tle/
Chica-
go

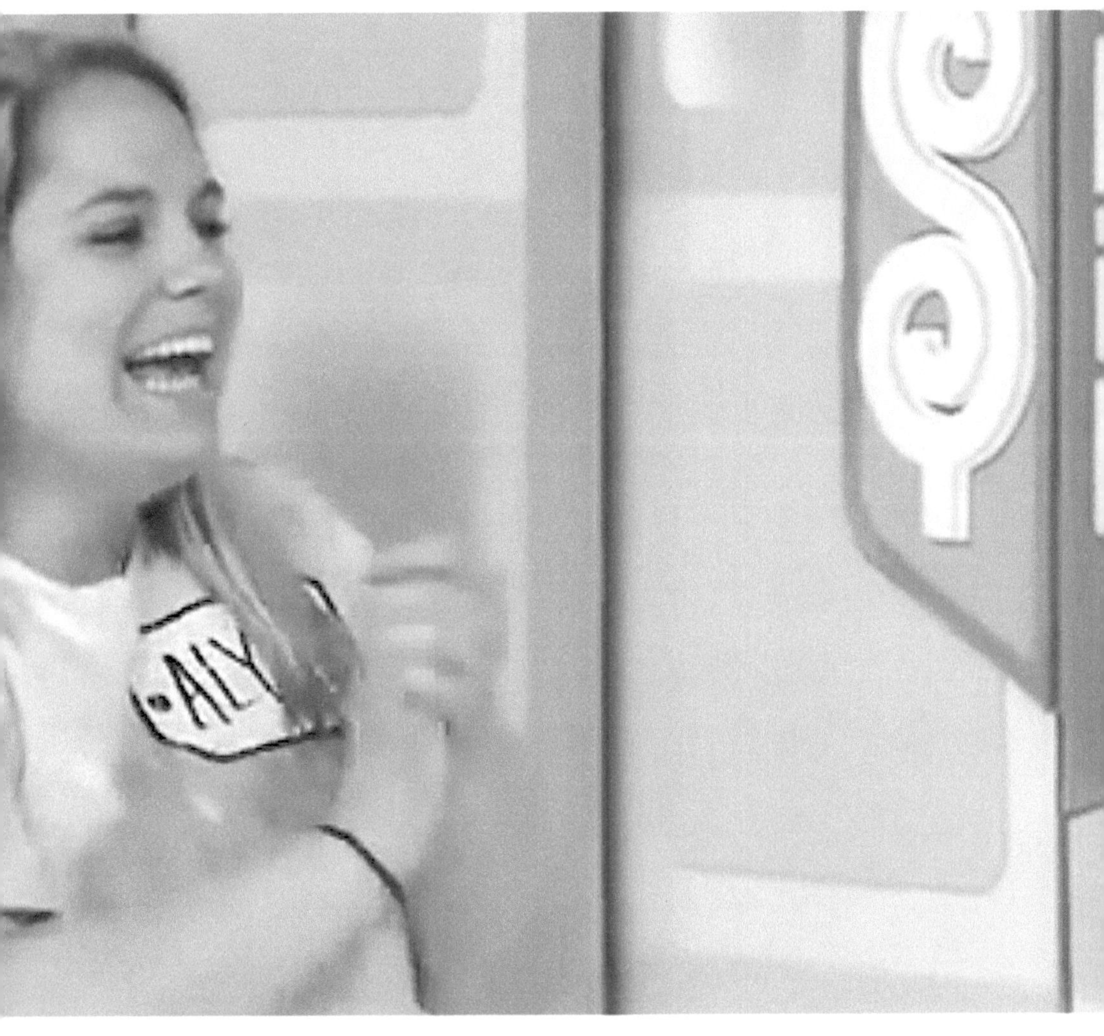

ALY

Seattle/Italy

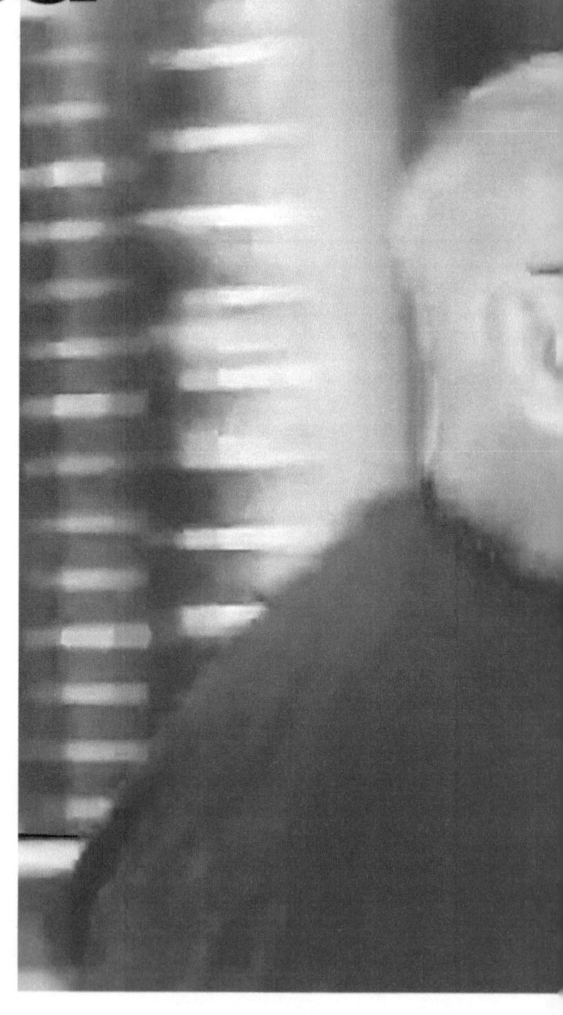

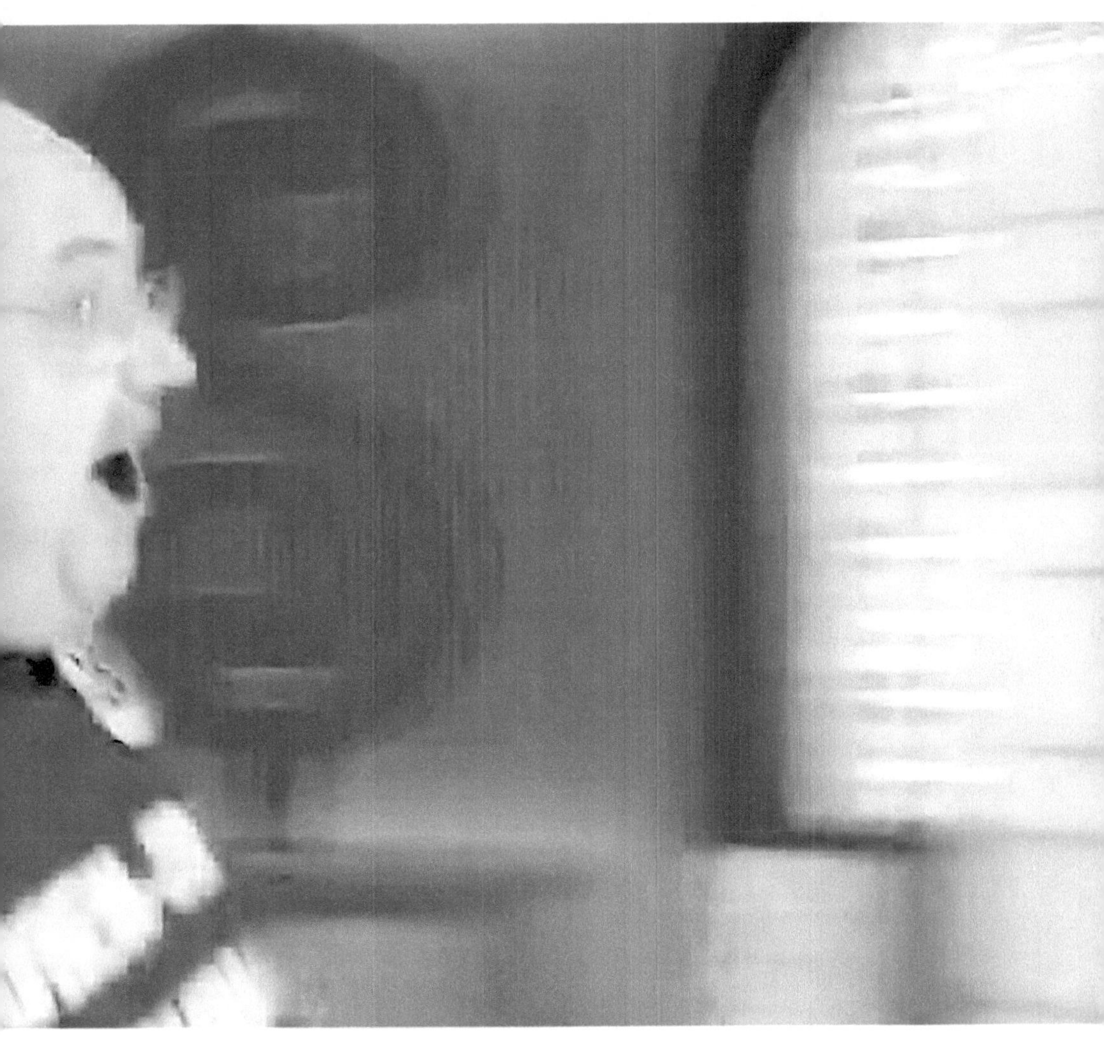

Sequoia Park

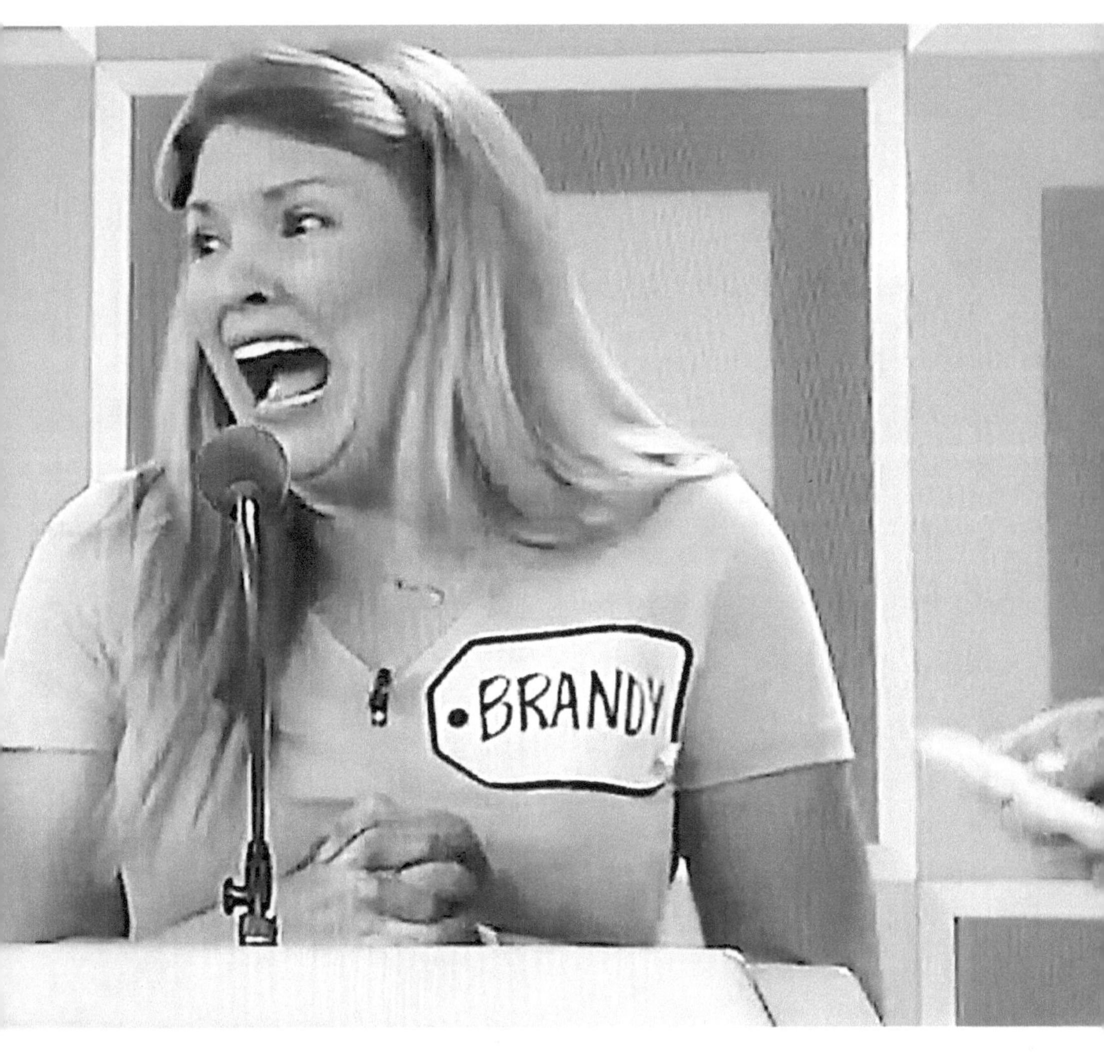

•BRANDY

Sicily

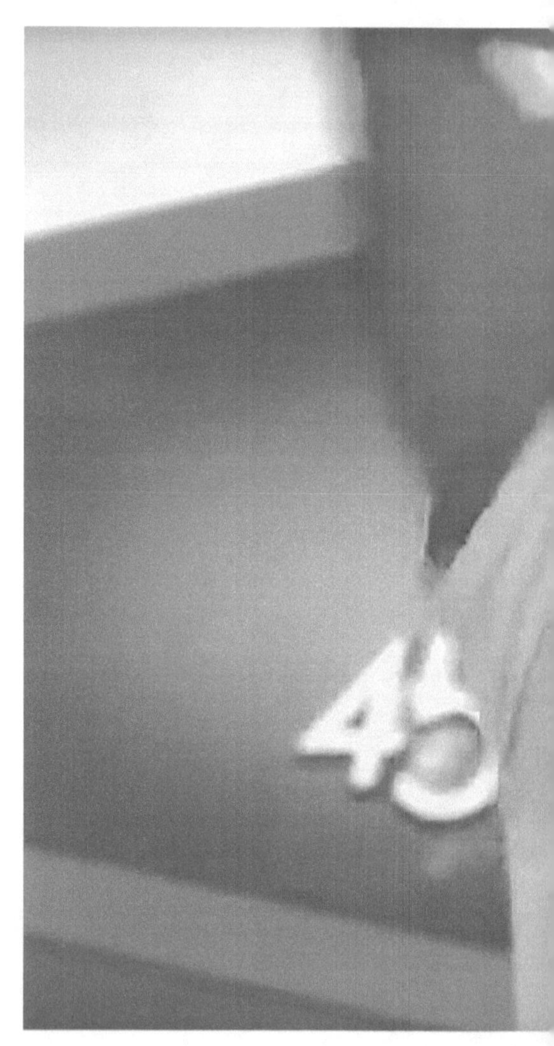

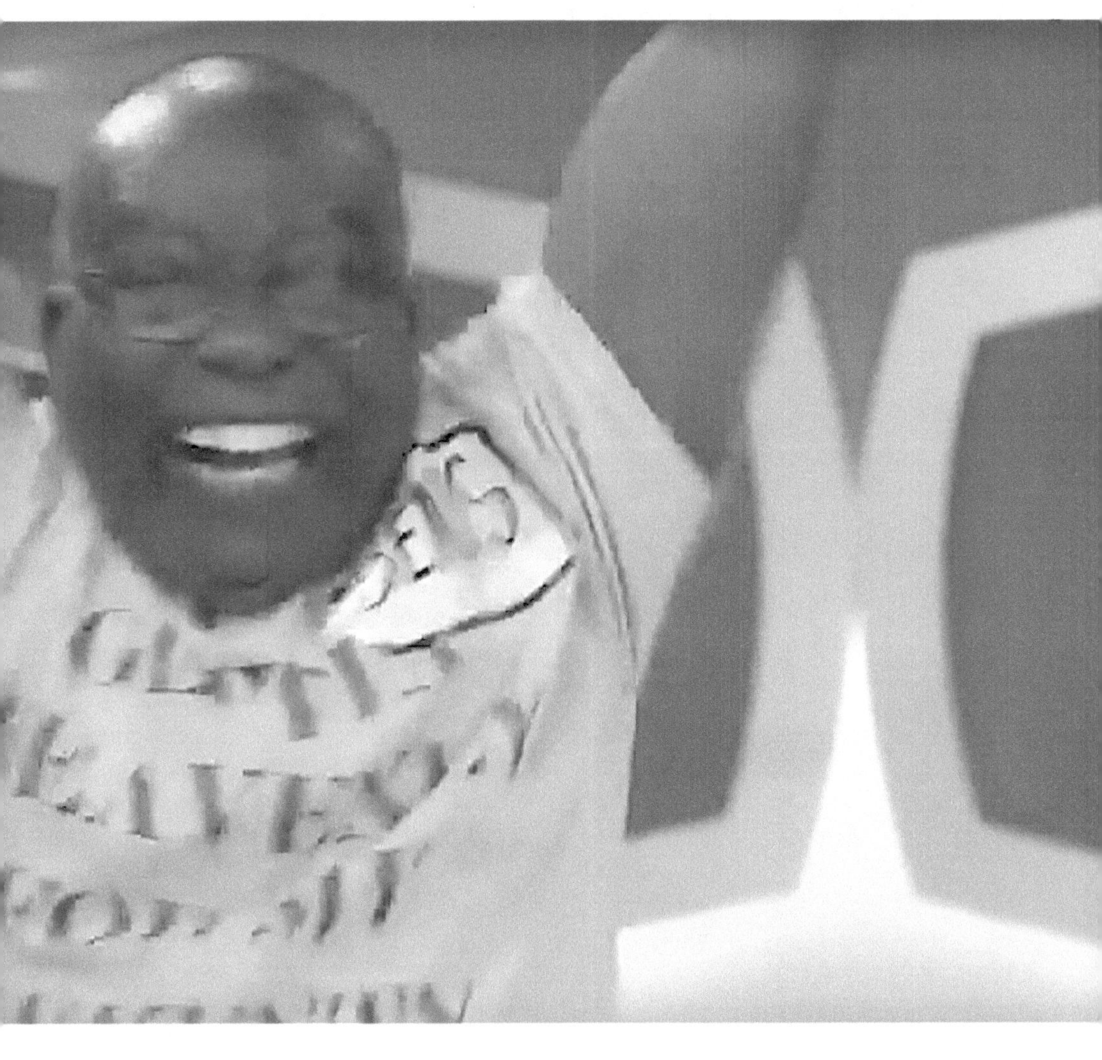

South America

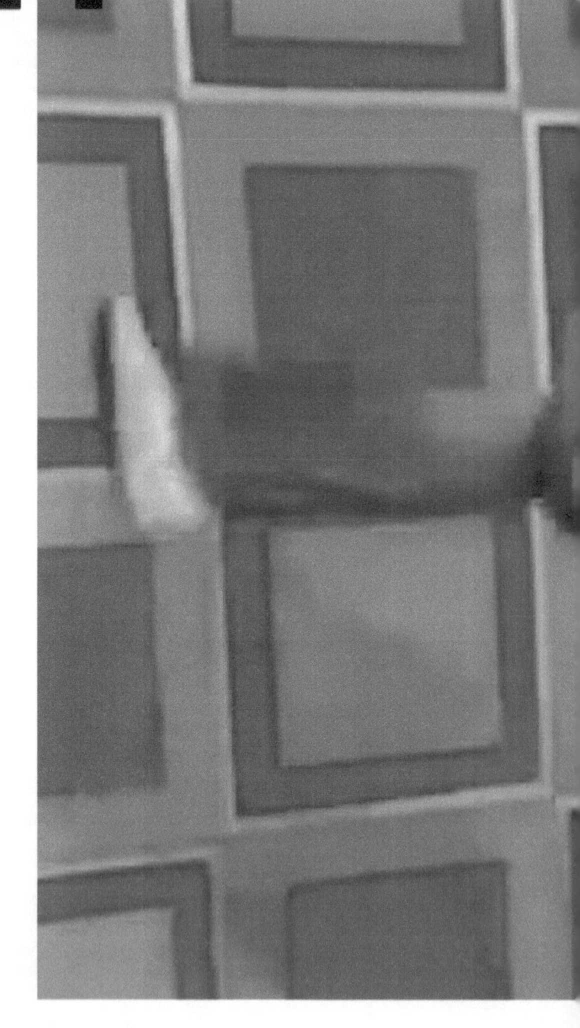

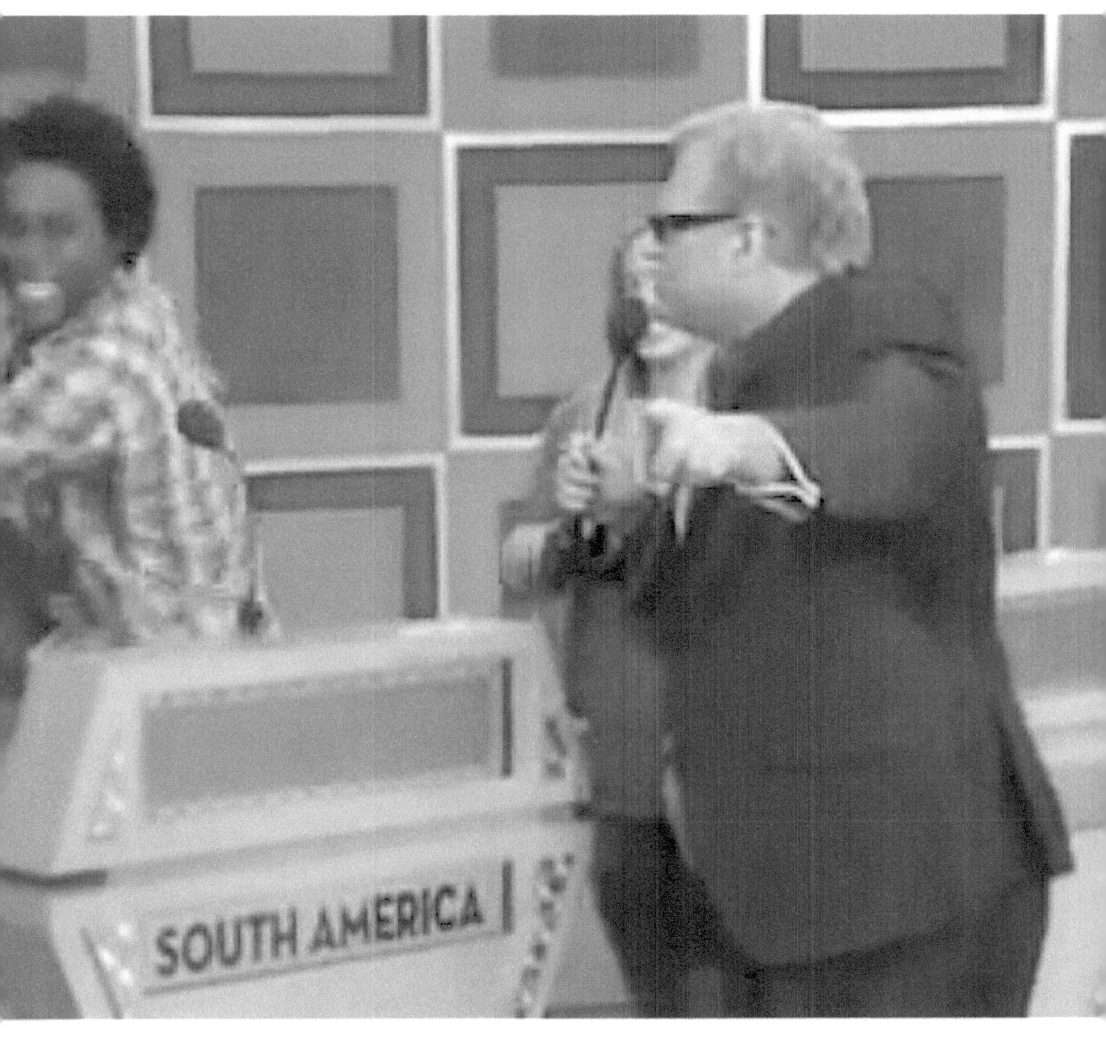
SOUTH AMERICA

South Beach

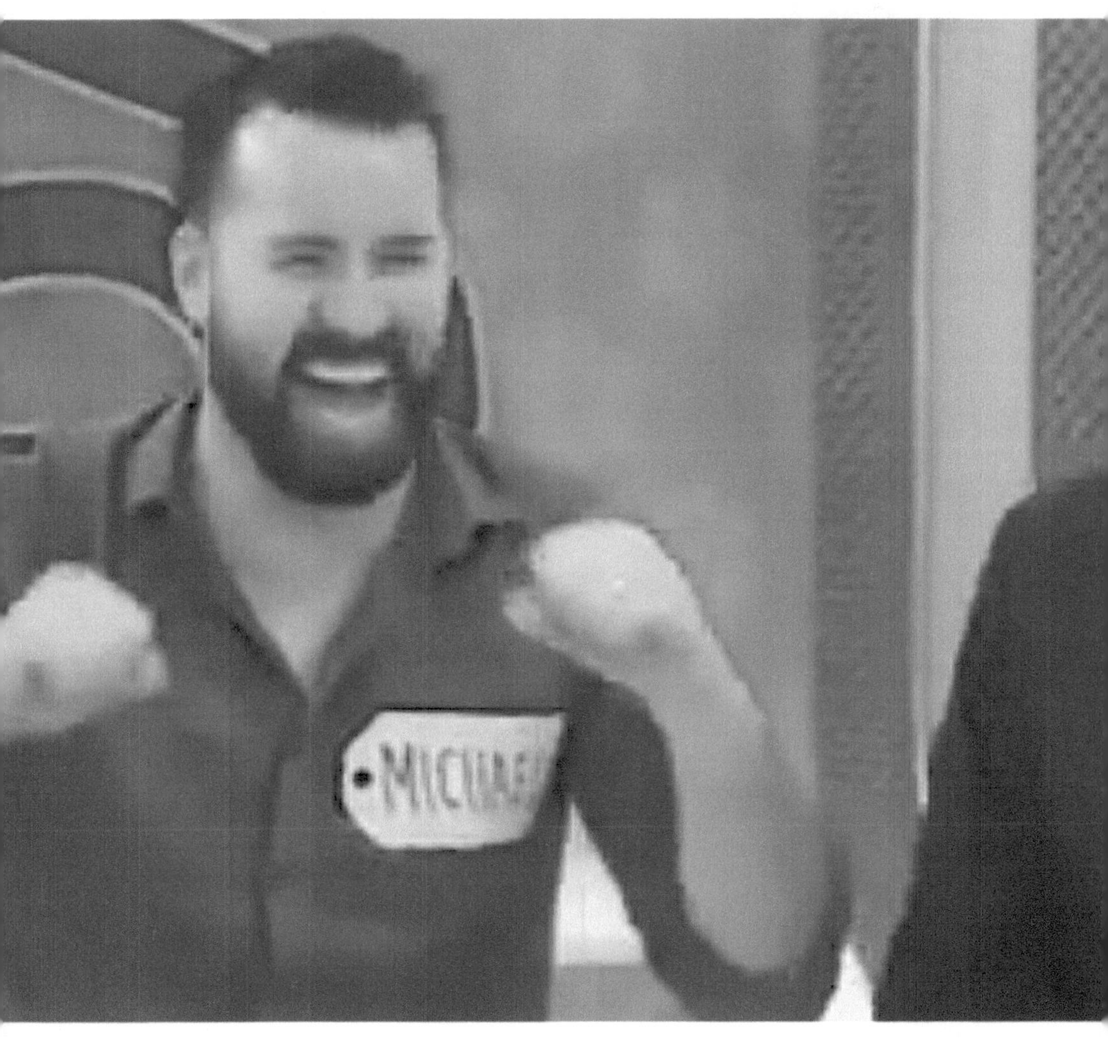
MICUN

Switzerland

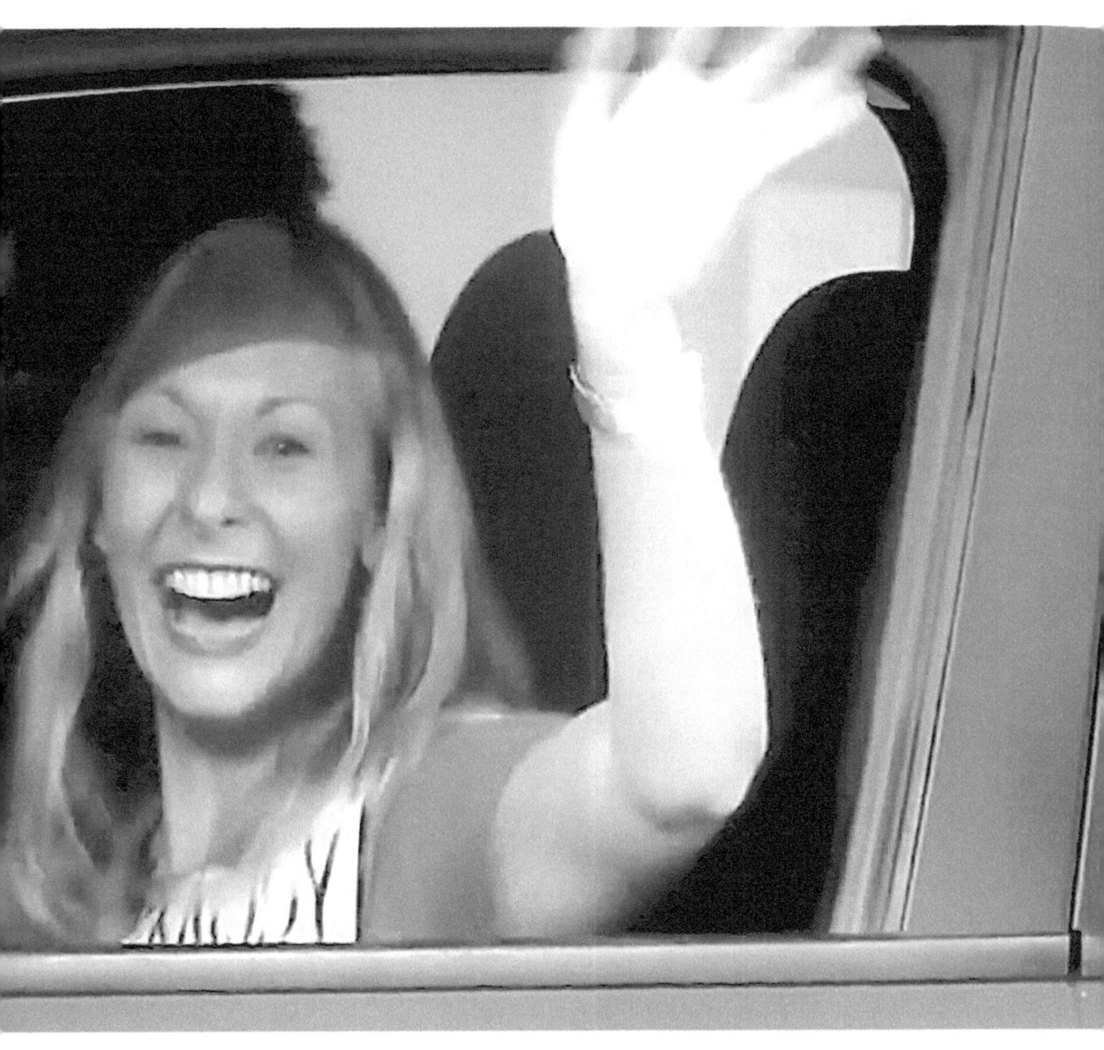

Thai-
land

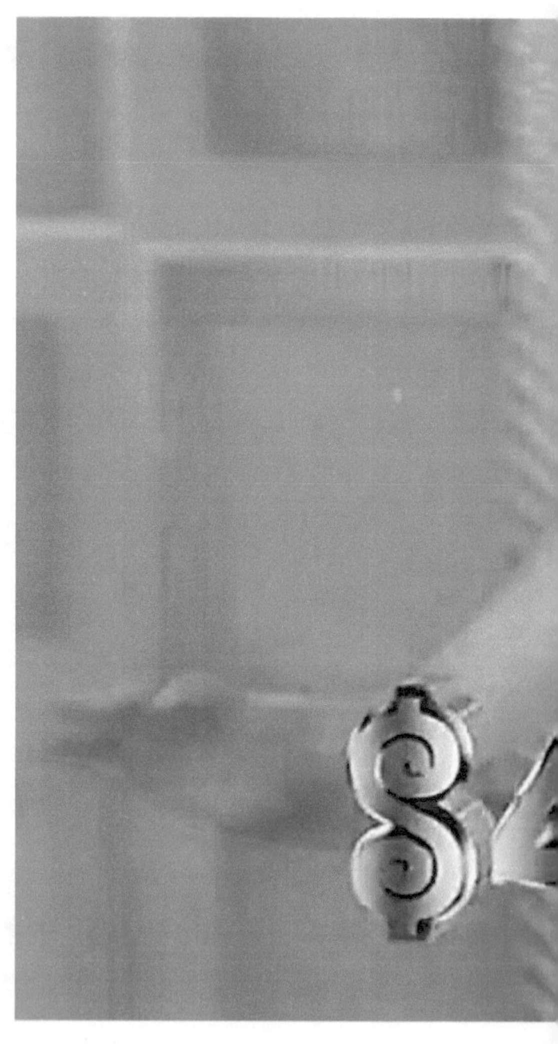

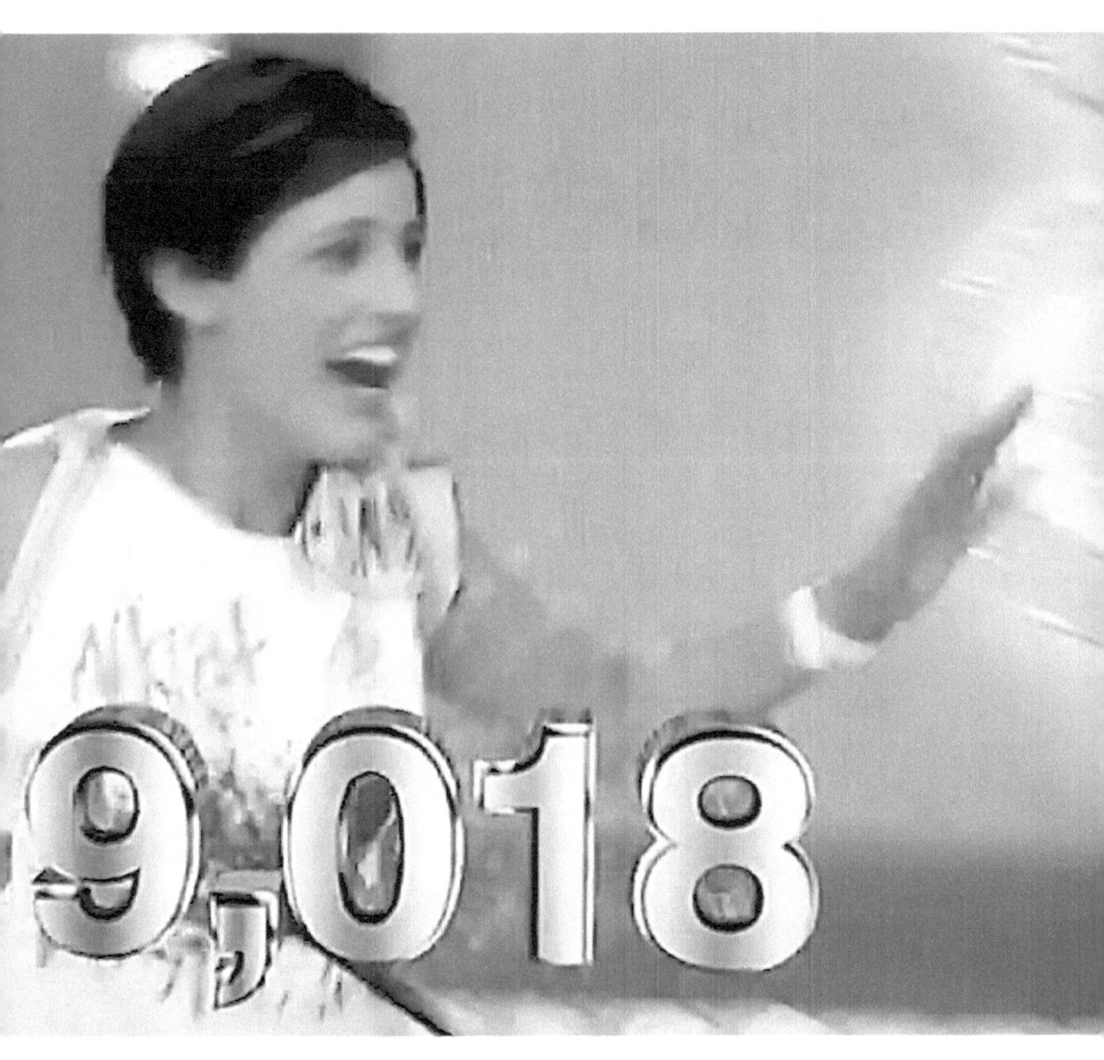
9,018

Turks and Caicos

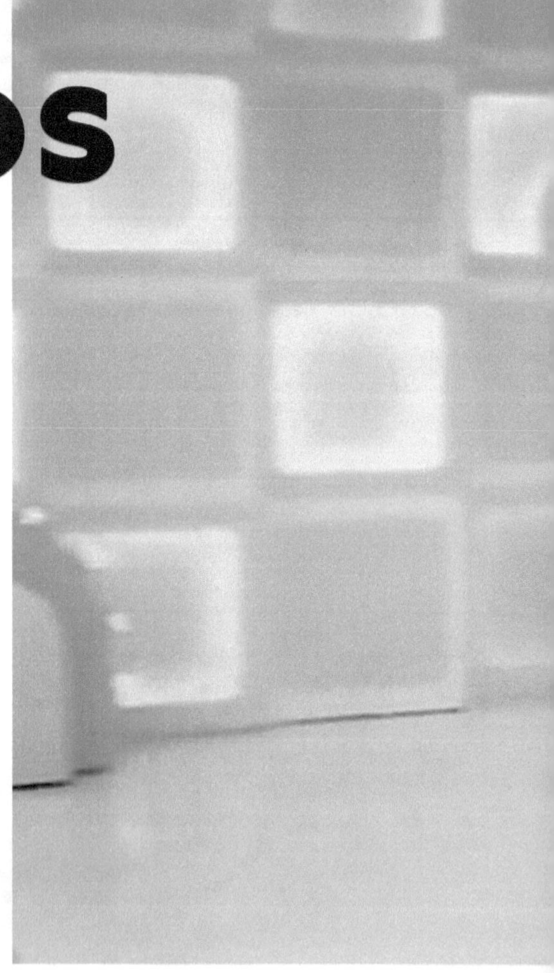

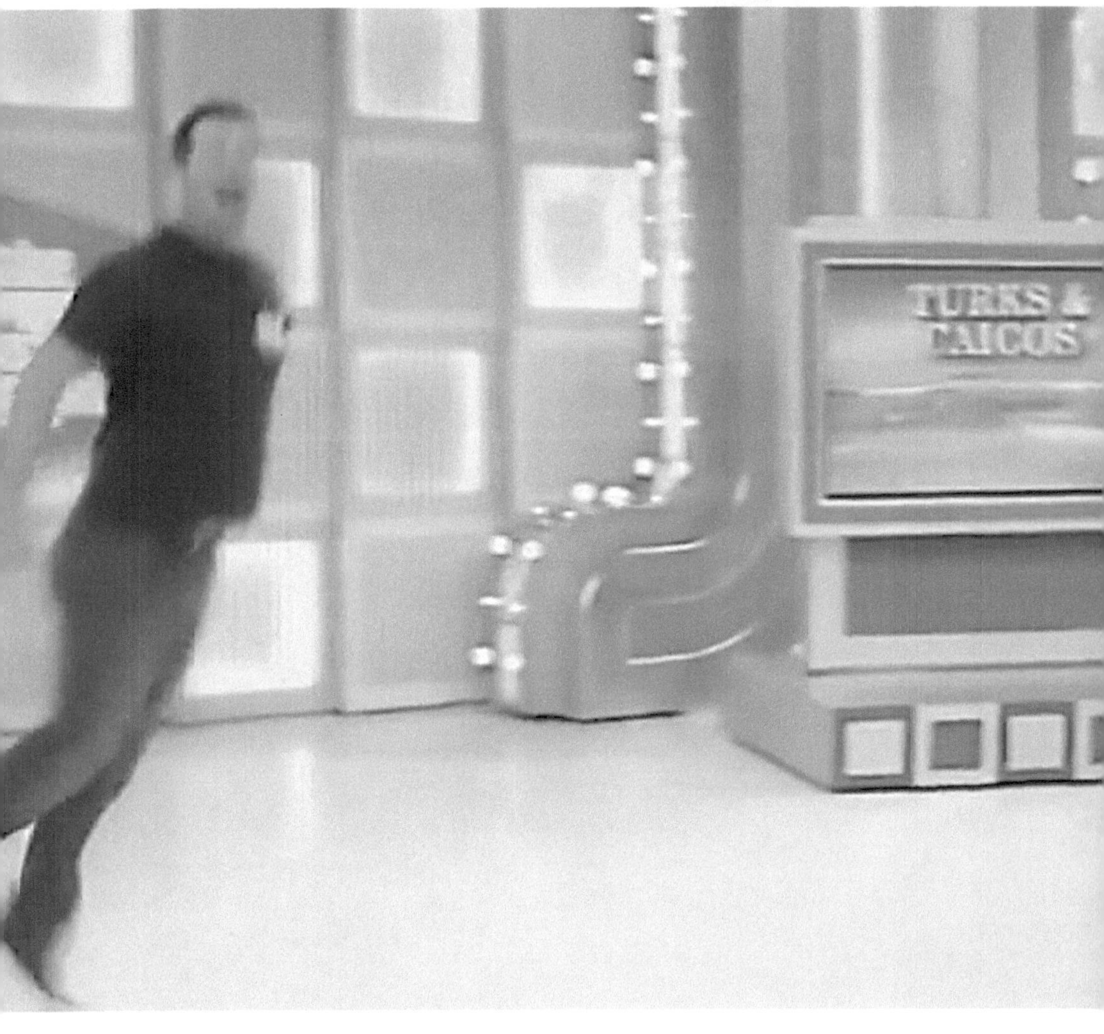
TURKS &
CAICOS

Turks and Caicos

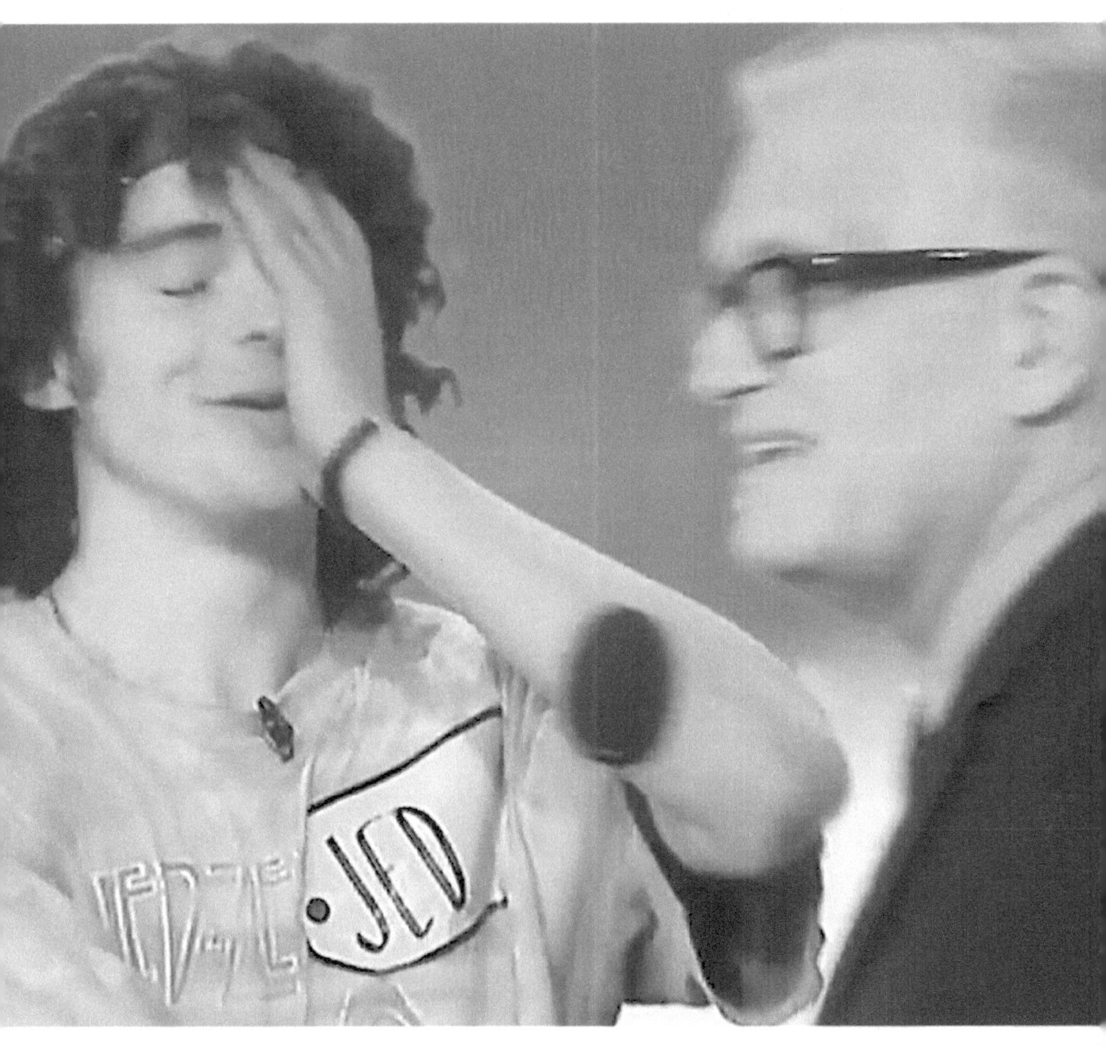

183

Van-
cou-
ver/
France

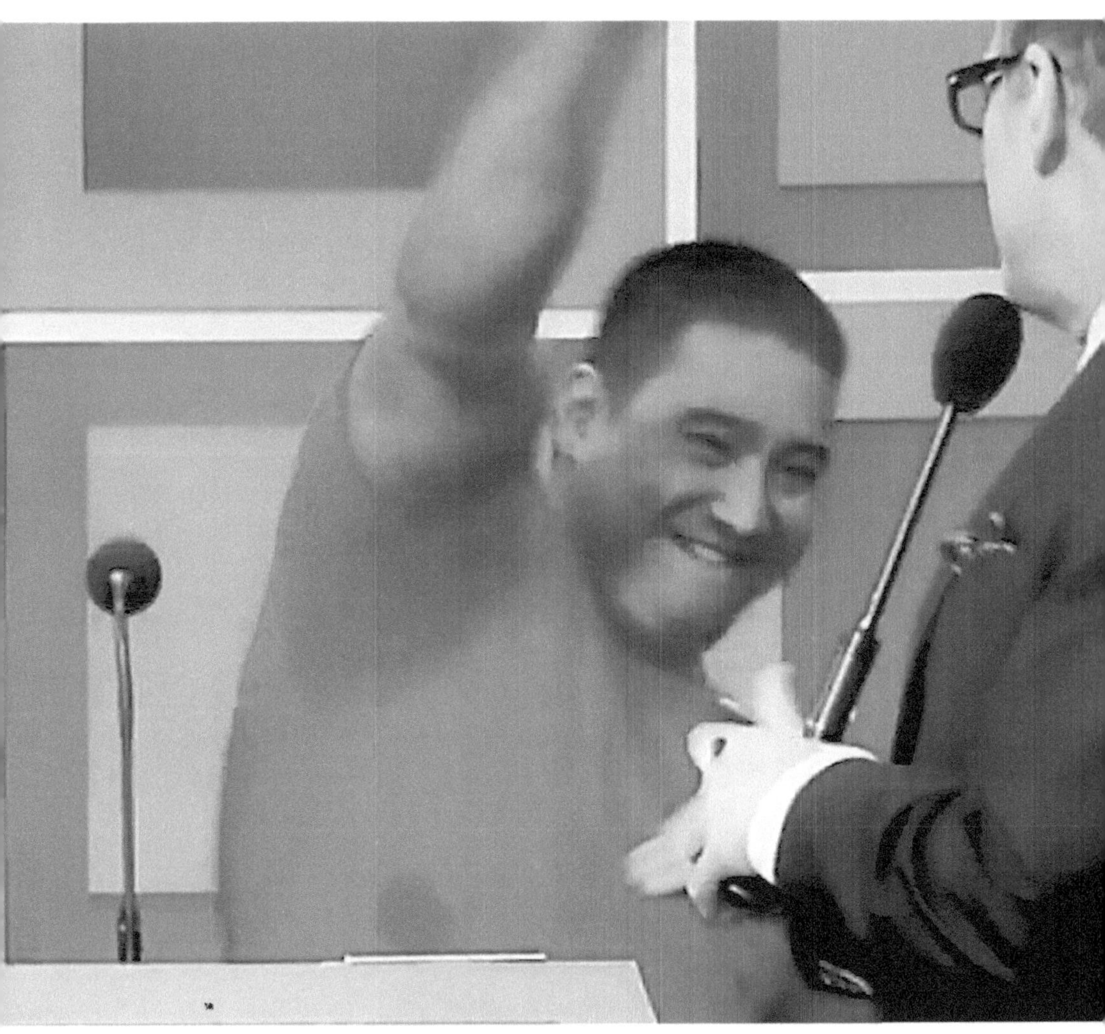

Venice

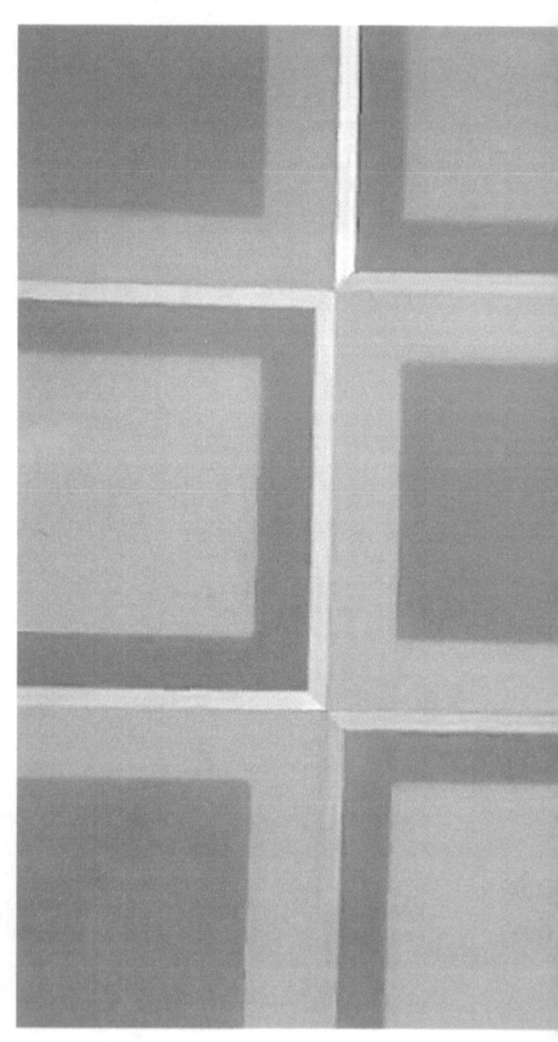

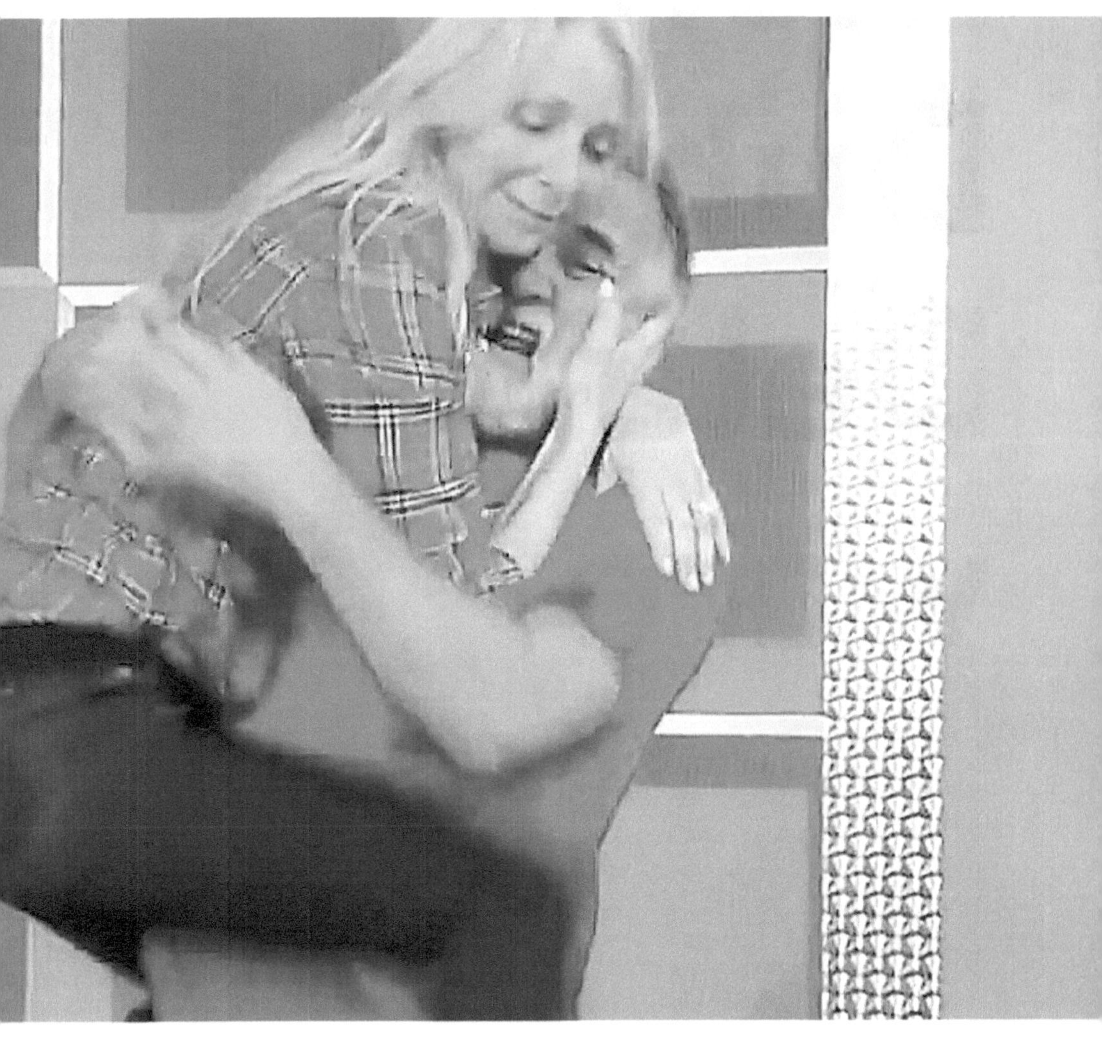

Vermont/ Dubai/ Delaware

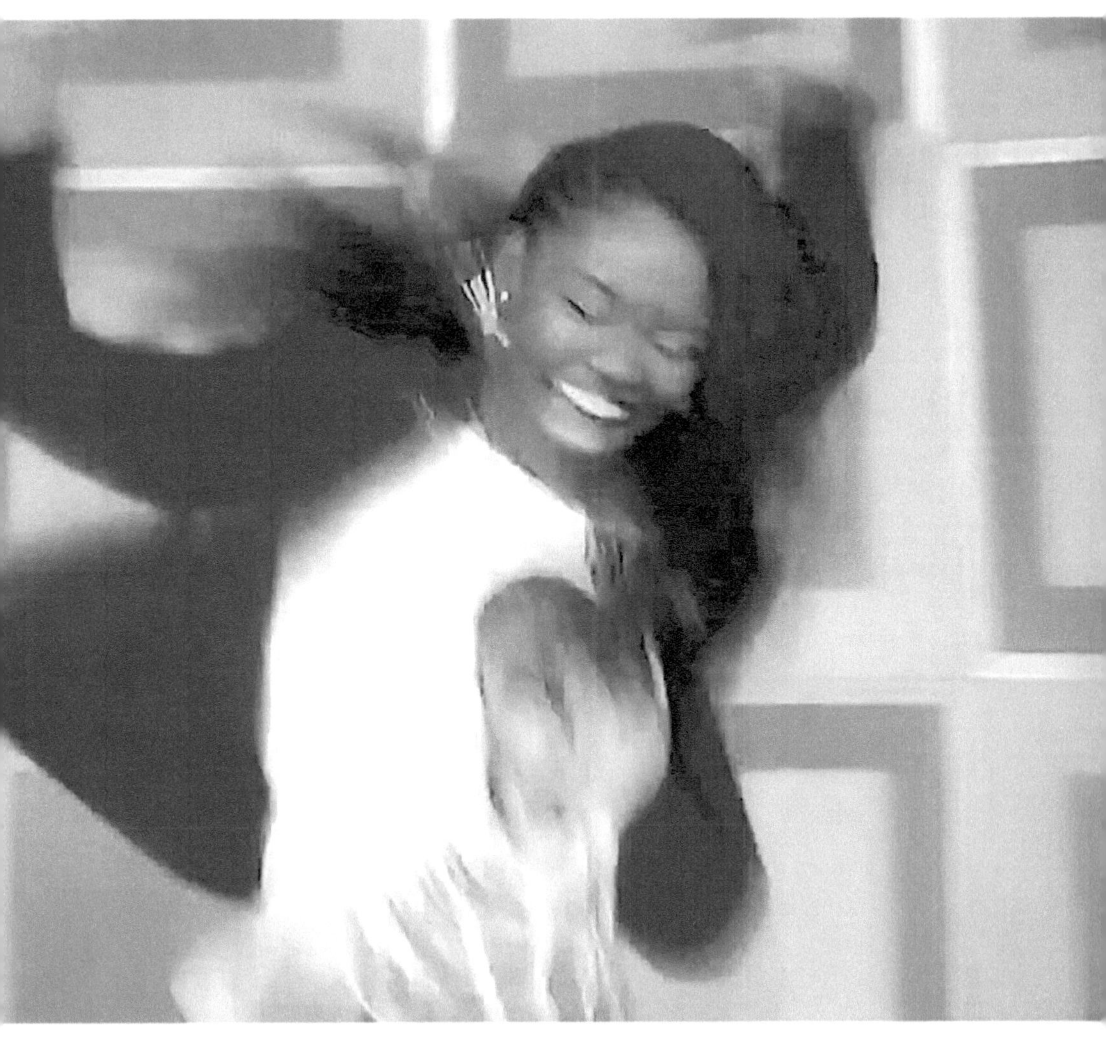

Wash-
ington
D.C.

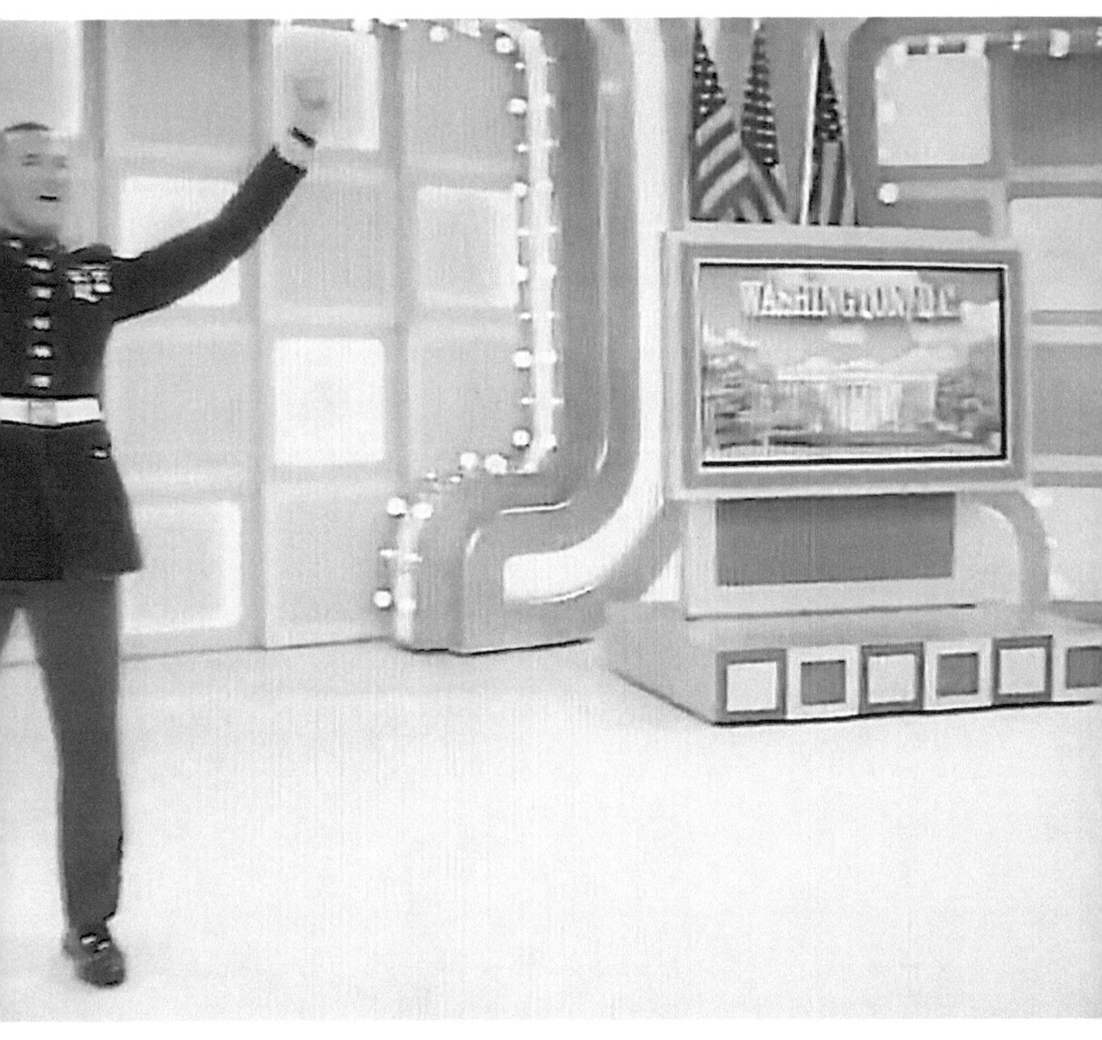

WASHINGTON D.C.

Wis-
consin

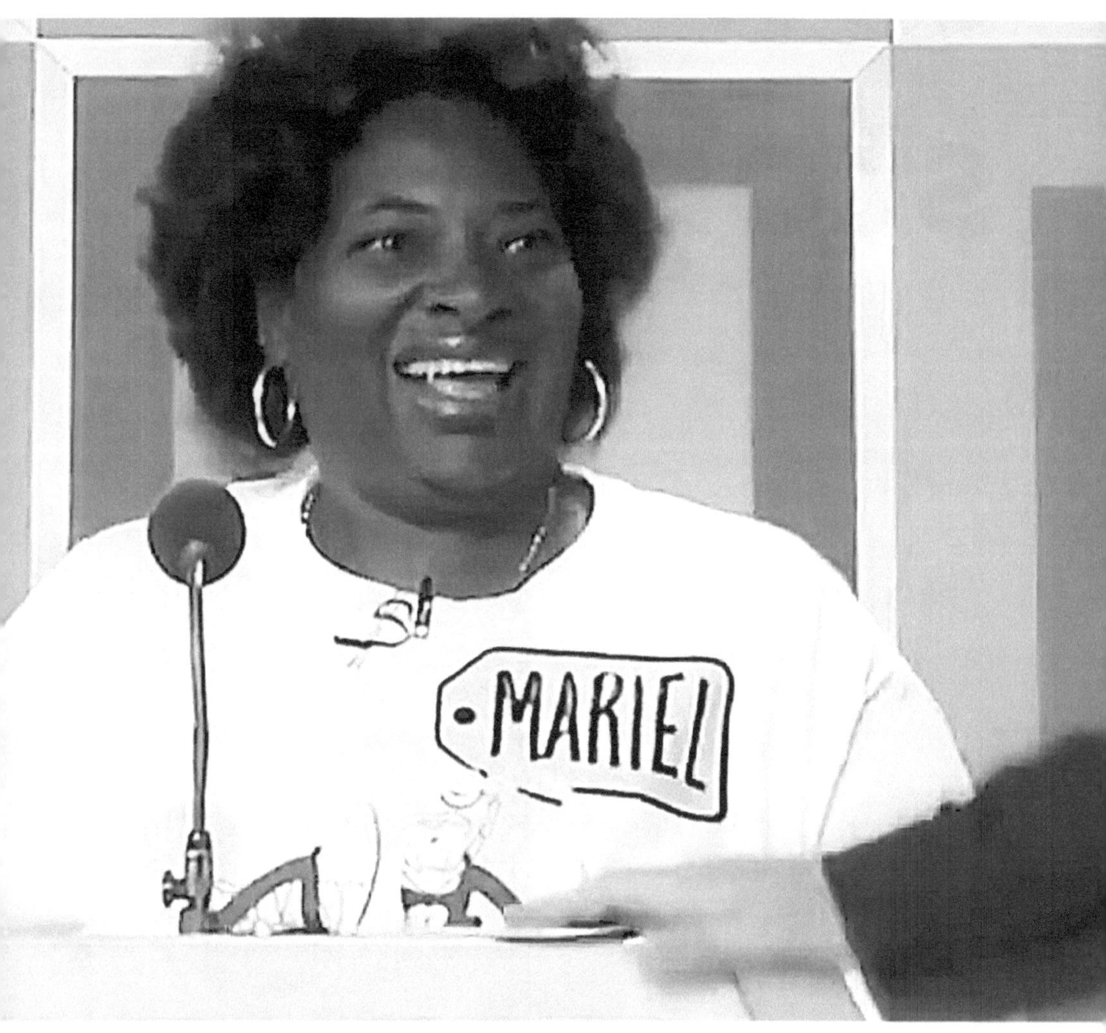

MARIEL

Yel-
low-
stone

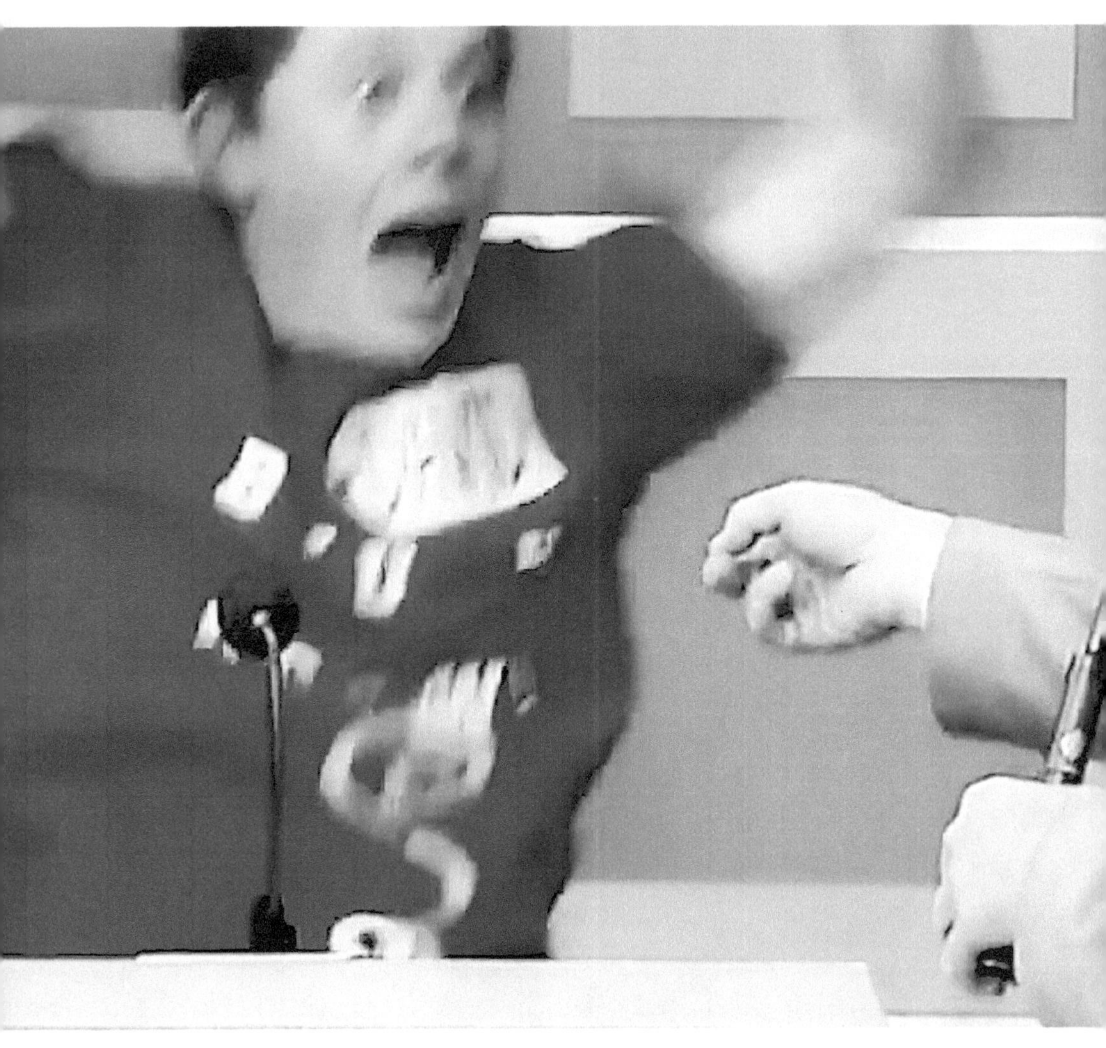

Yo-semi-te

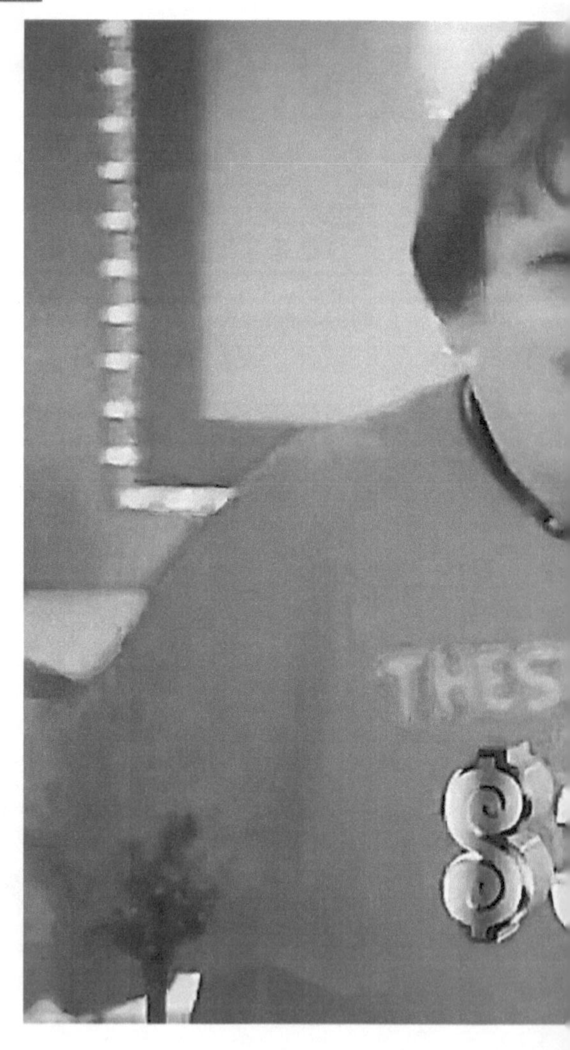

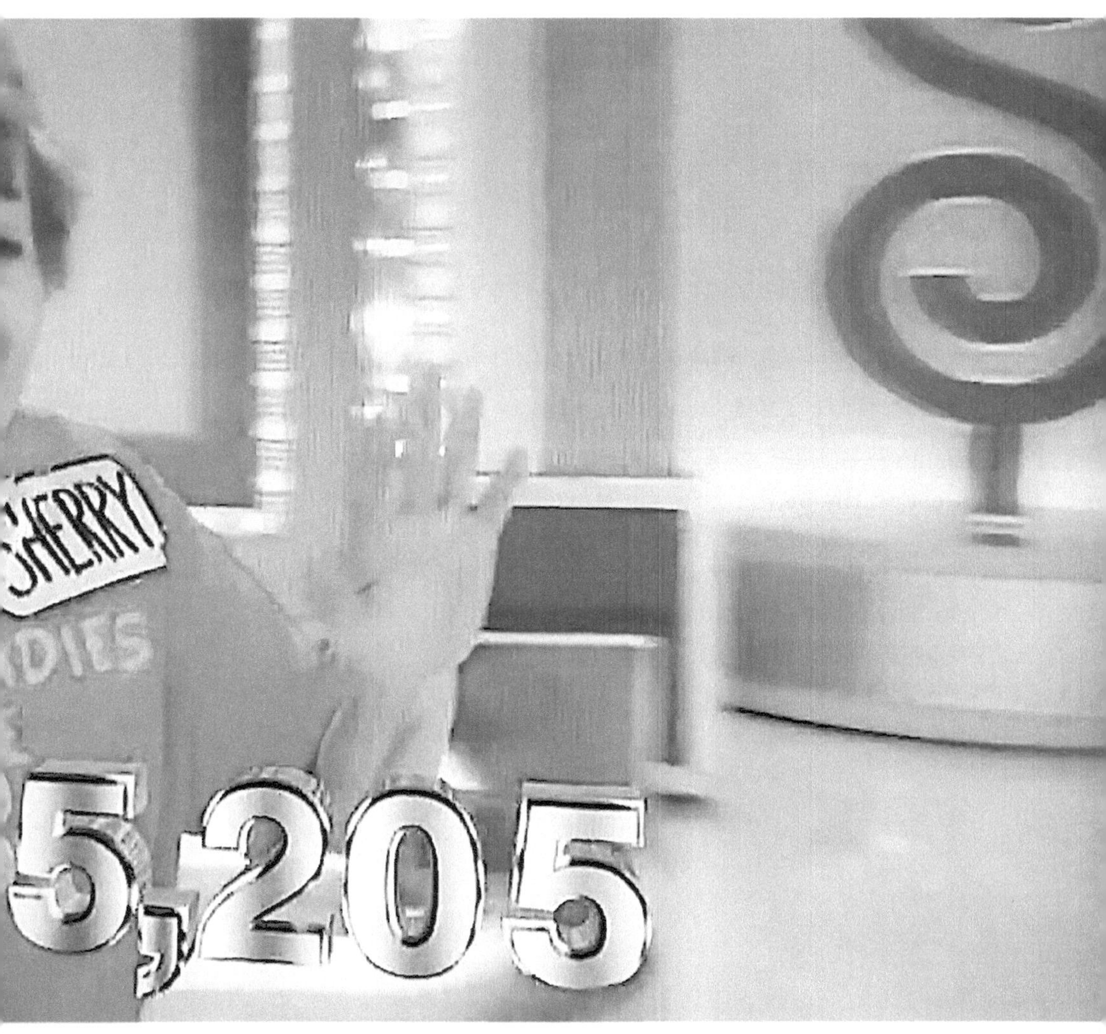
SHERRY
DIES
5,205

Edited, written and designed
by Dimitry Tetin

Published by Track and Field, Austin, TX
trackandfield.pub

Typefaces used:
P22 Underground and OkayD

© 2024 Track and Field
First Edition, Second Printing 2024
ISBN: 978-1-7374831-1-3

All rights reserved. No part of this
publication my be reproduced, stored
in a retrieval system or transmitted, in
any form or by any means, mechanical,
photocopying or otherwise, without
prior permission in writing from
the publisher.